Rebecca West's Subversive Use of Hybrid Genres

Also Available from Bloomsbury

H.D. and Modernist Religious Imagination,
Elizabeth Anderson
Djuna Barnes's Nightwood,
Bonnie Roos
Katherine Mansfield and Literary Modernism,
Janet Wilson, Gerri Kimber and Susan Reid
Reading Mina Loy's Autobiographies,
Sandeep Parmar
Virginia Woolf's Late Cultural Criticism,
Alice Wood

Rebecca West's Subversive Use of Hybrid Genres

1911–41

Laura Cowan

Bloomsbury Academic
An imprint of Bloomsbury Publishing Plc

B L O O M S B U R Y
LONDON • NEW DELHI • NEW YORK • SYDNEY

Bloomsbury Academic
An imprint of Bloomsbury Publishing Plc

50 Bedford Square
London
WC1B 3DP
UK

1385 Broadway
New York
NY 10018
USA

www.bloomsbury.com

First published 2015

British Library Cataloguing-in-Publication Data
A catalogue record for this book is available from the British Library.

ISBN: HB: 978-1-4411-4417-1
ePDF: 978-1-4411-9746-7
ePub: 978-1-4411-1739-7

Library of Congress Cataloging-in-Publication Data
A catalog record for this book is available from the Library of Congress.

Typeset by Deanta Global Publishing Services, Chennai, India
Printed and bound in Great Britain

To Richard and my bluebirds, Allyeshka and Cole

Contents

Acknowledgments viii
List of Abbreviations x

1 The Wide Interstices between West's Genres 1
2 "The Wild Eye of the Artist": Early Journalism, *Henry James*, and *The Return of the Soldier* 13
3 "The Miraculous Beauty of the Common Lot": New Woman Meets Female Gothic in *The Judge* 47
4 "A Mystical Confusion of Substance": Satire and Fantasy Fuse in Rebecca West's *Harriet Hume* 67
5 Art's "Blazing Jewel" in *The Strange Necessity* 87
6 "The Tragic Spirit has Come Back into Life": West's Works of the 1930s, *A Letter to a Grandfather, St Augustine, The Thinking Reed,* and *The Harsh Voice* 107
7 "To Cast Away All Acquisitions and Certainties": *Black Lamb and Grey Falcon* Combines Travel Genres and the Epic 133

Notes 167
References Cited 181
Index 191

Acknowledgments

Part of Chapter 2 on *The Return of the Soldier* appeared in *The Centennial Review* 42:2 (Spring 1998) 285–307. I thank *The Centennial Review* and the Michigan State University Press for their permissions.

The work for this book was supported by a summer grant from the University of Maine Women in the Curriculum Program in 2010 and by Incentive Release Time for Research awarded by English Department Chair Naomi Jacobs in Spring 2009.

I am grateful to the International Rebecca West Society—and especially its officers—for sponsoring scholarship and interest in West and for providing a forum for many of the ideas espoused in this book at Bi-Annual International Rebecca West Conferences. The West Estate and, especially, Helen Macleod Atkinson and her parents Norman and Marion Macleod have been remarkable in their encouragement of scholarship on West.

Thanks go to Bloomsbury Senior Editor David Avital for validation of my work, to Academic Editor Mark Richardson for his professionalism and capabilities during the initial stages of this project, and to Production Editor James Tupper for his conscientious work on the next stage. Deanta Project Manager Grishma Fredric and her team are amazing. Her intelligent grasp of ideas and her meticulous attention to production result in a work of integrity and quality.

Deep gratitude goes to Hansie Grignon and Jody Crouse for their invaluable help as research assistants. The University of Maine's Fogler Library and its able staff—especially Reference Librarian Mel Johnson and the Interlibrary Loan librarians—also facilitated my work. This book would not have been possible without the heroic teaching efforts of Orono teachers, Christina Jimenez and Rose Scheidt.

I am indebted to many friends, students, and colleagues—particularly the following colleagues: Pat Burnes for her help with my theoretical frame; Naomi Jacobs for encouraging my scholarship while she was Chair of English; Richard Brucher for evaluations of my work on West and travel genres; Howard Segal for professional advice; and Deborah Rogers for her intellectual, professional, and personal guidance during every stage of this project—and especially for reading several draft chapters.

My husband, Richard May, has given generously in order for me to work on this project. I am grateful to him for his devotion and for his attention to copyediting. Thanks to Kolya for his technical assistance. My sons Allyeshka and Cole give meaning to all my endeavors.

List of Abbreviations

Works by Rebecca West frequently cited*

Title	Abbreviation
Black Lamb and Grey Falcon	*BLGF*
The Court and the Castle	*CC*
"Elegy"	*EL*
Ending in Earnest	*EE*
The Judge	*TJ*
Harriet Hume	*HH*
The Harsh Voice	*HV*
Henry James	*HJ*
A Letter to a Grandfather	*LG*
The Return of the Soldier	*RS*
St Augustine	*SA*
The Strange Necessity	*SN*
The Thinking Reed	*TR*
The Young Rebecca (edited by Jane Marcus)	*YR*

* Bibliographical information about the editions of these texts can be found in "References Cited."

1

The Wide Interstices between West's Genres

Part 1 West's variety of genres

Rebecca West's humility about the volume and multiplicity of her work would puzzle many. Although *Time* magazine proclaimed her "the world's number one woman writer" in 1947, West was "appalled" when a university student wanted to write a thesis on her work: "I was naturally appalled. I explained that I was a writer wholly unsuitable for her purpose" (*BLGF* 1084). According to West, her individual works might "severally play a part in theses" on different subjects, but her entire *oeuvre*'s variety defied the purposes of a coherent thesis; her works "could not fuse to make a picture of a writer, since the interstices were too wide."

West's generic diversity has figured prominently in discussions of West and her legacy. Her works include political journalism, literary criticism, biography, satire, war fiction, fantasy, art history, melodrama, travel chronicles, epistolary novels, realism, epics, a detective novel, autobiography, and magic realism. Nothing seems to exceed her grasp. Scholar Samuel Hynes echoes West's self-description in his introduction to *Rebecca West: A Celebration*: "Few writers can match her range, or her steady moral seriousness." While Hynes praises West's infinite variety, he nonetheless regrets that West's multiplicity confounds literary critics: "Dame Rebecca's work has not fused in the minds of critics, and she has not a secure literary status—the interstices between her books ... are too wide; she is too difficult to define" (Hynes 1977: xviii).

Not all West's critics applaud her variety. Although Peter Wolfe was one of her early apologists, he deplores the generic eccentricity of *Harriet Hume*:

> Unfortunately, the fantasy in *Harriet Hume* falls short of [West's] critical requirements. Of all the early fictions, it is the most artificial and the most arbitrary. An academic exercise, it says nothing new about its subject and does nothing exciting with its materials. (Wolfe 1971: 42)

While a contemporary *New York Times* reviewer called West's *Black Lamb and Grey Falcon* "not only the magnification and intensification of the travel book form, but, one may say, its apotheosis" (Woods 1941: 4), Jan Montefiore comments on the same features and condemns them as "irretrievably hybrid" and "a loose baggy monster" (Montefiore 1996: 179, 183). William Carlos Williams criticizes West's essay "The Strange Necessity" because of its hybridity: "Here is a mixing of categories, a fault in logic—that is unimaginable in a person of orderly mind" (Williams 1929: 83).

Even West's champions—like Hynes—regret the scholarly consequences of her generic variety. Bonnie Kime Scott complains that modernist scholars in particular neglect West because of her "versatility. Many of her best critical judgments reside in works that can be assigned to the unfashionable genres of journalism and travel literature" (Scott 1991: 267). Carl Rollyson comments on its effect on scholarly books that treat West:

> The few introductory studies of Rebecca West tend to chop her up, assigning separate chapters to the different genres of her work. Consequently the development of her career, and the way her fiction and nonfiction relate to each other, have barely begun to be understood. (Rollyson 1995: i)

As my discussion of West's manipulations of genres will demonstrate, such "chopping" misses vital connections between her works.

My book solves the generic conundrum that plagues West studies by focusing comprehensively on West's manipulations of genres in a majority of her works from 1911 to 1941. None of her works fit neatly into a taxonomy of literary types; they are all in their own way sui generis. West deliberately manipulates, distorts, or subverts generic conventions and expectations throughout her career.

Part 2 Scholarly context

Several critical works about West call attention to her manipulation of genres. Bernard Schweizer, in particular, has advanced scholarship on West by focusing on West and genres. His *Radicals on the Road* argues that West and many of her fellow travelers in the 1930s "pioneered a new tradition" of travel writing (Schweizer 2001: 3). While Schweizer's interest in "new traditions" of travel writing has helped establish the importance of genre study to modernism, this book turns to West's use of "old traditions" of travel writing. Schweizer's examination of several of West's works as epics in *Rebecca West: Heroism,*

Rebellion, and the Female Epic (2002) is one of the most important general studies of West. I draw on Schweizer's work and its insights, but his generic focus is narrower than mine.

No matter what her thesis, Debra Rae Cohen's scholarship often has a "generic twist" to it. Cohen repeatedly makes a virtue of West's generic hybridity. Her analysis of West's novel *Harriet Hume* anticipates my anti-taxonomic bias. In an analysis of West's nonfiction, Cohen uses Kristen Bluemel's ideology of "intermodernism" to draw attention to West's disruptive use of genre: "West ... by employing multiple subject positions and generic lenses—disrupts those readerly certainties that attach to genre and implicitly interrogates the cultural apparatuses that produce them" (Cohen 2009: 150–1). Cohen celebrates West's "genre-bending" in *Black Lamb and Grey Falcon,* but regrets that it is "still largely untheorized" (Cohen 2009: 151). This book draws upon and continues Cohen's discussion and theorizing of West's use of genres.

Patrick Collier is another scholar who has championed West's hybridity for the qualities that early critics condemned. He praises both *Black Lamb and Grey Falcon* and *The Strange Necessity* for their variety: "Rebecca West's *Black Lamb and Grey Falcon* is full of surprising stylistic and generic shifts. ... West signals the hybrid nature of the nearly 1,200 pages" (Collier 2006: 169). Collier revisits West's relationship to her Edwardian predecessors and praises the Edwardians as "useful exemplars for West's own genre-straddling career" (Collier 2006: 186).

West quoted Bernard of Chartres to explain literature's cumulative powers: "We are like dwarfs ... seated on the shoulders of giants" (*CC* 4). This book is indebted particularly to Margaret D. Stetz's work on West, genre, and literary tradition. An analysis of genre inevitably involves an examination of a writer's relationship to history and to literary tradition. Several works by Stetz treat West's place in modernism and her relationship to literary traditions. Stetz argues that West was always acutely aware of how "creative works of the past and present were ... bound together in a fruitful alliance" (Stetz 1994: 45). My study of genres proves Stetz's filiative claim that "neither as a critic nor as a writer of fiction did Rebecca West seem to find it necessary to repudiate whole movements and eras or to deny affiliations between her own work and that of romantic or other artists" (Stetz 1994: 47). Stetz's analyses often implicitly or explicitly treat the hybridity of West's works. She says of *Harriet Hume,* for example: It (and other modernist texts) "utilized the forms of fiction but ... [were] nonetheless, also works of aesthetic theory" (Stetz 1994: 54). In *British Women's Comic Fiction, 1890-1990: Not Drowning, But Laughing,* Stetz examines a previously undiscovered 1929 short story by West to portray a woman using genre expectations to subvert patriarchy. This introduction builds upon Stetz's insights about "Elegy" to develop a model for West's subversive hybridity. I also draw on Lyn Pykett who echoes Stetz: "[West's] modernism is not predicated on that rupture with the ... past ... but rather it remains in dialogue with the writing of the nineteenth century" (Pykett 2000: 120).

West argues that cultural traditions are essential to healthy individuals and healthy countries. She does not believe in blind adherence to totalitarian systems, but she does believe that cultures, countries, and individuals need vital traditions. She condemned imperialism because it denies countries their own traditions. She groups James Joyce with Al Capone, St Augustine, and Hamlet because they are all "deracinated." "When Hamlet fails to obey [his father]," West argues, "he rejects the accumulated experience of his race; he has refused to aid society by transmitting a message; and he has taken as his government his individual impulses" (*CC* 16). Saint Augustine is also at a disadvantage because he lived in exile: "Augustine was at nature an artist who was unable to develop his true genius because he was alienated from his native culture" (*SA* 21). West honors literary tradition while recognizing that new situations demand new interpretations of traditions.

Although I share Stetz's and Pykett's view that West saw alliance and continuity where others saw rupture, I believe that West's use of tradition is often disruptive and subversive. As we see in her discussion of modernist painting, she believes that one can draw from tradition to revolutionary effect: "In the landscapes of Cezanne and Van Gogh we recognize a quality which comes from a novel and valid way of regarding matter, a manifestation that by following the tradition of art the artists have pushed on into a new phase of sensibility" (*EE* 210).

West views genres as processes with conventions to be deployed strategically to transformative and transgressive political ends: "It is obviously regrettable when state machinery which is working well is smashed by rebellion, but then if it has not worked well there is a reasonable case for dismantling it" (*CC* 59). Even more important than the variety of genres that West employs is the "impurity" of her works. All of her works are hybrids.

Part 3 West's short story "Elegy" as exemplary West hybrid

Part 3A Summary of "Elegy"

Stetz has focused on the short story "Elegy" in her discussion of comedy in modernist literature. Many of her interpretations of "Elegy" are pertinent to my concern with West's use of genres and her relation to tradition—always subjects prominent in Stetz's analyses. West's short story "Elegy" can serve as an emblem for West's subversive manipulation of multiple genres in all of her works. The narrator tells a story about a trick her mother (hereinafter referred to—as in the story—as simply "Mother") played on her stodgy uncle—for humanitarian reasons. Uncle John Cassilis, the director of the Museum of Colonial Antiques, had an honorable and conscientious employee whom he hired because of a letter of recommendation from Mother (who is deceased when the narrator tells the story). The letter's goals were moral, but its contents were—technically—immoral. Unemployed for six months, John Lumsden had tried to steal the gold watch of the narrator's father in order to feed his family. Seeing the man's good character, Mother wrote a letter of recommendation that resulted in Mr Cassilis's hiring Lumsden. Lumsden served Cassilis dutifully until retirement.

Part 3B Analysis of "Elegy"

Stetz points out that West has given us an example of a woman who manipulates a genre to subvert patriarchy:

> The mother plays deliberately upon masculine expectations about writing—the belief, for instance, that a letter of recommendation is an objective, factual document rather than a fictional text which one must decode carefully—as well as masculine assumptions about women, who are expected to side with the interests of their own ruling social class. (Stetz 2001: 56)

Stetz's discovered story and her analysis demonstrate that West conceived of genres as pliant. Mother enlisted a traditional, patriarchal genre (a letter of recommendation) in a typical Westian fashion for transgressive goals (employment for a man who attempted to commit a crime).

Although the variety of genres in this short story is not relevant for Stetz, the letter of recommendation is not the only genre invoked in this short story. The story is entitled, "Elegy." Just as Uncle John sat down with generic expectations when he read the letter, we readers bring generic expectations to the word "elegy." The short story both fulfills and contradicts these expectations. It honors and immortalizes the dead, but in a comic, satiric form. The story honors both Mother and Mr Lumsden (who is also deceased at the time of the story). It pays homage to Mother for saving Lumsden and his family and for raising a daughter with exemplary morals and insight. It pays homage to Lumsden for his devotion to his family, his service as an employee, and his generosity in bequeathing porcelain figures to his benefactress. While immortalizing the deceased, the elegy also mocks John Cassilis for his high seriousness. It also questions a social system whose laws need to be contravened in order to allow an honorable man to support his family and a society whose virtuous people are socially isolated when alive and gain full appreciation only after they are in the grave. The story also refuses one of the primary functions of the elegy, consolation. Stetz analyzes "Elegy" in a book about comedy: she points out that the narrator's laugh and Mother's chuckle do prevail. Nonetheless, as Stetz recognizes, melancholy and regret also inform the tone. The story is very much about loss: the death of remarkable people while "people like Uncle John go on and on living" (*EL* 224); the grandchildren Mother never had; the independent lives Mother's daughters lack; and the passion that Lumsden had for his wife, which Mother felt she never received. The story also subverts social hierarchies. The reader expects an elegy to the narrator's mother, an upper-middle-class woman. The reader is surprised to find that the story also pays respect to the employee, John Lumsden. West's readers would have been uncomfortable to have a man and a woman with tenuous connections to each other from different social classes commemorated in the same elegy.

West believes strongly in the transformative power of art:

> A major work of art must change the aspect of reality, for it is an experience of the order which breaks up the present as we know it, transforming it into the past and giving us a new present, which we may like better or less than we like the one just taken from us. (*CC* 5)

Mother's letter "changed the universe" by winning a job for an unemployed man. It also achieved social justice by rewarding a good man for devotion to his family while too fine a regard for the technicalities of the law might have punished him for attempted theft. The elegy also disrupts English gender protocols and classism by commemorating Mother and Mr Lumsden.

Part 4 Theoretical construct for West's subversive hybrid genres

Like this short story, all of West's texts are hybrid genres that create transformative spaces in the "interstices" between genres. Concepts from cultural studies and rhetorical studies of genre can illuminate West's transgressive fusion of genres. Key to Mary Louise Pratt's understanding of interactions between the different cultural groups in a colonized country is her "contact zone." In *Imperial Eyes: Travel Writing and Transculturation*, Pratt defines "contact zones" as "social spaces where disparate cultures meet, clash, and grapple with each other" (Pratt 1992: 4). It is a creative space characterized by interaction or exchanges rather than traditional notions of domination and subordination: "A contact perspective emphasizes how subjects are constituted in or by their relations to each other ... copresence; interlocking understandings and practices" (Pratt 1992: 7). Pratt sees travel writing as the scene for a productive encounter in the contact zone. I see all of West's works as "contact zones" where different genres meet. For example, the interaction between different genres in West's story "Elegy" creates a generative "contact zone" (of genres rather than of cultures). Pratt's theories are especially apt for West because a critique of imperialism is central to all her works from 1911 to 1941. West decries the cultural as well as the political and social consequences of imperialism. Her works argue for the kind of fruitful interactions between cultures that Pratt's "contact zone" promotes.

The subversive nature of West's generic hybrids can be further explained with rhetorician Anne Freadman's concept of "uptake." Freadman shares West's belief that genres are scenes of "action" and not fixed entities: "A genre does not inhere in its more or less standardized morphology, but in the dynamic of what Carolyn Miller calls 'social action'; that is, what it gets people to do with one another, and what they do with it" (Freadman 2002: 40). The letter in "Elegy" results in "social action": John Cassilis hires John Lumsden. According to Freadman, "Uptake is what happens when you accept an invitation to a conference, or agree to rewrite a paper" (Freadman 2002: 39). When John Cassilis sits down to read the letter of recommendation, "uptake" occurs. When we readers start a short story named "Elegy," "uptake" occurs. For Freadman and West, uptake is "productive when applied to the interaction of minimally a pair of texts" (Freadman 2002: 40). West's combinations of genres in all of her works achieve what Freadman calls a "bidirectional relation" (Freadman 2002: 42). Uptake can be subversive because it crosses a boundary. It crosses a boundary, but it does not destroy the boundary; rather it "mediates": "Translation is the mediation of a boundary, not its obliteration ... 'uptake' is the local event of crossing a boundary" (Freadman 2002: 43). West does not "obliterate" genres—rather she manipulates them. West's "Elegy" immortalizes Mother and John Lumsden and celebrates their roles in society just as it simultaneously interrogates the laws of society, social hierarchies, gender roles, and poverty.

West treats genres as texts with common discursive and interpretative strategies, not as collections of textual features. West's dynamic view of genres anticipates and endorses contemporary scholars who are exploring ways to go beyond a taxonomic view of genre. West was ahead of even twenty-first century theorists. Even a critic like Wai Chee Dimock who argues that our analyses would profit from a more "open" sense of genre, still maintains a bias toward genre as "catalog" (Dimock's term) or "product" in her definition of a genre as a "database" (Dimock 2007: 1377).

West's subversive aims call into question her use of genres. Can one use genres—which are defined by strict adherence to form or rules and are in some ways inherently conservative—to advance a liberal agenda? Stephen Owen recognizes genre's conservative threat when he states, "Genre is the discourse of total order, where everything has its place" (Owen 2007: 1393). To Stephen Heath, genre is "necessarily conservative" (Robbins 2007: 1645). Bruce Robbins calls attention to metaphors which compare genres to the "police" who enforce society's laws: "In limiting literature's possibilities, genre is seen as complicit with the larger culture; it is a social institution, burdened with the weight of social interests and constituencies" (Robbins 2007: 1646). Rhetoricians have been particularly sensitive to the possibility that a conservative ideology governs all genres—and particularly certain "masterful" genres. They ask if a writer/practitioner of a genre is unavoidably shaped by the ideology the genre embodies or if a writer can both use and subvert a genre's inherent ideology. Do "conservative," hierarchical genres oppress the very students who "master" their conventions and seek to be "empowered" by them or are the students empowered by their mastery? Anthony Pare recognizes that the normative power of a genre can make their implicit ideology "immutable" (Pare 2002: 59). He cites Richard Coe, who believes that one is shaped by the genre one employs: "Coe (1994) argues that 'genres embody attitudes' and adds that 'since these attitudes are built into generic structures, they are sometimes danced without conscious awareness or intent on the part of the individual using the genre'" (Coe et al. 2002: 183). West's position as a woman and her feminist goals further problematize her manipulation of genres. Carol L. Snyder captures women's problematic relationship to genre. Historically genres that have been gendered male can marginalize women and women's issues. Other genres that are gendered female can themselves be marginalized or dismissed:

> If genre is a particularly suspect term in post-modernist criticism, that is in good part because feminist theories have exposed some of the ways in which

> supposedly value-free literary classifications actually privilege male discourse. They have allowed us to see genre as the authorizing and valorizing instrument of the male canon, a grillwork barring women entrance, or a ladder on which women's writing occupies the lower rungs of the sub-genres. (Snyder 1991: xi)

While West is aware of the implicitly coercive power of genres, she manipulates different genres to her own ends throughout her career.

Central to West's dynamic manipulations of genres is a promotion of "process" over "product." The totalizing potential of genre that Owen recognizes is genre as "product." In a conversation in *Black Lamb and Grey Falcon,* West's husband decries those who value "product" over "process" (*BLGF* 800). He condemns their traveling companion Gerda because she has "no sense of process … [she] wants the result without any of the work that goes to make it" (*BLGF* 799). West sees genres as "process[es]"—which are mutable and variable. The importance of "process" is key to the liberating potential of the "generic counterpoint" of bidirectional uptake in the contact zone of hybrid genres that this book analyzes.

In their discussions of genre and composition studies, Richard Coe, Lorelei Lingard, and Tatiana Teslenko credit Kenneth Burke and Mikhail Bakhtin for a more "active" sense of genre as a strategy rather than a catalog: "This central notion of discourse as strategic response to situation is indebted not only to Burke, but also to Bakhtin's conceptualization of the 'dialogism' and 'addressivity' of the utterance" (Coe et al. 2002: 6). Bakhtin's notion of "dialogism" is key to my understanding of West's sense that genres have strategies that involve their audiences and also to West's "deployment" of a sort of generic counterpoint which creates subversive spaces in her text.

West believes she can manipulate "conservative" genres (such as letters of recommendations and elegies) to "liberal" ends (such as breaking patriarchal law for humanitarian reasons and criticizing class systems) or potentially "oppressive" forms (such as travel literature that demeans third world countries) for "revolutionary" results (such as undermining imperialism). Art always works to transformative purposes for West. She describes a "dual process in art" that resembles Bakhtin's dialogism. The "dual process in art" has "two parts of which we call romanticism and classicism" (*EE* 304). She rejects the notion that romanticism and classicism are opposite kinds or impulses in art. Rather she insists that they are two parts of the same process. Romanticism, which is based on an artist's encounter with "novelty," "breaks the mould of the universe" (*EE* 304). Classicism incorporates the disruption caused by romanticism and "reestablish[es] order" and harmony (*EE* 305). The two impulses are inextricably bound and therefore every work of art involves change and disruption.[1] Some works stay in the romantic phase; others move to the harmony of classicism. In each case, the artist "finds expression for his new reaction" (*EE* 304).

Part 5 Features of West's hybrid genres

Part 5A Feminist goals

As Mother's letter in "Elegy" demonstrates, feminist goals often motivate West's manipulation of genres. West's standing as a feminist is controversial, but I argue that a feminist agenda motivates all of her work. Her fight for women started early in her articles for Dora Marsden's *Freewoman* (which was to become *The New Freewoman* and *The Egoist*). As Jane Marcus remarks, "Vera Brittain, author of *The Testament of Youth*, saw Rebecca West ... as the embodiment of the feminist cause, the twentieth-century successor to Mary Wollstonecraft" (*YR* 11). According to Marcus,

> It was the dead souls of women she [West] wanted to resurrect. As she herself put it, feminism was "something more than a fight for the vote. It was a fight to grow in art, in science, in politics, in literature: it is a fight for a place in the sun." (*YR* 3)

One way to accomplish feminist goals is to subvert patriarchal genres or to celebrate genres that have been derogatively gendered as feminine.[2]

Part 5B Inclusion of at least one "unreal" genre

West's transformative goals are assisted by the nature of the genres that she combines. All of her hybrids include at least one genre that could be labeled "poetic," "fantastic," "mythical," or "unreal." *The Return of the Soldier* fuses a war novel with the pastoral. *The Judge* joins a New Woman novel to the gothic. *Harriet Hume* combines a political satire with a fantasy. *A Letter to a Grandfather* combines an epistolary novella, political journalism, and a mystical vision.[3] *The Thinking Reed* merges tragedy and farce. *Black Lamb and Grey Falcon* unites a travelogue and an epic. As we have seen, "Elegy" amalgamates letters and elegies. (Elegies were originally mythic and developed to incorporate pastoral idylls and symbolic uses of nature.) The transformative potential of these hybrids lies in their dialogue between genres. One of the short stories in *A Harsh Voice* is called "There is No Conversation." For West's hybrids to work, there *must* be a conversation. Having an imaginative or supernatural genre "converse" in the "contact zone" encourages the resulting work to interrogate "laws of reality" and transform prevailing worldviews. Jean-Paul Sartre declares that "fantasy assumes its proper function to transform the real world" (qtd Jackson 1981: 18). All of West's generic combinations resemble magic realism that "combines fantasy with ... physical reality or social reality in a search for truth beyond that available from the surface of everyday life" (Mellen 2000: 1).

Part 5C All works treat social class issues

British classism and the importance of social class to all aspects of life—including love, marriage, work, politics, and art—inform all of West's works. West was a socialist and wrote for socialist journals in the early years of her career. Although her investment in exploring class issues was not as explicit later in her career, these concerns continued to preoccupy her. We have already discussed the importance of class to "Elegy." *The Return of the Soldier,* as another example, describes a love affair between an upper-middle class man and a working-class woman. It also blames the Great War on class issues. West argues in *The Strange Necessity* that middle-class writers are the source of literature's transformative powers. The Yugoslavian peasants in *Black Lamb and Grey Falcon* are the epic chorus and the epic hero(es) of this work.

Part 6 Scope and goals

This book is an inclusive examination of West's subversive, generic hybrids during the first half of her career—from 1911 to 1941. I choose the first half of her career (just as her first biographer Victoria Glendinning chose the first half of her life) because West's output is too prodigious for one work to cover all of her career. As we have seen, the result of this prodigiousness means that other authors "chop" up her work by genres (Rollyson 1995: i). Debra Rae Cohen criticizes this "tendency to practice a kind of horizontal or vertical dissection of West's extended, contradictory, and extraordinarily varied oeuvre, slicing up West's career so as to quarantine [her works]" (Cohen 2006: 143). As my discussion of West's manipulations of genres will demonstrate, such "slicing" decimates where it should illuminate. Some critics might call 1911–41 West's "modernist" period, but West's hybrid tendencies cannot be compartmentalized into periods. These years conveniently end with *Black Lamb and Grey Falcon*, which is arguably West's "masterpiece" and certainly one of the greatest hybrid works of the twentieth century.

My generic lens is broad enough to provide my audience a sense of West's place in historical and literary traditions and specific enough to allow my study the coherence that books about specific topics in West's works or essay collections about her works cannot offer. This provides a coherent examination of her work and lays the groundwork for further examinations of her later career or more specific aspects of her work with a similar thesis.

My analyses of West's works proceed more or less chronologically according to dates of publication. Since West's works respond to their historical situation, a chronological organization makes sense. My argument is in no way teleological; I do not believe that West's talents for creating hybrid works started with callow ventures that crescendo to full magnificence in *Black Lamb and Grey Falcon*. I argue that an impulse for hybridization characterizes all her works—some more and some less, perhaps, but there is no discernable development. West was prolific and often published several works in one year. Since some works were written quickly and others took years, dates of publication capture only a snapshot of West's career. Although *Harriet Hume*, for example, was published in 1929 and *The Strange Necessity* in 1928, *Harriet Hume* usefully comments on many features of *The Strange Necessity*, so the chapter on *Harriet Hume* in this book precedes the one on *The Strange Necessity*. Each chapter focuses mainly on one work and sometimes includes abbreviated analyses of several other works—which help frame the chapter's main topic or help substantiate my claims on the value of examining all West's works as hybrids. I do not give full attention to posthumously published unfinished works such as *Sunflower*, *The Sentinel*, and *Adela*. Although I do not treat West's journalism (which includes political analyses, personal essays, and book reviews) as one or several coherent works, I do comment on their hybridity. I examine West's collection of essays *The Strange Necessity* as one work which fuses several genres. This general study of West's work aims to provide a comprehensive sense of West's place in her time and culture and of her contributions to an international modernist literary movement.

2

"The Wild Eye of the Artist": Early Journalism, *Henry James*, and *The Return of the Soldier*

Early journalism

The remarkable magnitude, variety, and scope that distinguish West's entire *oeuvre* also mark her early writing. Between 1911 and 1928, West published more than three hundred essays. Jane Marcus has collected many of her finest articles from 1911 to 1917 in *The Young Rebecca* (1989). These were heady years in both politics and the arts and West's works respond to and mark these tumultuous times. Her youth and her controversial subject matters spurred Cicely Isabel Fairfield to adopt the pen name "Rebecca West"—the name of a character she had played in an Ibsen play. This would remain her pen name and her public name for the rest of her life. Her essays about women's suffrage, socialism, and the Great War remind us of the political roots of the modernist literary revolution. The caustic wit, vivid language, and assertive style which delivered penetrating analyses of contemporary issues soon earned West renown. G. B. Shaw remarked, "Rebecca can handle a pen as brilliantly as ever I could, and much more savagely" (*YR* ix).

The feminist essays from *The Freewoman*, *The New Freewoman*, the socialist *Clarion*, and the liberal *Daily News* articulate West's evolving feminist politics. She insists on women's equality to men in abilities and entitlements. While she recognizes certain biological differences between the sexes, she will bridle no social discrimination: "There seems no difference of mentality. There is no study mastered by men, that women cannot master and no virtue honorable to men that dishonours women" (*YR* 163). She deplores the traditional roles assigned to women who have been forced to be "doormats," "parasites," or "prostitutes" and is particularly strident in her criticism of the tendency toward either self-sacrifice or sloth among her contemporary women. She, however, does not dismiss men wholesale, but rather labels a hatred of the opposite sex, by either men or women, "sex-antagonism" which she believes is a "neurosis which revolts against the difference of the sexes" (*YR* 248).

Although she fights valiantly to improve the status of women, she feels that any victory for women would be hollow in her contemporary authoritarian and oppressive social or political order which needs to be transformed radically. She warns suffragists that their fight for women's rights must go beyond the vote: "It is strange that the middle-class woman, who forms the backbone of the suffrage societies, should believe that one can superimpose the emancipation of women on the social system as one sticks a halfpenny stamp on a postcard" (*YR* 111). Even employment is not enough if it perpetuates a patriarchal system: "One would not wish women to become the kind of bureaucrats that the men's unions have in certain cases brought upon themselves, for it is one of the chief dangers to feminism that women may learn to play the fool as successfully as men" (*YR* 154). Rather women should refuse to become "competent wage-slaves" and "fight ... the capitalist and turn ... him out of the workshop" (*YR* 104). "When women came out of the home," West proclaims, "she came bringing not peace but a sword. Great things depend on how she uses that sword" (*YR* 115).

The corollary to these revolutionary tenets is that men can be feminists and that women can be patriarchs. Her fiction will portray many patriarchal women who perpetuate what she coins as the oppressive "masculinist and capitalist" order just as it will include men who resist that order (*YR* 245). Her feminism rests fundamentally on a desire for a transformed world that allows both men and women to realize themselves to the utmost and to lead rewarding, productive lives. "Life ought to be a struggle of desire towards adventures whose nobility will fertilize the soul and lead to the conception of new glorious things," she argues, and it should be everyone's goal to create a world in which such a life is possible. "We cannot bring this tragedy to a happy ending by hating a bad man here and a bad man there. We must design life anew as though we love all men" (*YR* 210).

West understands the rhetorical imperative behind her transformative ambitions in these essays. It is in many ways harder to write a subversive essay than it is to write subversive poetry or fiction. Any extreme departure from an audience's traditional generic expectations risks losing that audience and hence losing the point altogether. For example, T. S. Eliot's poetry of this time was challenging many poetic conventions, but his essays were fairly orthodox. West wants to transform her contemporary world through subverting conventional journalistic expectations or through blending hybrid elements into her essays.

Her methods are subtle but effective. The essays are unmatched in their vitality which move them beyond normal polemic into an "uncharted" realm/genre of their own. West's exuberance proclaims the inadequacy of traditional rhetoric and is a constant reminder of the drive to inspire adventurous, vital living that motivates all her works. Part of this forceful prose is a strident irony designed to shock and outrage her audience. Her irony is sometimes so extreme that readers have read her comments straight and misinterpreted her position. Irony is, of course, a hallmark of modernism[1] and it is an age-old rhetorical device. Patricia Meyer Spacks, however, makes special claims for irony as a subversive feminine device:

> A new category suggests itself for her: not the passivity of formlessness or the purposelessness of instability, but the feminine resource of evasiveness. The opponent who would presume to attack her finds her not where she was when he took aim. She embodies women as quicksilver, always in brilliant, erratic motion. (qtd Moi 1985: 36)

Irony underlines the absurdity of the opposing point of view, disarms your opponents, and also calls into question the rigid dualities that an authoritarian, patriarchal regime depends upon.

Another aspect of West's exuberance is her vivid metaphors—the most oft-noted feature of her writing. Many critics praise the metaphors for their lyrical vibrancy, but others criticize them as extravagant, irrelevant, or out-of-place. This is part of West's hybridity. She is blending conventions from fiction or poetry with essayistic conventions. The reader expects a formal, rational essay organized by reason. Readers are caught unawares in generic "uptake": this forces them to reexamine their assumptions. Extravagance and irrelevance are precisely the point. Because it distracts from the purely denotative, logical function of language, figurative language subverts any symbolic order and calls into question the super-rationality and utilitarianism that West ascribes to men. Metaphors transport the reader into an imaginative space—a generic contact zone—where logic and the imagination encounter each other to foster the transformative potential of art.

Although her political essays express the most explicit revolutionary and subversive views, West's hybrid book reviews employ some of the most antiauthoritarian devices. The narrator of West's reviews enters into the books themselves and treats the characters in the books as detached from the books' authors. The narratives and characters take on lives of their own. West's narrators often criticize the authors for misunderstanding or inappropriately assessing the characters they have created. In her review of H. G. Wells's *Marriage*, for example, West's narrator discusses Wells's characters Marjorie Pope and Trafford as if they have their own autonomy and criticizes Wells for his attitudes toward them:

> For the sake of sideboards and prestige she [Marjorie] was willing to give herself to a fool and transmit folly to her children. ... And the really fine and encouraging thing about the book is that Mr Wells sees that Marjorie is a thorough scoundrel. The horror of it is that, confused by her clear eyes and copper hair, he accepts her scoundrelism as the normal condition of women. (*YR* 65–6)

West's hybrid story/book review shatters the authoritarian presumptions behind traditional concepts of the author or creator as the sole locus of power and anticipates many premises of postmodern literary theory.

Henry James (1916)

West was attempting to write and complete a novel at least as early as 1909. It is not surprising, given West's hybrid inclinations, that the first complete book she published is not a novel, but a critical biography of Henry James. James is an apt subject for many of West's interests and a critical biography is in its nature hybrid. *Henry James* includes biography, history, psychology, art history, cultural analysis (especially of the differences between Europe and the United States), and literary criticism. The success of this work proves West's essentially hybrid imagination. She would go on to create hybrid genres out of works that are not traditionally hybrid for the rest of her career. She would also continue to excel in genres (like critical biography) that are inherently hybrid.

West begins with an examination of James's background and his early life in both Europe and America. She then divides his career into four phases: The International Situation, Transition, The Crystal Bowl, and The Golden Bowl. The study is one of West's first elaborations of art and culture's centrality to a fulfilling life. A thirst for their enrichment led Henry and his brother William to Europe where "there were many mines of treasure which they must find and rifle if they hoped for the health of their minds and the salvation of their souls" (*HJ* 14).

Art, however, is inextricably bound to history and politics for West. This conviction causes her to reproach James for frequently neglecting politics and history. She criticizes *The Bostonians* for its "nagging hostility to political effort" (*HJ* 72).

West enters into modernist literary debates even this early in her career. For example, T. S. Eliot's theory of "impersonality" would appear in his 1919 essay

"Tradition and the Individual Talent." West recognizes the source of this theory in French criticism at the turn of the century. She chides James for his reluctance to commit to his subjects emotionally: "The profound truth that an artist should feel passion for his subject was naturally distasteful to one who wanted to live wholly without violence even of the emotions; a preference for passionless detachment was at that date the mode" (*HJ* 52).

West's sense of the intrinsic connection between art and politics led to a typical modernist desire to wed imagination and vision with fact and reality and to her elevation of James's fiction of the 1890s. She also celebrated this fiction because of James's total commitment to their creation. "The state of genius," she explains, "consists of an utter surrender of the mind to the subject" (*HJ* 87).

> These wonderful stories, these exquisite vessels that swaggeringly hold and clearly show the contained draught of truth, like tall-stemmed goblets of Venetian glass. ... They are so truthfully conceived that one could compare them only to some nobly infrangible substance, so realistic and yet so charged with significance by their fashioning that their likeness must be something which is transparent and yet gives the light a white fire as it passed through. It is of crystal they are made, hard, luminous crystal. (*HJ* 94)

This "surrender to his subject" accounts for James's brilliance and also for the transformational power of his art.

In spite of her commitment to fact, West recognizes that many crucial incidents and scenes are trivialized by representation and are better served by leaving them out and depicting their consequences or the characters' reactions to them. James had mastered the suggestiveness of indirect representation. West employs the principle of presence through absence throughout her career. It accounts for the centrality of the Great War to *The Return of the Soldier* which never describes a war scene and the importance of fathers to *The Judge* even though none of them appear in the book.

The Return of the Soldier (1918)

The Return of the Soldier combines a war novel with the pastoral in order to criticize early twentieth-century Great Britain's values, to highlight women's roles in shaping and defining culture, and to insist upon the crucial importance of art in our personal lives and in our politics. It has become a historical commonplace that the First World War was the pivotal event in modern history which irrevocably changed the course of "culture," "civilization," and human consciousness.[1] The literature of the war is a rich source for understanding these changes. Paul Fussell's *The Great War and Modern Memory* is among many books that have explained the war's prominence. He describes the "simultaneous and reciprocal process by which life feeds material to literature while literature returns the favor by conferring forms upon life" and shows that "at the same time the war was relying on inherited myth, it was generating new myth, and that myth is part of the fiber of our lives" (Fussell 1975: 1).[2]

Part 1 Woman's war novel

Because of the number of educated men who directly participated in the war, we can measure the cultural effects of the war's devastation through writings (both autobiographical and fictional) by people who had first-hand experience of the war (Fussell 1975: 157). This advantage, however, led to a scholarly neglect of noncombatants, their experiences of war, and the ways in which their experiences can help us understand the First World War and our contemporary existence. Of course noncombatants can assimilate a combatant's experience. Nonetheless, probably because war has traditionally been viewed as a male domain, noncombatant men more readily identified with or sympathized with those who fought. Our disregard of noncombatants resulted in a marked neglect of women. Men and their consciousness may have dominated Western culture, but women's experience and consciousness have also shaped the world we live in.

Several studies have remedied the early critical neglect of women's experiences of the Great War. Claire M. Tylee's *The Great War and Women's Consciousness* (1990) is an explicit rebuke of Fussell's omission of women.[3] Rosa Maria Bracco argues in *Merchants of Hope: British Middlebrow Writers and the First World War, 1919-39* "that the popular literature of the Great War reveals the reality and the strength of the resistance against an ironic interpretation of the war" (Bracco 1993: 3). Susan R. Grayzel has two studies. *Women and the First World War* uses a cultural and historical approach to the Great War. *Women's Identities at War: Gender, Motherhood, and Politics in Britain and France during the First World War* claims "that the First World War does constitute an important arena for studying collectively the largest group of adult non-combatants' efforts to make sense of their gender and national identities at a pivotal moment of the modern era" (Grayzel 1999: 2). Grayzel reminds us that "the term 'home front' entered into common English usage during the First World War" (Grayzel 1999: 9). Grayzel and Debra Rae Cohen examine both the significance of the "home front" as a zone distinctly different from the military front and suggest that the designation of a "home front" means that the domestic sphere participated in the war in a new way.[4] Cohen's *Remapping the Home Front* examines women's literature written during the Great War to argue for "the Great War's importance to feminist revisionism ... in texts ... [where] the negotiations with narrative form mirror the uncertain reinvention of women's role in a war that marked the conflict" (Cohen 2002: 3).

The role of West's *The Return of the Soldier* in understanding the war and its myths is manifold. West's view of the war corroborates many of the myths male novelists created even as it offers its own original feminist perspective. Its date of composition contributes to its relevance. Fussell, Hynes, and Cohen remind us that our cultural understanding of the Great War—our "collective narrative of significance" (Hynes 1991: xii)—emerged some time after the war's end: "The Myth of the War was given its fullest definition in the years around the end of the Twenties, when the great war memoirs and novels ... were published" (Hynes 1991: xii). Virginia Woolf's *Mrs Dalloway* came out in 1925. Siegfried Sassoon's *Memories of a Fox-Hunting Man* in 1928, his *Memoirs of an Infantry Officer* in 1930, Radclyffe Hall's *The Well of Loneliness* in 1928, Robert Graves's *Good-bye to All That* in 1928, and Vera Brittain's *Testament of Youth* in 1933. It takes time for the imagination to engage with an event and come to terms with it. This means, however, that we are relying on *ex post facto* accounts—on imaginations which have already been distorted by the end of the war, its aftermath, and their consequent myths—for our sense of the *in medias* world. West conceived the plot of *The Return of the Soldier* in 1915 and the novel was all but finished in early 1916 (Rollyson 1995: 44). Written in the midst of the war by an acute mind grappling with immediate problems posed to both soldiers and civilians by the traumas and disruption of the war, *The Return of the Soldier* is propitiously situated to illuminate its problems and their consequences.[5]

The novel is about Chris Baldry, an upper-class soldier whose shell-shock causes him to forget fifteen years of his life. During these fifteen years his parents have died, he has taken over the family business, he has married, and his son has died. However, he remembers none of this and dwells in the halcyon days of a summer love affair with a lower-middle-class girl whose father owns an inn on a country island. The story is told by a Jamesian narrator, Chris's cousin Jenny, who lives with him and his wife Kitty. The novel is also very much about

Jenny's changing perceptions of Chris, Kitty, and Margaret, Chris's young love who has become a worn, poverty-stricken, middle-aged woman. *The Return of the Soldier* contributes to our understanding of the First World War and registers the importance of women's experience in our definitions of our modern culture and consciousness.

Although our twenty-first century interpretations of the Great War stress the war's brutality, soldiers' disillusionment, and an ironic stance toward existential problems, the art that emerged early in the war had not yet "learned" the "Myth of War." Hynes describes the early war novels that began "to appear early in 1915" (when West began her novel) as "recruiting tracts" (Hynes 1991: 43, 45) which celebrated the war: "It is the nature of war to diminish every value except war itself and the values war requires: patriotism, discipline, obedience, endurance" (Hynes 1991: 57). Grayzel reminds us that women's early war romances also promote the war and patriotic values. Nonetheless, like all of West's works, *The Return of the Soldier* subverts generic expectations to question and to criticize social norms. As our discussion will prove, the novel deplores the British values that led to the war and harshly judges people who subscribe to and perpetuate these values and their concomitant systems.

Critic Motley Deakin argues that the war is a "negative force" in *The Return of the Soldier* and that the novel is not a war novel. He dismisses the novel's treatment of the war because military scenes lack the prominence one expects in "war literature": "Despite its title, *The Return of the Soldier* does not give us any authentic sense of what war is about. ... For West, the war was a negative force that seems to be evoked simply to cause Chris's loss of memory. It was a contemporary convenience" (Deakin 1980: 132). Deakin and other critics discount *The Return of the Soldier*'s value as a war novel because of their "sense of what war is about"—which has been conditioned by the dominance of male authors and also by the priority given to battle experience—and also because war operates in the novel, as Deakin acknowledges, mostly as "a negative force." Jenny has several vivid dreams of Chris in battle, but aside from these, discussion of the actual war is little present. This should not be surprising: the story is really about absence—and primarily the absence that war creates.

In this sense, *The Return of the Soldier* conforms to many critics' sense that the "home front" and "military front" are separate zones. The war meant absence and emptiness to most women in Britain. Many husbands and sons were at the front and homes were empty. *The Return of the Soldier* begins with the theme of absence. It opens in the now empty, lifeless nursery that had once been filled with the activity of the Baldry's deceased child. Jenny's first reflections are on the irony between the beauty of the spring day and the emptiness of Jenny and Kitty's privileged lives because of Chris's absence:

> That day its beauty was an affront to me, because like most Englishwomen of my time I was wishing for the return of a soldier. Disregarding the national interest and everything except the keen prehensile gesture of our hearts towards him, I wanted to snatch my cousin Christopher from the wars. (*RS* 13)

Women's lives were empty with loss and waiting. The men's absence is more than physical because most women's identities depended upon the men in their lives. Without the roles of mother, wife, daughter, hostess, or housekeeper, many women had little left. If women's lives suffered a curious passiveness as servers in conventional Edwardian social life, this passivity was exacerbated by the war because it moved the focus of activity away from England (and home) to the war zone on the Continent. Hynes quotes Cicely Hamilton's description of the uselessness many women felt in their passivity:

> An idle, useless mouth,
> As cumbrous—nay, more cumbrous—than the dead ...
> That is my hurt—my burning, beating wound;
> That is the spear-thrust driven through my pride! ...
> Let me endure it then—I give my pride
> Where others give a life. (Hynes 1991: 93)

West portrays Jenny and Kitty's subordination to Chris in many ways. Jenny admits that Chris was "weighted by the needs of a mob of female relatives who were all useless either in the old way with antimacassars or in the new way with golf clubs" (*RS* 20–1).

The transcendent presence of the male signifier also accounts for what Deakin describes as the war's "negative presence" in this novel. A book written in 1915 and 1916 and published in 1918 does not need to make repeated direct references to the war because it was omnipresent at the time. The war is in everyone's minds. For example, Fussell describes "one of Kipling's most honorable and decent works, the two-volume history *The Irish Guards in the Great War* (1923) which is really a 'memorial to his dead son who had been in that unit'" (Fussell 1975: 171). Yet, "Kipling performs the whole job without mentioning his son, who appears only in the list of dead, wounded, and missing at the end together with hundreds of others." Just as Kipling's son, the real subject of his work, is barely mentioned, the war—which is the main subject of *The Return of the Soldier*—receives only passing reference.

West learned from Henry James that many crucial scenes and incidents are trivialized by representation and are better served by leaving them out and depicting their consequences or the characters' reactions to them. She says of Henry James,

> Certainly he invented a technical trick which in its way was as important as the discovery which Ibsen was making ... that if one had a really "great" scene one ought to leave it out and describe it simply by the full relation of its consequences. (*HJ* 95–6)

Another reason for the war's incidental presence is its unspeakableness. The horrors of the war left eyewitnesses speechless, unable to find in our traditional store of words signifiers equal to such unbelievable events. West's comments on May Sinclair's *A Journal of Impressions in Belgium* explain her own silence by implying that it would be offensive—even obscene—to elaborate upon these horrors: "The book [*A Journal of Impressions*] is given a solemnity by her sense that it is as indecent to intrude without cause upon the deathbed of Europe as it would be to intrude upon the deathbed of a neighbor" ("Miss Sinclair's Genius" *YR* 305). West's reticence and her refusal to adopt the "appropriate" reverence for patriotic values implicitly criticize the war.

The most obvious *absence* of the book and the ultimate declaration of the unspeakableness—indeed the unimaginability—of the war, is Chris's amnesia. This denial by someone as virtuous and upstanding as Chris is a definitive condemnation of the war: "His very loss of memory was a triumph over the limitations of language which prevent the mass of men from making explicit statements about their spiritual relationships" (*RS* 133).

West's war romance plot also contradicts generic expectations in order to underline the different priorities of her war novel. Grayzel describes some of the predictable plot lines and the predictable stock characters that emerge in early war romances. These works repeatedly condemn men who are "slackers," "shirkers," and "wasters" and refuse to enlist (Grayzel 1999: 24–5). Women's "war work" in these novels is to inspire these slackers to enlist. Grayzel explains that "the emotional work of loving the correct man so as to prompt him to correct actions was a constant refrain in the wartime romance novels" (Grayzel 1999: 26). In *The Return of the Soldier,* the heroic Chris—who has returned home from the war—is a potential "shirker" because of his shell-shock. Unlike the novelists that Hynes and Grayzel describe, West (through Jenny) praises Chris's rejection of his life as a soldier: "It became plain that if madness means liability to wild error about the world, Chris was not mad" (*RS* 133). Chris's "refusal to remember his prosperous maturity and his determined dwelling in the time of his first love ... showed him so much saner than the rest of us" (*RS* 134). All three women are complicit in deciding to bring Chris back to sanity and therefore conform to what Grayzel describes as "an important and repeated aspect of the British women's romance novel: the encouragement of women as crucial for men's participation in the war" (Grayzel 1999: 25). Nonetheless, Jenny and Margaret regret Chris's "draught of truth." Chris is rudely jolted back into reality rather than inspired by a beatified love. West is clearly writing a "counter-narrative" to the popular war romances of her day.

In denying fifteen years of his life, Chris explicitly rejects his wife Kitty for Margaret. The love triangle between Chris, Kitty, and Margaret allows West to explore the social and political causes of the war and also to critique the British class system. In many ways, Kitty and Margaret can symbolize two different worldviews. In simplest terms, Kitty stands for a "modern" materialistic worldview and Margaret for a "pre-modern" spiritual one. They also represent their two different classes.

Kitty is exquisitely beautiful. Jenny first describes her with the perfection of a "cover girl":

> And when I looked again I saw that her golden hair was all about her shoulders and that she wore over her frock a little silken jacket trimmed with rosebuds. She looked so like a girl on a magazine cover that one expected to find a large "7d" somewhere attached to her person. (*RS* 11)

To Kitty and Jenny this cultivated beauty—"whose law of life is grace" (*RS* 65)—is virtuous and makes them morally worthy. They create loveliness and adhere to rules of decorum in order to protect Chris and themselves from the unseemliness of nature—its hostility and cruelty. When Chris stumbles on the way to dinner, for example, "his hot consciousness of disorder" is redeemed by Kitty's "radiance" which is "a deep refreshment" (*RS* 57–8). This cultivation of grace is to them the essence of civilization. It gives their lives purpose and dignity.

Kitty and Jenny fill the void that Chris's absence creates through cultivating their private realm. Women have often compensated for their passivity in the public domain by a cultivation of the private life. Tylee feels that women's myths were transferred to the public sphere during the war, but West's portrait of Kitty and Jenny and British employment statistics prove that this is only partially true. According to Tylee,

> If we adapt the model used by Elaine Showalter in "Feminist Criticism in the Wilderness" (1981), we could say that women's writing of that period was not

> concerned with the "wild zone" of women's culture. Women were not then so concerned to express that imaginary area of their experience which was literally "no-man's land," off-limits to men and so outside the dominant culture. Rather their literature is concerned with women's entry into that exclusive part of the national culture which had previously been forbidden to women, all that area of public privilege and power to which men had access, and women did not, such as politics, the professions, skilled industrial work, sexual adventure. (Tylee 1990: 14)

Hynes contends that upper-class and upper-middle-class women were not as "activated" in the war by traditional male employment as myth would have it. Middle-class women, for example, did not "enter the labour market":

> Middle-class women were untrained to do any manual work, and they had been raised to think such work unsuitable for ladies. This did not change significantly during the war; statistics show that half of the ... women who came into industry—mainly munitions factories—during the war years left jobs in domestic service to do so. ... Most of the rest came from other kinds of factory work. (Hynes 1991: 91)

The Return of the Soldier refutes Tylee's claim and substantiates Hynes's argument. Jenny's, Kitty's, and Margaret's lives remain firmly rooted in their own women's sphere. We do not see any of these women outside of the home. Jenny's visions of the war are distinctively of "*No-Man's* Land," that marginal area between trenches where no soldiers dare venture. Even Jenny's imaginative engagements with the war exclude encounters with men. Although she sometimes adopts the same myths and tropes that men do in describing the First World War, West is intent on condemning the patriarchal Edwardian world—"that exclusive part of the national culture which had previously been forbidden to women." This book is firmly rooted in and promotes a feminist wilderness that is at odds with the "masculine" sphere.

Kitty and Jenny fill up the void in their lives through decorating and grooming the Baldry estate, Harrow-weald. Again Jenny's reflections explain that this is done in service of a male past or present:

> My eye followed the mellow brick of the garden wall through the trees, and I reflected that by the contriving of these gardens that lay, well-kept as a woman's hand, on the south side of the hill, Kitty and I had proved ourselves worthy of the past generation that had set the old house on this sunny ledge, overhanging and overhung by beauty. And we had done much for the new house. ... I was sure that we were preserved from the reproach of luxury because we had made a fine

> place for Chris, one little part of the world that was, so far as surfaces could make it so, good enough for his amazing goodness. (*RS* 15–16)

As in any logocentric, phallocentric system, the men have more "presence" in their "absence" than women ever have.

In describing Jenny's and Kitty's cultivation of their private realm which includes decorating the estate, West's story is typical of its contemporary war romances. However, readers of these romances would have learned to deplore such occupations as frivolous and self-centered in a wartime world. For example, the heroine in Jeanne Landre's *L'école des marraines* deplores the superficiality of women who could "still be amused" by non-wartime pursuits:

> She thought of other young, anguished spouses, of anxious mothers, or fiancées who dared no longer wait, of departed comrades, already mown down ... and she did not understand why some women could still be amused by everything, by nothing, like they had been in an era when the country was not in danger. (qtd Grayzel 1999: 32)

Because the story is told by a Jamesian narrator, cousin Jenny, the readers of *The Return of the Soldier* must do much of the work of interpretation. Jenny and Kitty believe that their attention to the beauty of the private realm is morally defensible, but that does not mean that West or her readers (or the general reading public) affirm Kitty and Jenny's values.

West's descriptions of the "deliberate delicacy of Kitty's car" (*RS* 101) and the forced beauty of Baldry Court make it clear that this beauty is superficial and contrived. It is unnatural and results in unnatural, false relationships. The description of Kitty's radiance as she waits for dinner on Chris's first evening home is telling—and again counters the tropes that Grayzel discovers in other early war romances. Kitty has dressed for dinner in an elegant white satin gown and is sitting by the hearth. The hearth is a repeated motif in early war novels.

> She frowned to see that the high lights on the satin shone scarlet from the fire, that her flesh glowed like a rose, and she changed her seat for a high-backed chair beneath the furthest candle sconce. There were green curtains close by, and now the lights on her satin gown were green like cleft ice. She looked cold as moonlight, as virginity, but precious; the falling candlelight struck her hair to bright, pure gold. So she waited for him. (*RS* 56–7)

Kitty's preoccupation with her own looks and with staging dinner—assuming the proper roles and giving the scene its proper look—leads her to shun the warmth (or passion) of the fire for a cold, perfect appearance. Kitty rejects "the hearth"—the locus of the security and safety of the home. This is a radical rejection in the context of the First World War when so many people were sacrificing for the preservation of the "hearth and home." Grayzel reminds us of the symbolic potential of the hearth in war literature in her description of Marcelle Tinayre's *La vieillée des armes* (1915). To Tinayre, women's "war effort" is different from men's "war effort," but not inferior: "Women's patriotism ... was 'not the same nature of that of men' because it was rooted not in the 'brutality of instinct' but in the love of '*hearth,* the husband, the child'" (Grayzel 1999: 26, emphasis added). Women similarly gain heroic stature in Ernest Stern's *Le baptême du courage* (1916) because of their dedication to preserving hearth and home. Stern's hero reflects, "However many sufferings and deprivations lie in wait for us, we will never know the long and powerful martyrdom of waiting in empty and abandoned *hearths*" (qtd Grayzel 1999: 34, emphasis added). In contrast, and in light of wartime attitudes described by Grayzel, Kitty's attempt to appear virginal and her valorization of her beauty above the warmth of the family hearth are reproachable. Grayzel's central point is that the war put the spotlight on women's role as mothers: "Women evaded their duty not by refusing to fight, but by refusing to produce future fighters" (Grayzel 1999: 2). Refusing to "be good mothers and send their sons to battle" is equivalent to "men refusing to fight" (Grayzel 1999: 38). Kitty—whose son, a potential soldier, has died—belies this expectation of what it means to be a good mother as the novel implies that she desires to seem "virginal" and not able to produce more offspring.

Kitty's emphasis on beauty, roles, and right behavior robs human relationships of true feeling. Jenny later describes "the blankness of [Chris's] eyes which saw ... Kitty ... as a stranger who had somehow become a decorative presence in his home and the orderer of his meals" (*RS* 133). And Chris remarks of Kitty, "[I remember her] in a sense. I know how she bows when you meet her in the street, how she dresses when she goes to church. I know her as one knows a woman staying in the same hotel" (*RS* 68). Chris's memories all depend on Kitty's social roles and do not include the intimacy one expects of a husband and wife. One wonders how much more he ever really knew Kitty.

Kitty's attitude toward Chris is materialistic and acquisitive. When she informs the psychiatrist Dr Anderson, "He [Chris] wished for nothing. He was fond of us, and he had a lot of money," it clearly does not occur to her that Chris could have other than material needs (*RS* 164). This materialistic attitude is revealed in her comment about the telegram Chris sent Margaret from the hospital: "If he could send that telegram he isn't *ours* any longer" (*RS* 39, emphasis added), and the "*possessive* fury" (*RS* 47, emphasis added) with which she bids that Chris be brought home. Instead of reacting to the revelations of his illness with concern or compassion, she responds with selfish resentment. One is reminded that "propriety" and "proprietary" have the same Latin root: *proprietat, proprietas.*

Margaret contrasts in every way with Kitty; this contrast makes it clear that what Chris "wished for" was a life of emotions and spirit instead of propriety. In her first appearance at Baldry Court, Margaret is an affront to Kitty and Jenny—and to their values. Her sickly yellow raincoat, her tawdry black plumes, and her cheap boots—"a spreading stain on the fabric of our life" (*RS* 37)—violate every principle they have dedicated themselves to and all the grace they have deliberately cultivated. Her "seamed red hand ... looked even more horrible [juxtaposed to their beauty] when she presently raised it to touch the glistening flowers of the pink azalea that stood on the table beside her" (*RS* 24–5). In spite of her physical repulsiveness, Margaret's "personality sound[s] through her squalor" even in our first encounter of her. "She lifted to Kitty a sallow and relaxed face whose expression gave me a sharp, pitying pang ... it was beautiful that so plain a woman should so ardently rejoice in another's loveliness" (*RS* 24). Although Jenny is initially disgusted by Margaret's shabbiness, she gradually comes to appreciate her kindness and her spirituality. The contrast between Kitty and Margaret is most explicit in Jenny's dream about Chris and an Olympian man behind the lines in France. Chris

> is looking down on two crystal balls. ... In one he sees Margaret; not in her raincoat and her nodding plumes but as she is transfigured in the light of eternity. Long he looks there; then drops a glance to the other, just long enough to see that in its depths Kitty and I walk in bright dresses through our glowing gardens. We had suffered no transfiguration, for we are as we are and there is nothing more to us. The whole truth about us lies in our material seeming. (*RS* 136–7)

Jenny later describes Margaret's greater depth through metaphors of radiance. Kitty is a "polished surface that reflected light, like a mirror hung opposite a window" and Margaret, "a lamp grimed by the smoke of careless use but still giving out radiance from its burning oil" (*RS* 155). Margaret's light is profound and stems from within, while Kitty's narcissistic beauty is superficial.

Margaret's greater depth results from and in a generosity that is the opposite of Kitty's materialistic acquisitiveness. As Jenny and Margaret enter Baldry Court for Margaret's first visit to Chris, Jenny's thoughts focus on Margaret's offense to the beauty of the estate: "Here we estimate only controlled beauty ... the wild ... must be delicate and decorated into felicity. Surely she must see that this was no place for beauty that has not been mellowed but lacerated by time, that no one accustomed to live here could help wincing at such external dinginess as hers" (*RS* 115). Margaret's thoughts are elsewhere, however: "She said, 'It's a big place. How poor Chris must have worked to keep it up'" (*RS* 115). Whereas Kitty felt Chris "wished for nothing," Margaret's first reaction to the magnificence of Chris's estate is pity and compassion.

Margaret's generosity is epitomized in the peace she bestows on Chris as he sleeps at her side on the hill:

> It was the loveliest attitude in the world. It means that the woman has gathered the soul of the man into her soul and is keeping it warm in love and peace so that his body can rest for a little time ... sleep was the least of her gifts to him. (*RS* 143–5)

Margaret's very being is an indictment of Kitty's and Jenny's devotion to the private sphere. West advocates a spiritual approach to the cultivation of the private sphere, rather than a materialistic, controlled approach.

The trauma of the war causes Chris to turn *from* Kitty *to* Margaret. Because of their materialistic values, Kitty and Jenny are convinced that when Chris sees Margaret who has been ravaged by poverty and by time, he will no longer love her. Jenny warns Chris, "She's seamed and scored and ravaged by squalid circumstance" (*RS* 90). Margaret's looks, however, are *immaterial* to Chris. When they meet, they embrace and "they stood with clasped hands, looking at one another (they looked straight, they looked delightedly!)." As Jenny reflects, "How entirely right Chris had been in his assertion that to lovers innumerable things do not matter" (*RS* 123). These things do not "matter" because theirs is a love of the heart and soul that does not depend upon material seeming.[6]

Chris's choice extends beyond a choice between Kitty and Margaret or a choice between two types of women. It is a choice made in an historical context. The war between the spiritual and the material was raging well before 1914 and is fundamental to modernism. The Great War, nonetheless, brought the conflict to a head. In 1900, W. B. Yeats describes the issues central to *The Return of the Soldier* in terms of the "divine life" and "our outer life." Using prophetic metaphors, he explains that

> because the divine life wars upon our outer life, and must needs change its weapons and its movements as we change ours, inspiration has come to them in beautiful shapes. The scientific movement brought with it a literature which was always tending to lose itself in externalities of all kinds, in opinion, in declamation, in picturesque writing, in word-painting or in ... an attempt "to build in brick and mortar inside the covers of a book." (Yeats 1961: 155)

This conflict between the "divine life" and "our outer life" is at the heart of many of the intellectual and esthetic movements of the modern era—such as symbolism and realism—and it also extends to social and political realms. Chris is, in essence, rejecting Yeats's "externalities of all kinds." On his first evening home, Jenny tries to convince Chris that fifteen years have passed, they have all aged, and he is married to Kitty. Chris "turned away with an assenting mutter. But I saw deep down in him, not to be moved by any material proof, his spirit was incredulous" (*RS* 69). Chris's spirit has rejected fifteen years and their physical realities and will accept only spiritual truths because of the horrors of the First World War. He, like Yeats, connects these horrors with "our outer life." This "outer life" has been shaped particularly by science and industrialism, forces that also shaped the ideology that sparked the war. When Chris renounces Kitty's acquisitive spirit, he is renouncing the imperialistic, acquisitive spirit that fueled the war. In an early essay, West describes these values and the society they inform as the "masculinist and capitalist world" (*YR* 247–8).

Chris's amnesia picks up on another trope familiar to First World War literature: the image of a dividing line or a gap. As Fussell explains, "Of course August 4, 1914, is the classical 'dividing line' but the image of time abruptly divided emerges everywhere" (Fussell 1975: 81). Hynes describes the image in the opening chapter of *Women in Love*:

> The two sisters discuss marriage, and find themselves "confronted by a void, a terrifying chasm, as if they had looked over the edge." ... All visions of the future in the book have that fearful quality, expressed in similar images, as an abyss, a chasm, a void. (Hynes 1991: 137)

Like these other gaps, Chris's amnesia marks the war as the dividing line between a time of virtue and innocence and that of disillusionment and bitter wisdom.

Since he was wounded in the summer of 1916 and recuperated in a hospital in Boulogne, West implies that Chris was wounded in the Battle of the Somme. Many historians contend that the carnage and horrors of the Battle of the Somme transformed British soldiers' view of the war. According to Fussell, "The innocent army fully attained the knowledge of good and evil at the Somme on July 1, 1916.[7] That moment, one of the most interesting in the whole long history of human disillusion, can stand as the type of all the ironic actions of the war" (Fussell 1975: 29). *The Return of the Soldier* supports this sense of the Battle of the Somme and declares that it was a turning point for those on the home front as well.

If the Battle of the Somme was the trigger to Chris's recognition of the malevolence of war and the society that spawned it, the source of this recognition was much deeper. Chris forgets not two, not six, not ten, but fifteen years. This is a radical rejection. And it says that innocence and virtue were lost, not, as Fussell maintains, in 1914 when the war started, or in 1910 as modernists, following Virginia Woolf's lead,[8] suggest, but in 1901. Chris rejects the war and his wife (whom he married in 1910), but also two historical periods: the Edwardian and Georgian eras—an entire century. (Queen Victoria died in 1901 and Edward in 1910.)

The source of Chris's trauma lies fifteen years before the action of this novel. Misha Kavka focuses on Dr Anderson's discussion of Chris's past to find the source of his trauma. Kavka recognizes that the war trauma that caused Chris's amnesia is not the "originary" traumatic event. If it were, Chris would have forgotten two years, not fifteen: "Only a psychoanalyst, in this case a literary representative of Freud, would look past the precipitating event of a war trauma and search instead for a 'suppressed wish'"(Kavka 1998: 159). The revelation of Oliver's death triggers both Dr Anderson and Margaret to look beyond the war for the source of Chris's trauma. Kavka argues that "the death of the child" is the "proper" precipitating trauma (Kavka 1998: 159).

Nonetheless, Oliver died only five years before the action of this novel. The fact of Oliver's existence is staggering enough to shake Chris out of amnesia, but the loss of fifteen years points to a different originary trauma. Chris's denial of fifteen years blames the prewar years for the catastrophe of the war. Henry James too implicates the prewar period in a letter he wrote on the first day of the war. James implies that the industrial, economic, and social developments that followed the Victorian era caused the war:

> The plunge of civilization into this abyss of blood and darkness by the wanton feat of these two infamous autocrats is a thing that so gives away the whole long age during which we have supposed the world to be, with whatever abatement, gradually bettering, that to have to take it all now for what the treacherous years were all the while really making for and meaning is too tragic for words. (James 1920: 398; qtd Hynes 1991: 2)

Like James, West accuses "the treacherous years," the years before the war, for its catastrophe. Sir Edward Grey intoned at the beginning of the First World War, "The lamps are going out all over Europe. We shall not see them lit again in our time" (qtd Hynes 1991: 3). In *The Return of the Soldier,* West claims that the lamps had been out for fifteen years.

Chris is jarred into "reality" by a jersey and ball that belonged to Oliver, and not, for example, by the child's picture. In choosing the jersey and ball, West blames England's upper class and their values for Chris's trauma. Oliver's jersey and ball are metonymies for the British public schools and their "sporting" spirit. Fussell describes the metaphors from sports that permeated war rhetoric. The Battle of Ypres was called the "Race to the Sea," for example, "suggesting that what was happening was not too far distant from playing games, running races, and competing in a thoroughly decent way" (Fussell 1975: 9). So deeply inscribed was this equation between sports and war that "the English young man's fondness for [football] was held to be a distinct sign of his natural superiority over his German counterpart" (Fussell 1975: 26). The British carried their sporting spirit so far that they commenced an attack by kicking a football toward the enemy line. This obsession with sports betrays the war's roots in an upper-class public school, masculine ideology which Chris rejects. "Chris," Jenny asserts, in the opening of the novel, "was not like other city men" (*RS* 19). Kavka discounts Dr Anderson's questions about Chris's relationship with his parents, but these questions reveal the source of Chris's troubles. We discover that "his mother was not his sort. She wanted a stupid son who would have been satisfied with shooting" (*RS* 167). Even before the war, Chris had rejected his class and its values.

A condemnation of the "masculinist and capitalist world" grounds West's early feminism. Although this world is essentially patriarchal, *The Return of the Soldier* reveals that even in its beginnings, West's feminism did not insist on simplistic sexist binaries. "Life ought not to be divided into watertight compartments," she asserts in an essay of 1912 (*YR* 111). As West's early journalism explains, women such as Kitty can contribute to or perpetuate this masculinist and capitalist system. She remarks in a *Clarion* article of 1914, "One of the chief dangers to feminism [is] that women may learn to play the fool as successfully as men" (*YR* 154). In fact, part of the malignity of this world is that it can set women against each other. *The Return of the Soldier* again counters commonplace myths about the unifying powers of the war by showing the war—and the ideology that shapes it—pitting women against each other, instead of bringing them together for mutual support. On the other hand, men such as Chris can resist this masculinist and capitalist world. When they do, however, they usually prove "unmasculine" in any traditional Edwardian or Victorian sense.[9] Chris is distinguished by his sensitivity, not his courage. Chris's illness—shell-shock—was often associated with hysteria and considered feminine. Sue Thomas recounts that "witnesses before the War Office Committee of Inquiry drew parallels between shell shock and what one witness summed up as the 'usual feminine outbursts of hysteria'" (Thomas 1987: 50).

Chris rejects his upper-class wife and her values as well as his upper-class education and its training. He chooses instead a lower-middle-class woman and her generosity and spirituality. In spite of Jenny's appreciation of Margaret's character and her recognition that in Chris's rejection of fifteen years, Chris has attained a superior "sanity" that belies the values of their upper-middle-class world, all three women decide, "The truth's the truth ... and he must know it" (*RS* 184). Using Oliver's jersey and ball, Margaret "brings [Chris] from various outlying districts of the mind to the normal" (*RS* 168).

The ending of *The Return of the Soldier* is ambiguous and controversial. Margaret and Jenny decide to jolt Chris's memory by reminding him of his lost son. Some critics feel that returning Chris to sanity compromises the values the novel has promoted. Deakin and Tylee both see the ending of the novel as an abdication to patriarchal, materialist values. Deakin dismisses it as "stock formulae" (Deakin 1980: 132) and Tylee calls it "a classic example of the way in which popular literature attempts to reconcile the implicit contradictions of false consciousness" (Tylee 1990: 143). She believes that "Chris's return to sanity is a resumption of the materialistic values of the bourgeois marriage, which have never really been at risk. ... The war is never questioned" (Tylee 1990: 145). Douglas Mao also reads the ending as an affirmation of the war. Critics fail to see the conclusion's irony partly because they confuse Jenny (the unreliable narrator) with West. Jenny has accepted Chris's fate, but West has not. West's condemnation of Chris's "return" to normality is clear in her description of him when he approaches the house. "He was looking up under his brows at the overarching house as though it were a hated place to which, against all his hopes, business had forced him to return" (*RS* 187). The word "business" blames the capitalist forces that caused the war for Chris's regrettable return to sanity. Kitty rejoices that Chris is "cured," but Jenny reminds us that the "cure" will lead him "back to that flooded trench in Flanders under that sky more full of flying death" (*RS* 187).[10]

Part 2 Pastoral

Even though West—and her readers—regret Chris's return to sanity, the novel's ending can be disappointing, even disheartening. One of the reasons that critics misunderstand *The Return of the Soldier* is that they fail to recognize its "hybrid" nature. West's feminist critique of the First World War is clear if one interprets *The Return of the Soldier* as a subversive war romance. The novel, however, is more than this. West believes that art—especially literature—can be transformative. Her first complete novel is no exception. West's war novel combines with a pastoral to condemn the Great War and the values that led to it, but also to give us hope for a different world order. The pastoral carries readers beyond the impasse they feel at the end of the novel to a revelation of the possibilities inherent in a transformation of this world.

The pastoral is one of the oldest literary genres or modes. Its critical history is equally long and complicated. Most claim that the pastoral began with the Greek poets Hesiod and Theocritus and was further modified by the Roman poet Virgil. Sir Philip Sidney and Edmund Spenser were two early British practitioners of the mode. Many critics treat William Shakespeare's pastoral plays (*As You Like It*, *Midsummer's Night Dream*, and *The Tempest*) as the high point of the genre.

The pastoral is variously defined by recurrent stock features or—more liberally—according to recurrent and more general dynamics or attitudes. Some of its stock features include the following: shepherds as main characters, a Golden Age, a *locus amoenus*, and the personification of nature. Some of the broader themes or dynamics of the pastoral include an idealization of nature, the elevation of the humble or the mundane, a nostalgia for country ways, placing the complex into the simple, a unification of opposites, a proletarian spirit, a tension between the country and the city, and a highly artificial natural world.

Almost all of West's works valorize nature and manipulate conventional attitudes toward and literary interpretations of nature. *The Return of the Soldier* exploits two different pastoral traditions: a nostalgia for rural life typical of many war novels and a Renaissance and Enlightenment pastoral garden.

Part 2A Pastoral as nostalgia for rural life

Fussell's examination of war literature finds frequent occurrences of what he calls "the pastoral." Fussell uses the term "pastoral" liberally. His recognition of the pastoral strain in many works of the Great War, nonetheless, enlarges our understanding of the literature of this war and of the British culture. Fussell devotes a chapter of *The Great War and Modern Memory* to "both a highly sophisticated literary pastoralism and what we can call a unique actual ruralism" (Fussell 1975: 231). Fussell cuts a broad swath. Descriptions of nature in everything from Edmund Spenser's *Prothalamion* to William Wordsworth's transcendentalism to the British periodical *Country Life* fall under his sway as "typical" of the English elevation of and nostalgia for nature: "What other literature has in it a Herrick, a Cowper, a Clare, a Cobbett, a Wordsworth, or a Blunden—all types and classes embrace it" (Fussell 1975: 233). For Fussell the pastoral provides a counter-narrative to the war that measures the war's extent and protects against the war's violence: "Recourse to the pastoral is an English mode of both fully gauging (through ironic contrast) the calamities of the Great War and imaginatively protecting oneself against them" (Fussell 1975: 235). West employs the kind of nostalgia for ruralism that Fussell describes in her descriptions of Chris's estate Harrow-weald and the family manor, Baldry Court. The novel contrasts the "old" Baldry Court and the "new" Baldry Court. The old Baldry Court is the estate as Chris remembers it when Chris and Jenny were young; the new Baldry Court is the estate that Kitty has renovated with the "knowing wink of the manicurist" (*RS* 12). In her treatment of Baldry Court, West is drawing on a time-honored pastoral tradition of a paean of the English country estate—as established in the seventeenth century by Ben Jonson in "To Penshurst."

Chris finds himself lost and uncomfortable in his own home because Kitty redecorated Baldry Court after their marriage and he does not remember these changes. The new Baldry Court is an elegant commodity, the product of "architects who had not so much the wild eye of the artist as the knowing wink of the manicurist, and between them they massaged the dear old place into matter for innumerable photographs in the illustrated papers" (*RS* 12). These contrivances rob Baldry Court of spirit and make it pure decorative matter which recall West's *Clarion* description of the sterility of the rich woman: "brittle beautiful things" (*RS* 15). Jenny comments upon Baldry Court's denial of the natural in her description of the border of scillas and crocuses which line the driveway:

> There is no aesthetic reason for that border; the common outside looks lovelier where it fringes the road with dark gorse and rough amber grasses. Its use is purely philosophic; it proclaims that here we estimate only controlled beauty, that the wild will not have its way within our gates, that it must be made delicate and decorated into felicity. (*RS* 115)

The scilla is native to southwestern Russia, the Caucasus, and Turkey. The crocus is native to southern Europe, North Africa, the Middle East, and islands in the Aegean. With its cultivated flowers of foreign origin, the new Baldry Court "exerts its will" over nature and forces it under control: this is the imperialistic, domineering philosophy that brought on the war. The new Baldry Court is a product of industrialism and "business"—all that Kitty embodies in the novel. Debra Rae Cohen reminds us that the Baldry's money has been gained through industrialism and business. (Chris was sent off to rescue the family's imperialist endeavor in mines in Mexico.) Jenny reveals the threat inherent in this philosophy in the contrast between the untamed nature beyond Baldry Court and the estate's artificial beauty:

> The house lies on the crest of Harrow-weald, and from its windows the eye drops to miles of emerald pastureland lying wet and brilliant under a westward line of sleek hills blue with distance and distant woods, while nearer it ranges the suave decorum of the lawn and the Lebanon cedar whose branches are like *darkness made palpable,* and the *minatory gauntnesses* of the topmost pines in the wood that breaks downward. (*RS* 12–13, emphasis added)[11]

The suave decorum of Edwardian manners is lifeless, evil, and threatening. Jenny makes this clear in the parallel she draws between the crocuses, the larch, and the searchlights of the war:

> Why had modern life brought forth these horrors that make the old tragedies seem no more than nursery shows? Perhaps it is that adventurous men have too greatly changed the outward world which is life's engenderment. There are towns now, and even the trees and flowers are not as they were; the crocuses on the lawn ... should have pierced turf on Mediterranean cliffs; the golden larch beyond should have cast its long shadows on little yellow men as they crossed a Chinese plain. And the sky also is different. Behind Chris's head, as he halted at the open window, a searchlight turned all ways in the night like a sword brandished among the stars. (*RS* 63–4)

The "foreignness" of the crocuses and the larch emphasize their artificiality and their alienation and also the acquisitive impulses behind imperialism. The sword-like searchlight explicitly connects "modern life's horrors" and the war. By comparing the new Baldry Court to the old Baldry Court we can measure the corrupting influence of modernity; or we can find out, as James put it in his comments on the outbreak of the war, "what the treacherous years were all the while really making for and meaning."

Since Chris is the novel's hero, his rejection of the new Baldry Court indicts it. He refused to identify with it even before the war and his traumatic injury. Dr Anderson reminds Kitty and Jenny that "the reason the War Office didn't wire to you when he was wounded was that he had forgotten to register his address" (*RS* 165). Chris's affinity with the old Baldry Court, however, suggests that the "dear old place" built "before modern life brought forth these horrors" had values and integrity. Chris's reaction to Baldry Court on his first night back suggests the true nature of the renovations: "[Chris] looked up the staircase and would have gone up had I [Jenny] not held him back. For the little room in the south wing with the fishing-rods and the old books went in the rebuilding, absorbed by the black and white magnificence that is Kitty's bedroom" (*RS* 53). In casting aside the fishing rods and the old books, twentieth-century industrialism destroyed nature and learning. Chris is baffled and appalled by the new house. "This house," he notices upon first arriving, "is different" (*RS* 54). And Jenny comments, "If the soul has to stay in the coffin till the lead is struck asunder, in its captivity it speaks with such a voice." Chris's voice registers the shock of the devastation that the masculine and capitalist ideology has wreaked upon the world because his spirit is in the world of the old Baldry Court (and Monkey Island). Jenny's reflections continue and she remarks, "Strangeness had come into the house and everything was appalled by it, even time." The strangeness is the dissonance between Chris's perspective gained from the war and the values of the twentieth century. Jenny's observations of Chris's attraction to the old things echo Henry James's realization that the epoch preceding the war had been false and had led to the war:

> Whenever he thought himself unobserved he looked at the things that were familiar to him. ... He would glance sideways at the old oak paneling. ... It was his furtiveness that was heartrending; it was as though he were an outcast and we who loved him stout policemen. Was Baldry Court so sleek a place that the unhappy felt offenders there? Then we had all been living wickedly and he too. (*RS* 59)

Chris is nostalgic for eighteenth-century and nineteenth-century values that prevailed before "strangeness had come into the house" and the modern world partook of "minatory darkness." The descriptions of landscapes in *The Return of the Soldier* condemn the twentieth century as exploitative and power-hungry. However, the descriptions of the estate's grounds named "Harrow-weald" implicate the upper class for centuries of exploitation. As Jenny reflects, "Then we had all been living wickedly and he too." "Weald" means a "heavily wooded area: forest" or "a wild or uncultivated area." "Harrow" means "to pillage or plunder" or "to cultivate with a harrow ... an implement set with spikes, spring teeth, or disks used primarily for pulverizing and smoothing the soil." Nature at the Baldry estate has been "pulverized" even as it was "smoothed."

The contrast between Kitty and Margaret is an implicit condemnation of the British class system. West's use of the conventions of a war romance lends itself to this censure. Analyzing the novel's manipulation of pastoral conventions emphasizes the class critique implicit in the contrasting descriptions of the two women. This is no sentimental celebration of the poor, however. West makes the misery of the poverty that wears down the poor clear in her portrait of both Margaret and Wealdstone where Margaret lives. "Wealdstone" implies a hardened or reified wilderness presumably due to the poverty of the suburb. The similarities and the differences between Harrow-weald and Wealdstone censor the upper class. And, of course, Margaret does not really "belong" to Wealdstone. She "belongs" to Monkey Island.

West describes rich and poor women in a 1912 *Clarion* article. Both types of women are "failures," but she clearly blames the upper class for the degradation of the poor:

> Both [rich and poor women] are failures. The rich woman is the most expensive luxury the world has indulged in. She is the most idle human being that has ever secured the privilege of existence, and, with her furs and jewels and silks from strange places, commands more service than any emperor of the past. And her achievements are nothing. Art and science are beyond her grasp, and her growing sterility stultifies the last reason for her dependence. Perhaps she feels the tragedy of her incompleteness, but luxury has bred a hard pride into her.
>
> And hard work has made the poor woman ugly and clumsy. The working woman, whom childbearing and continual drudging have made a bruised and withered thing at forty-five, feels herself an offence against beauty and life. She is too weak, too tired to shift the blame to those who ought to bear it, and feels humiliated. (*YR* 130)

If *The Return of the Soldier* is read as a war romance, it is a scathing critique of the Great War and the social, economic, and political values which led to the war. West's subversive war romance valorizes spirituality and deplores materialism within an implicit criticism of the British class system. If the war romance reading expands to include a nostalgia for rural ways and values, the novel's critique of "modern" values and its condemnation of British classism are much more explicit. While condemning the "modern" world, West's depiction of the Baldry estate and its grounds further emphasizes her critique of the class system. It is not just the last fifteen years that have been "horrific." Harrow-weald has been exploitative since its inception. Harrow-weald is a metonomy for the British upper-middle class and its values. As I said, Cohen reminds us that the Baldrys are not an aristocratic family with landed estates, but rather members of an industrial and business class that is in its own way more exploitative than the landed gentry. This sense of the war as a result of an inequitable social structure was intensified by the growing division between businessmen at home and soldiers at the front. W. H. Auden remarked that "World War I was a retribution visited upon Western Europe for the sins and omissions of its ruling class, for which not only they, but also the innocent conscripted millions on both sides, must suffer" (Auden 1961: 3).

William Empson captures the importance of class to the pastoral in his classic study *Some Versions of the Pastoral* which was inspired by Empson's determination to explore the possibility of a proletarian literature. Empson declares that "good proletarian literature is usually Covert Pastoral" (Empson 1974: 6). Although general, Empson's analysis of the pastoral can help delimit Fussell's discussion of the pastoral. Empson argues that humble figures in pastoral (e.g. shepherds) meet more sophisticated figures and that a better understanding of both classes results. Empson's approach would highlight the importance of Monkey Island in *The Return of the Soldier.* Upper-middle-class Chris meets lower-middle-class Margaret on Monkey Island in a harmonious relationship whose "utter difference was a healing, and [they] settled down happily in a green silence" (*RS* 103).

Part 2B Renaissance pastoral

West turns to the conventions of a Renaissance or Enlightenment pastoral in her portrait of Monkey Island. The use of the Renaissance pastoral underlines even more the novel's critique of class systems and also reveals the transformative intentions of West's novel. The features of the pastoral on Monkey Island differ from the features of rural nostalgia in Baldry Court in crucial ways. The old Baldry Court provides an escape from and a measure of the "modern" world. Monkey Island provides a transformative "pastoral sojourn" that Michael Squires describes as "at bottom ... not an *escape* from, but an oblique *exploration* of the world" (Squires 1974: 8, emphasis added).[12]

Monkey Island has many features of Renaissance pastorals. For example, they usually feature a *locus amoenus,* a pleasant place in a rural or wilderness setting. Nature in this setting is both "natural" and the height of artifice.

David Young describes "the heart's forest" in Shakespeare where "so closely are nature and art intertwined ... that to speak of one is to speak of the other" (Young 1972: 188); "subjectivity, artificiality, and mannerism were their stock in trade" (Young 1972: 31). Harold E. Toliver explains that "pastoral nature is more ceremonial than useful; it has no need of planting, cultivation, or harvest, and its periodic renewal is less economic than symbolic or miraculous" (Toliver 1971: 4). Prospero's island in *The Tempest* or the magical forest in *A Midsummer's Night Dream* are classic examples of this pastoral space where nature is idealized or enchanted. Naïve or humble people of unusual sensitivity and perception usually inhabit this space. The *locus amoenus* is a transitional space where opposites conjoin harmoniously. Young describes the tripartite structure of most pastorals: "The pattern ... begins with one or more groups of characters who leave the normal world ... to take up residence in a rural or wilderness setting, and ends with their restoration and return" (Young 1972: 20). The "sojourn" offers a "perspective on sophisticated life" and results in a "reassessment of values and a reorientation towards society" (Toliver 1971: 9). For example, Shakespeare's characters are transformed by their experiences on Prospero's magical island in *The Tempest* or the fantastic forest with its fairy inhabitants in *Midsummer's Night Dream*. These characters recognize the magical elements of their experiences, but they return to the "real world" with a new perspective and a commitment to the ideals of virtue and social harmony enshrined in their pastoral visits. Thomas McFarland comments on what he calls the "necessity" of pastoral ideals as a virtuous "goal for struggling mortals": "So the pastoral ideal reveals itself as something far more necessary than a merely historical tradition in literature. ... It represents the deepest authentication of the meaning of human hope" (McFarland 1972: 159).

Monkey Island in *The Return of the Soldier* resembles these transformative and magical Shakespearean islands and forests. Jenny remarks that both Chris and Margaret "spoke of it as though it were not a place, but a magic state" (*RS* 102). It was his realization that he had been living falsely that sent Chris back to Monkey Island. In trying to persuade Chris that he is married to Kitty and that fifteen years have passed, Jenny inquires of Chris, "Tell me what seems real to you" (*RS* 69). He replies, "Why, Monkey Island's real" (*RS* 70).

As a young man, Chris sought out the simple truths of Monkey Island after his exams at college. Margaret's account stresses his sophistication: "Before the afternoon was out he had snared them all with his silken net of his fine manners" (*RS* 105). Margaret's purity and white dresses suggest the innocence of a shepherdess. Monkey Island is an idealized pastoral world where social class does not matter. The island represents a naturalness and innocence, a generosity and virtue which industrialism and capitalism have since destroyed. It contrasts in many ways with Baldry Court. One reaches it by a field path through a meadow and past cows. Indigenous trees such as alder, poplar, walnut, beech, and hawthorne and untamed animals such as ducks and rabbits flourish there in rich and disordered profusion.[13] It is a "gentle jungle" which refuses to be cultivated or domesticated. It and its inhabitants have the uncorrupted innocence typical of the pastoral which resists civilization's intrusions: "Margaret would sit quiet, round-eyed at the world's ways, and shy" (*RS* 76). By having it built in the eighteenth century, West is explicit about its connection with an earlier, premodern order:

> The third Duke of Marlborough had built it for a "folly," and perching there with nothing but a line of walnut trees and a fringe of lawn between it and the fast full shining Thames it had a grace and silliness that belonged to the eighteenth century. (*RS* 72–3)[14]

Unlike the "deliberate delicacy of Kitty's car" and the contrived, commercial beauty of Baldry Court, this grace and silliness are not forced—they are capricious and natural, deliberately non-utilitarian.

Chris turns naturally to this pastoral world. Monkey Island as well as Margaret obsesses him. Even in the hospital his mind turned to the island's wildlife. He betrays himself during his first dinner at Baldry Court: "'Funny thing. ... All the time I was at Boulogne I wanted to see a kingfisher. That blue, scudding down a stream. Or a heron's flight round a willow.' ... He checked himself suddenly; his head fell forward on his chest" (*RS* 60). The island's beneficent environment nourishes his spiritual love for Margaret which denies the practical and material aspects of life that constitute "business" and war. Jenny recounts, "That he loved her [Margaret], in this twilight [on Monkey Island] which obscured all the physical details which he adored seemed to him a guarantee that theirs was a changeless love which would persist if she were old or maimed or disfigured" (*RS* 78). In spite of the crystalline quality of this small masterpiece, Jenny's portrait of Margaret in *The Return of the Soldier* can seem hyperbolic or sentimental. If one thinks of this setting as a pastoral Golden Age, then this explains the idealized depiction of Margaret and we accept that "she is charity and love itself" (*RS* 79).

Chris also turns to the island's harmony which the grandeur of Baldry Court lacks. Things live at peace with one another. The last day in his memory epitomizes this harmonious reconciliation:

> The whole world seemed melting into light. Cumulus clouds floated very high, like lumps of white light against a deep, glowing sky, and dropped dazzling reflections on the beaming Thames. The trees moved not like timber shocked by wind, but floatingly, like weeds at the bottom of a well of sunshine. (*RS* 79)

The world merges harmoniously together here. Clouds high in the sky are reflected in the depths of the river and are equally brilliant in both domains. Trees participate in the characteristics of the water and clouds around them as they move "floatingly." The oxymoron "a well of sunshine"—which concludes the passage—combines depth, darkness, height, and light with joyous ease. This kind of synesthesia is not possible at Baldry Court or in the Edwardian system that is marked by opposition and division. Margaret and Kitty will always stand at odds; the material will not be able to combine with the spiritual; rich and poor are separated; men's and women's interests clash; young and old are in opposition; indeed, all contraries feud.

The pastoral allows the amalgamation of dualities which jar stridently in the masculinist and capitalist world because of the pastoral's essential generosity which does not impose itself like the world of business. Jenny senses this when she imagines Chris "who would have talked as he loved to do when he looked at leisure on a broad valley, about ideas which he had to exclude from his ordinary hours lest they should break the power of business over his mind" (*RS* 128). The pastoral essence has been destroyed by this "power of business," but it is not exclusive to Monkey Island. It can exist in this broad valley, and Chris and Margaret create their own pastoral even at Baldry Court. Chris instinctively goes to the "pond on the hill's edge" (*RS* 88) his first morning home because it is a spot that refused to be cultivated—"everywhere but this wet intractable spot bore the marks of Kitty's genius" (*RS* 89). Chris and Margaret retreat here every day. This is where they create their own pastoral, their own globe of peace "as in a crystal sphere" where Margaret's generous spirit prevails. The magic moment on the hill discussed earlier is a pastoral moment. Jenny compares the lovers' bodies to

> kneeling worshippers, their bodies bent stiffly and reluctantly and yet with abandonment as though to represent the inevitable bending of the will to a purpose outside the individual, or when under any sky one sees a mother with her child in her arms. (*RS* 143)

The "abandonment" and unselfish release are essential to the natural world of pastoral. Commenting on the peacefulness of the lovers' merged souls which results from Margaret's generosity,[15] Jenny says,

> That is a great thing for a woman to do. I know there are things at least as great for those women whose independent spirits can ride fearlessly and with interest outside the home park of their personal relationships, but independence is not the occupation of most of us. What we desire is greatness such as this which had given sleep to the beloved. (*RS* 144)

The choice of metaphor in this description of pastoral relationships is apt: human relationships should be a "park"; not a "mansion" or even a "garden," but in fact a pastoral: a natural environment enriched by, but not oppressed by, human cultivation.

Human beings have intervened in a park and they are also very much part of the pastoral. West does not want a "wilderness of personal relations." When Fussell discusses the First World War's authors' use of the pastoral, he sometimes confuses the use of pastoral conventions with an unalloyed celebration of nature. Many writers—especially under the influence of nineteenth-century Romantic poets—have tended to do the same. (There is a tacit implication that the Golden Age existed.) But this is false to the spirit of the pastoral. Monkey Island is not a Rousseauian (or even a Wordsworthian) worship of nature. As *The Princeton Encyclopedia of Poetry and Poetics* explains, the pastoral includes artifice: "The pastoral imitates rural life, usually the life of an imaginary Golden Age. ... Only when poetry ceases to imitate ordinary rural life does it become distinctively pastoral."[16] Monkey Island is not a wilderness, but rather a gentle jungle with its fair share of artifice. It was, after all, built as a folly and Chris and Margaret's climactic love scene takes place in "a small Greek temple, looking very lovely in the moonlight" (*RS* 85). West's deliberate implementation of many pastoral conventions, such as the symbolic use of flowers and the personification of nature[17] also draws attention to the artificiality of her creation.

In contrasting Monkey Island with Baldry Court, West is not juxtaposing civilization and wilderness or art and nature, nor recommending one over the other. While she celebrates the island's wild abundance, for example, she stresses that it was fabricated in the eighteenth century, the most "civilized" and conventional era of English history (which revered Classical Greece and Rome). The pastoral contains these antinomies. The pastoral offers an alternative to the compelled "brittle" order that modern civilization has imposed upon nature's disorder.[18] Capitalism has forced and distorted nature's capacities without redeeming them. In trying to control and master its inevitable flux and disorder, it has only intensified its destructive fury and the preeminence of matter. West stresses the artistic as well as the natural aspects of Monkey Island to insist that it is a product of the imagination working in harmony with nature. The pastoral is an imaginative vision that combines matter—the natural world—and the spirit.

It is an artistic creation whose purpose is to transform humans. Prospero's art in Shakespeare's *The Tempest*—which harnesses both Ariel and Caliban—is paradigmatic of the pastoral. Prospero and Shakespeare both create art—plays and islands—which order and interpret nature and help their characters and their audiences understand the real world they live in. Commenting on the masque that Prospero produces for Ferdinand and Miranda, Young emphasizes the parallels between actors and audience in *The Tempest*: "We recall how Prospero's shows tend to blur the line between actor and spectator" (Young 1972: 190). The characters in Shakespeare's play are compared to the real world audience throughout the play. The goal is transformation of the characters and of the audience:

> All the characters who are washed ashore ... undergo an experience of self-knowledge, which may or may not change them. Any given audience is in a sense washed ashore. ... In both cases the experience will be illusory—the result of art, shadowy, an insubstantial pageant—but that will not make it less valuable. (Young 1972: 190)

West also aims for a parallel transformation between the characters in *The Return of the Soldier* and its audience. She has created an island which orders nature—albeit benignly and generously—to help her readers understand the real world they live in. Monkey Island's role in *The Return of the Soldier* is similar to Prospero's island in *The Tempest.* The young Chris was transformed by Monkey Island and Margaret's spirituality and love. Then fifteen years later, Chris and Margaret both become pastoral characters in the novel's account of Chris's return. Margaret is the pure and ideal shepherdess and Chris becomes a humble pastoral character in the tradition of Bottom of *Midsummer Night's Dream.* Empson stresses the importance of a "mystical respect for poor men, fools, and children" in the pastoral's humble setting (Empson 1974: 21). Jenny is transformed—in her own way—by "Monkey Island" as it is embodied in Chris and Margaret's story. West wants her readers to identify with Jenny and to imagine a world order in which humans integrate, share, and participate with nature and with each other.

West's attitude toward the war and its causes in this novel is typical of her stance toward the central social issues of her time. For example, in demanding suffrage she insists that one cannot "superimpose the emancipation of women on the social system as one sticks a halfpenny stamp on a postcard" (*YR* 111). Nothing less than a new social system is necessary. She announces her transformative aims in an early article that blames evil systems, not evil individuals for the tragedy of modern life (*YR* 210). If the war is going to end and people are to live in peace and harmony with each other, nothing less than a new social system will be required. This social system will demand a new imaginative vision of its citizens—which West delineates in the details of her pastoral.

By subverting many of the conventions of a traditional war novel, West condemns the values that have led to the Great War and that prevail in early twentieth-century society. By combining this subversive war romance with two versions of the pastoral, West places her readers in a generic "contact zone" where they interpret the novel according to the conventions of war novels and also according to West's use of a nostalgia for rural life and its values and West's creation of a Renaissance pastoral that demands transformation of its world, its characters, and its readers. The "contact zone" resembles a Renaissance pastoral in that clarity and change emerge from confusion.

The novel's ironic ending and the reader's regret that Chris must know the truth insist on a new world. That the world in 1918 is inadequate—and that West would like to distance herself (if not Jenny) from it—is partly evident by the inadequacies of all the women characters in *The Return of the Soldier.* Neither Kitty nor Margaret are apt or workable models or ideals of female identity. Jenny—who reconciles some qualities of the two extremes that Kitty and Margaret represent—comes closer to a conceivable model of womanhood. But either she or her world are indelibly flawed: she remains "unattached" to anyone and even more "parasitic" than the other women. There is no depiction of a woman who in any way resembles Rebecca West herself or the type of woman that she was championing in her feminist essays of this time. Like the shell-shocked Chris, such a person could not survive in the society that *The Return of the Soldier* portrays.

A full vision of West's work requires a serious consideration of the pastoral and its potential. West uses the pastoral in order to make radical social commentary palatable. Other works critical of the war were being censored by the Defence of the Realm Act (Grayzel 1999). The pastoral tradition has long been a mode where "you can say everything about complex people by a complete consideration of simple people" (Empson 1974: 11). Because it is not an "elevated" mode, its audience is not as threatened by potentially subversive claims. The Renaissance scholar Puttenham commented on this capacity of the pastoral: "under the vaile of homely persons, and in rude speeches to insinuate and glaunce at greater matters, and such as perchance had not been safe to have disclosed in any other sort" (Puttenham 1936: 43).

West demonstrates that the world as it exists in 1916 will not allow Margaret's spirituality or the harmony of the pastoral *and* social responsibility. Far from being the book's weakness (or internal contradiction), that is its point. Chris's finer self cannot inhabit the masculinist and capitalist world. The characters in the novel are condemned to a war-torn, materialistic world. Nonetheless, West hopes that her audience will be transformed. She insists—and wants her readers to realize—that the modern, industrial, classist world and its citizens need radically to revise their concept of society—and the ideology that shapes it—in order to achieve a livable world. Notions of male-female relationships, class, sanity, "normality," and social responsibility all must be revised to create an inclusive rather than an exclusive world. We need new vision and West hopes that art, including her novel, can inspire it. West's only explicit mention of art in the novel reflects upon her own work. She contrasts the "wild eye of the artist" with the "knowing wink of the manicurist" who whittled the new Baldry Court (*RS* 12). This alludes to the "fine frenzy" of the eyes of the artist in Shakespeare's pastoral vision in *A Midsummer's Night Dream*. *The Return of the Soldier* blends Shakespeare's trinity "the lunatic, the lover, and the poet" into one. With this achievement it also reconciles Showalter's "wild zone of women's culture" with the traditional artistic inspiration of the pastoral to create its uniquely resonant and perceptive vision of the First World War and its place in our modern consciousness.

3

"The Miraculous Beauty of the Common Lot": New Woman Meets Female Gothic in *The Judge*

Part 1 The New Woman and the hybrid imperative

Rebecca West's portraits of the three women characters in *The Return of the Soldier* draw attention to her deliberate representations of different "female types" in her first published novel. Jenny describes herself and Kitty as the "parasite" women that West portrayed in her early journal essays. These women "weigh" Chris Baldry down: "At his father's death, he had been obliged to take over a business that was weighted by the needs of a mob of female relatives who were all useless either in the old way with antimacassars or in the new way with golf clubs" (*RS* 20). Just as Jenny and Kitty are typical women of their upper class, Margaret typifies a lower-middle-class woman of new suburban London—Wealdstone is called "the red suburban stain which fouls the fields three miles nearer London than Harrow-weald" (*RS* 22). Margaret, "repulsively furred with neglect and poverty" (*RS* 25), is repeatedly described in terms of her class: "She was not so much a person as an implication of dreary poverty, like an open door in a mean house that lets out the smell of cooking cabbage and the screams of children" (*RS* 141). West also classifies the three women in terms of their spirituality, placing them on a scale from gross materiality to utter ethereality:

> I suppose that the subject of our tragedy, written in spiritual terms, was that in Kitty he had turned from the type of woman that makes the body conqueror of the soul and in me from the type that mediates between the soul and the body ... and had given himself to a woman whose bleak habit it was to champion the soul against the body. (*RS* 134–5)

Even though none of the women have living children, Margaret's nurturing ability to replenish Chris makes her an archetypal maternal figure. Jenny describes Margaret with Chris asleep beside her on a grassy slope:

> It has sometimes seemed to me that there was a significance about it ... when ... one sees a mother with her child in her arms, something turns in one's heart like a sword ... when it was my dear Chris and my dear Margaret who sat englobed in peace as in a crystal sphere, that I knew that it was the most significant as it was the loveliest attitude in the world. (*RS* 143)

Kitty, of course, is the perfect upper-class wife and hostess and Jenny is a stereotypical upper-class spinster.

West's effort to comprehend so many "types" of early twentieth-century women in her depictions of Kitty, Jenny, and Margaret underlines her omission of any "type" of woman who resembles Rebecca West herself: a professional journalist and artist, an active supporter of woman's suffrage, a socialist and Fabian Society member, and a single mother with a son born out-of-wedlock. *The Return of the Soldier* calls for the transformation of West's contemporary world into a world where an enlightened, sensitive Chris can thrive and not be enslaved by a masculinist and capitalist system or slaughtered in a senseless war. West omits a character that resembles herself in *The Return of the Soldier* because its culture does not provide a viable space for her type of woman.

Women like West—an intelligent, self-supporting, politically involved, sexually liberated woman—existed in early twentieth-century Great Britain, Europe, and America. Patricia Raub attests that this was a time "in which women were beginning to try on new social roles" (Raub 1994: 111).[1] She elaborates, "Even if historians have been forced to accept the notion that women made relatively modest political and economic strides ... many scholars still maintain that women gained substantially greater personal freedom" (Raub 1994: 109). According to Bonnie Kime Scott, "West had all the independence, motivation, and intelligence as the fin de siècle new woman" (Scott 1991: 170). This new type of woman was also prominent in literature starting in the 1880s and 1890s "New Woman" fiction.[2] A. R. Cunningham describes New Woman fiction as "a series of novels, mainly by women, which set out to attack marriage, to break the bonds of censorship which tacitly forbade the treatment of sexuality in fiction, and above all to argue ... the feminist case" (Cunningham 1973: 178). In defining different categories of the New Woman, Cunningham acknowledges the variety of New Woman heroines but argues that they all "rejected some features—though by no means always the same ones—of the feminine role as then [1890s Great Britain] defined" (Cunningham 1973: 178).

Although West excludes the New Woman from *The Return of the Soldier*, the New Woman engaged her as early as 1909 when she began her first (unfinished) novel, *The Sentinel.* West attempts to portray different versions of the New Woman in five novels over twenty years.[3] *The Judge* (1922) is her first published depiction of the New Woman. West's struggle to write (and complete) a New Woman narrative and the flaws critics are quick to remark in these works reveal the challenges all women faced in trying to redefine gender stereotypes and to negotiate the social, economic, and political obstacles that faced women before and after the First World War.

Drawing on Susan Stanford Friedman's models for genetic readings of feminist texts, Kathryn Laing treats *The Sentinel, Adela*, and *The Judge* as one "composite, palimpsestic text" (Laing 2006: 171). She interprets *The Judge* by reading it intertextually with these early works as the "textual unconscious" of the later work. These three works are inextricably bound. Reading these three texts together can also reveal the "hybrid imperative" in all of West's works. *The Sentinel* and *Adela* posed problems in the depiction of the New Woman that West was unable to resolve until she developed hybrid strategies in *The Judge* (and subsequently *Sunflower* and *Harriet Hume*). By combining the conventions of two popular and gendered genres—the New Woman novel and the gothic novel—West was able to overcome some of the obstacles she could not surmount in her attempts to depict the New Woman in *The Sentinel* and *Adela. The Judge* not only combines two different genres; it also draws on the conventions of two subgenres of each of these two genres.

Part 2 *The Judge* as hybrid of two New Woman novels

The two heroines named Adela Furnival in *The Sentinel* and in *Adela* and Ellen Melville in *The Judge* share many traits. They are all intelligent, independent, career-minded young women active in women's suffrage. All three heroines' lives and ambitions are complicated by romantic relationships with older men. All these qualities are typical features of a common brand of New Woman heroine. The plot surrounding Ellen in *The Judge* further resembles a New Woman novel because it critiques marriage. Unlike the "Adelas" who have no parents, Ellen lives with her mother whose marriage to an alcoholic deserter has left her impoverished.

Both Shirley Peterson and Lyn Pykett label Ellen Melville a New Woman heroine and analyze *The Judge* as a New Woman novel.[4] They also recognize Marion Yaverland's commonalities with New Woman heroines—especially in her sexual freedom and in her persecution by Victorian/Edwardian ideals of marriage and femininity. Peterson examines *The Judge* with a political lens and sees Marion and Ellen as two generations of the woman's movement: "From a political perspective, Ellen and Marion become allegorical figures of the women's movement itself as it undergoes a generational change" (Peterson 1997: 111). Pykett defines New Woman fiction of the fin de siècle as an "exploration of the material, psychological and ideological conditions in which female/feminine desires and aspirations are constructed and constricted, and its focus on the ways in which a domestic existence and the patriarchal family produce female hysteria" (Pykett 2000: 112). She views Ellen as "one kind of New Woman": "the feisty suffragette ... a vivid representation of the excitement of the young woman drunk on the ideas of socialism and feminism" (Pykett 2000: 117–18). Marion, on the other hand, "is the heroine of another kind of New Woman tale; she is 'a woman who did,' and spent the rest of her life paying for it" (Pykett 2000: 118).[5] Marion's affair with the local squire produces Richard (Ellen's lover) and leaves her to live in ignominy.

If Marion's acts qualify her as a New Woman, West's depiction of Marion's sexuality is even more reminiscent of the "forensic sexual frankness that was often seen as shocking" (Pykett 2000: 112) frequent in New Woman fiction. In order to save face, Marion marries her lover's butler, Peacey, who promises never to consummate their marriage. West's description of his rape of Marion is spine-chilling:

> His fleshy fingers, pink with constriction, terrified her. ... He desired they should know each other only as animals and enemies. ... She watched his face grow yellow ... and moaned. ... Then in the blackness his weight threshed down on her. Even his form was a deceit, for his vast bulk was not obesity, but ironhard strength. All consciousness soon left her, except only pain and she wandered in the dark caverns of her mind. Her capacity for sexual love lay dead in her. She saw it as a lovely naked boy lying with blue lips and purple blood pouring from his side, where it had been jagged by the boar who still snuffled the fair body, sitting by with its haunches in a spring. (*TJ* 287)

When Peacey departs, Ellen views the landscape which connects the violence of her rape with the violation of her maternity: "The eastern sky was inflamed with such a livid scarlet dawn as she had never seen before, and the full tide was milk streaked with blood, and the sails of the barges that rode there were as rags that had been used to staunch wounds" (*TJ* 288).

West's unabashed depiction of the sensuality of Marion's breast-feeding is also reminiscent of the sensuality of New Woman novels:

> She bent over him, enravished by the brilliant bloom of his creamy skin and the black blaze of his eyes. ... She became vexed with love for him, and longed to clasp him, to crush him as she knew she must not ... a wave of love passed through her and she took him to her. They were fused, they were utterly content with one another. He finished, smacking his lips like an old epicure. (*TJ* 285)

Peterson and Pykett interpret *The Judge* as a hybrid New Woman fiction. The tales of two different types and two different generations of New Woman heroines meet in West's generic adaptation of Mary Louise Pratt's "contact zone." This dialogic encounter is at the heart of their interpretations of *The Judge*. As we have seen repeatedly in West's works, her hybridizations undo dualism at all levels. Ann Ardis sees New Woman texts' challenge to their contemporary culture's worldviews as fundamentally anti-dualistic. *The Judge*'s hybrid of two New Woman texts in a dialogic contact zone is even more strenuously anti-dualistic than most New Woman texts. Ardis's explanation of the New Woman novels as "radical threats to the Victorian social order" (Ardis 1990: 26) dramatizes the anti-dualistic projectory of *The Judge*:

> The New Woman's claim to the right of self-definition should be recognized ... as a challenge to the tradition of liberal humanism ... they challenge not only the bourgeois Victorian social order's prescriptive definition of "correct" female behavior but also the pattern of thinking in hierarchically organized binary oppositions that pits men against women, "good" women against "fallen ones," the middle class against the working class, and European against non-European cultures. (Ardis 1990: 27)

These interpretations of *The Judge* as a Georgian redaction of New Woman novelistic conventions have helped to redeem West's work's critical reputation. Peterson and Pykett imply that West scholars—like feminist scholars of New Woman fiction—have condemned *The Judge* because its New Woman conventions do not "fit" with prevailing esthetics of "feminist" or "modernist" literature. As Pykett recognizes, "It is a loose, baggy, melodramatic novel of ideas" (Pykett 2000: 117).

Part 3 Gothic connections

Like Pykett's and Peterson's revisionary generic readings, Philip E. Ray's interpretation of *The Judge* as a gothic novel gives method to West's madness by interpreting what has seemed "incompetence" as purposeful manipulation of gothic conventions. According to Ray, critics have been "applying ... the wrong kind of standards. ... The standards appropriate to the discussion of the Gothic romance have the advantage of making *The Judge* ... a competently constructed work of literature" (Ray 1988: 297).

West solves the dilemmas posed by writing a New Woman novel by incorporating two New Woman novels into one and also by joining her New Woman novel to a gothic novel. This fusion of genres differs from many of West's hybrids because it combines two inherently subversive—and often gendered—genres. Many of West's hybrids subvert patriarchal values as they adapt patriarchal conventions to her transformative ends. Both the New Woman novel and the gothic novel interrogate social, political, economic, and esthetic mores of their times. This marriage of two transgressive genres can in part account for *The Judge*'s hostile reception. Nonetheless, the structural dynamic common to all of West's hybrids works to open a transformative space where new values can prevail. New Woman hybrid meets gothic hybrid and a full understanding of West's text emerges in this encounter. Turning to a gothic interpretation of *The Judge* demonstrates that the New Woman novels' intersection with gothic conventions is not "monstrous" as many critics contend, but—as we shall see—"marvelous" and "sublime."

Part 4 A male gothic reading of *The Judge*

Ray's article "*The Judge* Reexamined: Rebecca West's Underrated Gothic Romance" introduced a new, influential perspective on West's novel. Gothic conventions explain some of the most troublesome features of the novel, including the change in style and narrative manner between Parts I and II and Ellen's character change from a self-assertive, independent suffragette to an "enervated," "passive witness" (Orel 1985: 127, 130; qtd Ray 1988: 297). According to Ray, "such transitions from an orderly universe in which virtue and sanity prevail to a nightmare universe in which vice and madness undermine all order are a primary characteristic of Gothic fiction" (Ray 1988: 298). It is also typical of the gothic for the "heroine to experience a ... diminution of personality" (Ray 1988: 300).

In Ray's eyes, Marion's family home—Yaverland's End—is the "impregnable, rude, and barbarous" gothic castle—the "dynamo of cruelty" (Hallie 1982: 68; qtd Ray 1988: 298) where the tragic gothic tale unfolds. Ray identifies Marion with her demonic castle and as "lord of the castle" she becomes the villain of the story.

Ray's gothic reading rescues *The Judge* from "the charge that it is ... an incompetent literary production by a major literary artist" (Ray 1988: 305), but more importantly it invites further explorations of West's manipulation of gothic conventions in the context of her generic hybridity. A gothic frame suits *The Judge* in many ways.[6]

David Punter "reads the original Gothic novels as literary manifestations of deep social anxieties" (Punter 1998: 236–7). These anxieties stem from social, civil, economic, political, and philosophical changes with their concomitant unrest.[7] *The Judge* also reflects its contemporary social and political anxieties. Published in modernism's *annus mirabilis* 1922 (the same year as T. S. Eliot's *The Waste Land* and James Joyce's *Ulysses*), the gothic elements register well the post-Great War, prefascist angst of this era. Women's issues were also a ripe source of anxiety at this time. The 1918 Representation of the People Act enfranchised women over the age of thirty who owned a certain amount of property. Nancy Paxton reminds us that although this was a significant gain for women's rights, "Ellen as a poor, unmarried woman under thirty, still could not vote, nor could West herself" (Paxton 2006: 194). More importantly—as Paxton emphasizes—the right to vote does not solve many other women's problems such as job equality or sexual freedom. The novel's anxious gothic atmosphere insists on social problems in a way that a romantic, realistic novel, or even a New Woman novel would not.

Even more important for West's transformative ambitions, the gothic has been inherently subversive since its inception. It draws on the political, revolutionary fervor of the eighteenth century and it forefronts everything that neoclassical society regarded as "the other." The Marquis de Sade believed that the gothic's assault on hierarchy and reason were linked to the French Revolution: this "genre [is] the inevitable product of the revolutionary shocks with which the whole of Europe resounded" (qtd Hogle 2002: 13). Fred Botting describes the gothic as a "counternarrative displaying the underside of enlightenment and humanist values" (Botting 1996: 2). As the following analysis will prove, most of the dominant ideologies or discourses available to the characters in *The Judge* are not capable of comprehending the complex tangle of forces that embroil them. Scottish rationalism, Scottish pragmatics, suffragist ideals, Christian revivalism, and English aristocratic values are all trivialized by the enormity of the novel's problems. Richard—the novel's putative adventurer/hero—whose virility, vitality, good looks, passion, intelligence, and worldly success should qualify him as "conqueror" seems especially impotent. Ironically, Richard—a chemist who has lived abroad and has returned to start an explosives factory—embodies all the values and institutions which West's contemporary journal articles deplore: imperialism, capitalism, science, rationalism, and violence. Ray reads the novel's epigram to mean that Marion condemns her sons for their fathers' sins: "Richard for the sins of his father in declining to divorce his wife ... Roger for the sin of his father in raping her [Marion] in marriage" (Ray 1988: 303). Although Ray is not explicit about this, his interpretation indicts patriarchal exploitation of women and blames the patriarchy for both middle-class and working-class decline.

Ray's claims are based upon his general definition of a universal gothic. The gothic model that Ray employs, however, is what has commonly been labeled the "Male Gothic." All gothic tales share many conventions, but critics have differentiated between the "Male Gothic" and the "Female Gothic"—which have discernibly different traditions, conventions, and legacies. Although these paradigms were initially determined by an author's sex, they have more recently been socially and psychoanalytically constructed according to cultural scripts and models. An author's sex does not necessarily predict a gothic paradigm. West's complex plot draws upon both the male and the female gothic traditions.

Ray's emphases—which include the identity between the lord and his gothic castle, the oedipal plots, and the tragic ending—are all features of the male gothic. Ray cites the authority of critic Andrew Wright to claim that "the central Gothic feature is the castle ... there must be a lord of the castle ... [and] persons ... owing him obedience" (Ray 1988: 298). Contrary to most gothic tales, Yaverland End's "lord" is a "lady," but her power is still absolute. Casting Marion as the gothic villain condemns her overweening desire for power and control. Anne Williams describes the male gothic's "hero/villain" as "an isolated overreacher punished for his hubris" (Williams 1995: 103). Subverting gothic and patriarchal conventions by making a woman the all-powerful gothic hero/villain, West simultaneously criticizes the masculinist and capitalist values of power and violence which led to the First World War and which still prevail in this postwar world.[8]

Marion's "castle" reflects her character. Ray remarks on the ugliness of the "old" Yaverland's End and on the alienating "immensity" of Marion's new addition. Although it is not relevant to Ray's argument, when he describes Marion's "will to power" and identifies her with her "castle," he is referencing the presence of other prime gothic features in *The Judge:* gothic horror and terror. *The Judge* lacks ghosts, decaying corpses, or flesh-eating monsters, but a palpable atmosphere of menace and gloom permeates the second part of the book (and also informs Part I). A contemporary review in the *Times Literary Supplement* describes Part II as a "*milieu* of horror and lust" (*TLS* 1922: 427; qtd Ray 1988: 297). Drawing on distinctions made by Ann Radcliffe in her essay "On the Supernatural in Poetry," scholars describe gothic emotions as either terror or horror. David Cavallero explains that "terror [is] deemed intangible and resistant to definition, [while] horror [is] definable by virtue of its material nature" (Cavallero 2002: 2). Terror and horror—which are usually inspired by the supernatural—are keys to the gothic's interrogation of Enlightenment (and Post-Enlightenment) reason and morality.

Both Marion and her house are described in terms of extravagance and excessiveness that are typical of the male gothic and inspire horror. David B. Morris describes Walpole's architecture and its ideological foundations in terms similar to Ellen's perceptions of Yaverland's End: "As in the extravagant architecture of Strawberry Hill, Walpole's subversion of neoclassical proprieties depends upon finding unanticipated resources in material which an earlier generation would have dismissed as grotesque, excessive, and merely ornamental" (Morris 1985: 302). Ellen perceives Marion's extremity as extravagant excess. She reflects on Marion's new parlor: "Here in this room the inconceivable had happened, and she recognized that there was present an excess of beauty and an excess of being" (*TJ* 240–1). Even Marion's domestic tidiness is perceived as fearful and violent: "Ellen *shivered* ... and looked at the bookcases. The violent order characteristic of the household had polished the glass doors" (*TJ* 243, emphasis added). Ellen characteristically shivered at the material horror of Marion's house. Ellen also attaches excess to Marion's soul and vilifies it: "Ellen tried to rescue her mind from mersion into this excess of beauty ... it was lost as completely and disastrously ... in the not less excessive view of the spiritual world presented by this woman's face" (*TJ* 242). To Ellen, Marion's face and the atmosphere at Yaverland's End are "subtle as villainy" (*TJ* 242).

Examining the gothic horror in *The Judge* reinforces West's condemnation of the patriarchal features of her society. Oedipal plots commonly arouse horror in male gothic texts. Richard's horrific murder of Roger and his consequent doom (death by hanging) result from society's fear of a powerful woman. West exposes the horror implicit in patriarchy that Anne Williams describes: "Male Gothic expresses the horrors inherent in the premises of Western patriarchy—that 'the female' (the mother) is 'other,' forbidden, and dreadfully, uncannily powerful, a monster that the nascent self must escape at the cost of whatever violence seems necessary" (Williams 1995: 135). Both Richard's and Roger's devotion to their mother results in atrocious violence.

Marion inspires horror, but she is also the victim of "horrific acts": desertion by her lover, stoning by the local villagers, and marital rape by Roger's father. Reading *The Judge* as a hybrid of gothic conventions with New Woman conventions suggests that Marion is the victim of patriarchy as well as a perpetrator of patriarchal judgments. A reader of *The Judge* enters the "contact zone" where gothic conventions meet New Woman conventions. The reader's "uptake" of the different genres' conventions complicates Ray's male gothic reading to suggest another perspective on Marion. Jessica Bomarito explains the gothic's bias against patriarchy: "Authors employ horror and the Gothic to convey the horror of being perceived as freakish by society for engaging in or espousing ... pursuits considered outside of the traditional ... woman's realm" (Bomarito 2006). Although she can be thought of as the "lord of the manor" or even a "monster" in a male gothic plot, Marion also fulfills many of the requirements of a "suffering ... female heroine" in a male gothic text whose "virtue [is] threatened and often violated," according to Anne Williams (1995: 104). Marion's suffering at many hands and her suicide are typical of Williams's male gothic heroine who collides with a doomed New Woman: "Ultimately she may be (must be?) punished as a 'fallen woman'" (Williams 1995: 105).

Ray and many critics view Marion unsympathetically. The novel undeniably condemns her desire for control and her excesses. Nonetheless, as New Woman text encounters a male gothic text in a generic contact zone, a reader must deplore patriarchy's domination of women's sexuality and society's subjugation and persecution of strong women in its portrait of the horrors visited upon Marion.

By refusing to see *The Judge* in a dualistic way, this intersection of New Woman and gothic readings also reveals the "horror" in Ellen's life in Scotland in Part I of the novel. Ray's male gothic reading relies on a bifurcation of the novel. Part I, which focuses on Ellen Melville's story, is read as upbeat and cheerful in spite of Ellen's penurious circumstances. Part II, which focuses on Marion Yaverland, is read as monstrous and dark. Shirley Peterson's New Woman reading suffers from a similar bifurcation. Peterson reads Part I as a more or less lighthearted "depiction of Ellen's early development from innocence to experience" (Peterson 1997: 108). Recognizing Ellen's marginalization, Peterson comments:

> [Ellen] relishes her leisure time spent in subversive talk of suffrage and socialism. The matriarchal idols of both her community and her imagination seem to compensate for her absent father and to mitigate the humiliation and condescension this New Woman endures in her capacity as typist for a patronizing attorney and his son. Her biggest complaint is boredom exacerbated by the gloominess and the vague agitation of youth. (Peterson 1997: 108)

Viewing *The Judge* as more than Peterson's portrait of contrasting New Women novel "types" complicates Peterson's interpretation. Interpreting *The Judge* as a gothic hybrid insists upon the "horror" that Peterson's New Woman lens misses. Although Ellen's boss, Mr McTavish James is ("merely") condescending and avuncular, his son Mr Philip persecutes and psychologically abuses Ellen to the point that Ellen contemplates suicide in order to escape his sexual harassment. "A dark man shaking with a suppressed passion of malice," Mr Philip fills Ellen's workdays with anguish and her non-working hours with dread (*TJ* 108).[9] His presence haunts the office and Ellen's imagination.

> Mr Philip sat in the dark corner beyond the fireplace and showed by the way the whites of his eyes turned about that something bad had come into his mind ... and then it would come out suddenly, cool and as mean as mean could be and somehow unanswerable. (*TJ* 108)

The Judge vividly depicts workplace harassment in early twentieth-century England. A hybrid interpretation of *The Judge* as a female gothic novel as well as a New Woman novel brings attention to this important feminist and class problem.

Part 5 Female gothic: Terror and matrophobia reconciled

Turning from male gothic "horror" to female gothic "terror" can refocus our understanding of *The Judge*. This female gothic lens can also give us a way to look at Marion and Ellen's relationship beyond the fusion of two types of New Woman novels or Ray's reading of Marion as gothic villain.

As we have seen, gothic horror is distinguished by its material nature: it can be found in ghosts and corpses, but also in castles as well as sexuality and monstrous behavior. "Terror," which belongs to the female gothic, is intangible and transcendent rather than material. Ann Radcliffe's "On the Supernatural in Poetry" differentiates between the two emotions: "Terror and horror are so far opposite, that the first expands the soul, and awakens the faculties to a high degree of life, the other contracts, freezes, and nearly annihilates them" (Radcliffe 1826).[10] Terror in the female gothic is inspired by what Radcliffe called "the supernatural *explain'd*" (Ellis 2000: 66). Male gothics abound in ghosts or monsters which cannot be assimilated into our mundane world. The supernatural in the female gothic is finally explained: what seemed to be a decaying corpse was actually a wax figure, for example. Anne Williams, again, is useful: "Whereas Female Gothic is organized around the resources of terror, of an imagined threat and the process by which that threat is dispelled, Male Gothic specializes in horror" (Williams 1995: 104). The supernatural explained provides the possibility for a happy resolution or closure.

The explained supernatural can be seen in Marion's powers of perception—her uncanny ability to understand others. While these soothsaying powers seem magical or uncanny, they are based on her womanly experience and on careful observation. Ellen is struck by Marion's perspicuity in their first meeting when Marion quickly analyzes Ellen's character as well as her beauty: "I expected you to be beautiful. ... It's the other things I'm surprised at: that you're clever, that you're reflective, that you feel deeply" (*TJ* 214). Ellen exclaims, "But how do you know all that?" We see Marion's almost magical abilities in her insights about Roger's companion from the Hallelujah Army. Poppy Alicante pretends to be the essence of religiosity and purity in her uniform, circumspectness, and modesty. Marion discerns that she was a prostitute and has joined the Hallelujah Army in regret over her recently born child whom she "hated giving up" (*TJ* 395). Marion infers this from a brown stain on Poppy's face which is common to pregnant women and remains after birth. She hypothesizes that Poppy's love of beauty made her choose her name and resulted in "the handsome sailor [who] picked her up in Chatham High Street on Saturday night" (*TJ* 395). On the evening of Marion's death, Ellen and Poppy look across the river at the lights of Chatham and Poppy recognizes Chatham and weeps: "'Ah, Chatham's a nice place,' said Poppy in a surly voice. She pressed her face against the glass like a beast looking out of its cage. It was quite certain, as the silence endured, that she wept" (*TJ* 417). Ellen realizes, "Then Marion had been right." And a "wave of *terror* washed over Ellen" (emphasis added). Marion seems to have terrifying supernatural powers, but at the same moment that she experiences the terror, Ellen understands that Marion had been able to read Poppy's story because of a deep knowledge of her own sexuality, her intense experience of motherhood, and her profound empathy for others.

This terror realigns Ellen's relationship with Marion. Female gothic conventions can help us better understand Ellen's relationship to Marion, Ellen's own growth as a character, and the ambiguous—and much disputed—ending of the novel.

The patriarchal family is at the heart of both the male and female gothic. While the male gothic story in *The Judge* is oedipal and culminates in the death of the mother and both sons, the female gothic story in *The Judge* focuses on mother-daughter kinship relationships. As Deborah D. Rogers explains,

> Rejecting the traditional focus on patriarchal violence to stress the relationship between Radcliffean mothers and daughters is a recent development in feminist criticism. According to this view, starting with Ann Radcliffe, the Female Gothic has emphasized female kinship relations, especially the mother-daughter bond. (Rogers 2007: 57)

According to Rogers, the mother-daughter kinship relationship found in female gothic texts often is a relationship between the gothic heroine and an *absent* mother. Insofar as Mrs Melville dies at the end of Part I, *The Judge* conforms to this scheme. Ellen's relationship with her mother is critical to Part I, but it also triggers the climax of the novel in Part II and gives meaning to the novel's resolution.

Ellen and her mother have a close, loving relationship, but in many ways Ellen consciously chooses to carve an identity that will be different from her mother's—so that she can be spared her mother's suffering. Nonetheless, some of Mrs Melville's influences are positive. She bestows upon her daughter a love of nature and a transcendent Romantic esthetic which sees nature as the spiritual source of an "aspect more sublime" (Wordsworth 1798). Ellen shares a sensitivity to nature with Ann Radcliffe's female gothic heroines.[11] As many critics have recognized, Edmund Burke's theories of the sublime—which celebrate exalted emotions as more important than reason—informed the eighteenth-century gothic and subsequently Romantic nature poetry. West's Romantic esthetic is one of the most important—and neglected—aspects of *The Judge* and one that can be more deeply appreciated if one interprets *The Judge* in the context of the female gothic. Nature's spiritual powers are essential to an understanding of this work.[12]

The Judge celebrates untamed nature in the mountains of the Pentlands and also finally in the mudflats and the plains of Southern England. West is explicit about the Romantic esthetic that shapes her work in references to Romantic poets and in scenes that recall Romantic poems—especially Wordsworth's. These comparisons demonstrate Mrs Melville's importance in instilling a Romantic esthetic in her daughter. In fact, Ellen compares her mother to Romantic poets: "And she [Mrs Melville] was more than a romantic: she was a poet. What was there in all Keats and Shelley but just this same passion for unpossessable things?" (*TJ* 195). Ellen's mother takes her on holidays and weekend outings in the Pentlands where Mrs Melville nurtures a love of nature and its spiritual potential in her daughter and where Ellen learns a Wordsworthian ability to find consolation in nature. Wordsworth speaks of the power of memories of nature to restore our spirits in many poems. In "Lines Written a Few Miles above Tintern Abbey," he speaks of the river Wye's beauty and of the consoling, moral power of nature:

> Though absent long,
> These forms of beauty have not been to me,
> As is a landscape to a blind man's eye:
> But oft, in lonely rooms, and mid the din
> Of towns and cities, I have owed to them,
> In hours of weariness, sensations sweet,
> Felt in the blood, and felt along the heart,
> And passing even into my purer mind
> With tranquil restoration:—feelings too
> Of unremembered pleasure; such, perhaps,
> As may have had no trivial influence
> On that best portion of a good man's life. (Wordsworth 1798: ll. 24–36)

Wordsworth finds "tranquil restoration" and moral influence in these recollections of nature.

Ellen also seeks refuge in nature. As noted, she is tormented by sexual harassment at work. One evening Ellen breaks into tears at work and runs home filled with suicidal thoughts. At home, she is calmed by her familiar surroundings and she consoles herself in a Wordsworthian way with memories of her mother and herself in nature.

> Very vividly, for her mind's eye was staring wildly on the past rather than look on this present ... there sprung up before her on the bare plastered wall a potato-field she and her mother had seen one day when they went to Cramond. Thousands and thousands of white flowers running up to a skyline in ruler-drawn lines. They had walked by the River Almond afterwards, linking arms, exclaiming

> together over the dark glassy water, which slid over small frequent weirs, the tents of green fire which the sun made of the overarching branches, the patches of moss that grew so symmetrically between the tree-trunks on the steep river-banks above the path that they might have been the dedicatory tablets of rustic altars. (*TJ* 154)

The "thousands of white flowers running up to a skyline in ruler-drawn lines" recall Wordsworth's "ten thousand" daffodils "continuous as the stars that shine ... [which] stretch in never-ending line" (Wordsworth 1807). Wordsworth's daffodils "flash upon that inward eye/Which is the bliss of solitude" much like the white flowers restore Ellen and deter her suicidal thoughts.

A walk in the Pentlands also marks a crucial turn in Richard's and Ellen's relationship. Again, Ellen is beset by thoughts of Mr Philip's cruelty and she attempts to escape these thoughts by running into nature. In this scene Ellen is similar to Wordsworth's younger self who

> When like a roe
> I bounded o'er the mountains, by the sides
> Of the deep rivers, and the lonely streams,
> Wherever nature led; more like a man
> Flying from something that he dreads, than one
> Who sought the thing he loved. (Wordsworth 1798: ll. 68–72)

Ellen feels compelled to leap and to run in nature, searching for the consolation and fulfillment that she found on her trips with her mother.

> If she leapt from a height she might lift this curious burden from her heart. She scrambled up on the stone parapet ... and jumped back to earth. ... She must run about, or the beating of her heart would become an agony ... she ran round the stone spur of the bridge and crouched down beside the arch on the damp turf. (*TJ* 106–7)

Ellen's appreciation of and sensitivity to nature helps her transition in her visit to Essex and finally restores her at the close of the novel. Ellen finds the landscape in Southern England "illimitable" in a Burkean sublime way that threatens her sense of proportion. When she first views it from the train as she arrives to visit Marion and Richard, she observes,

> There stretched a great quiet plain. It stretched illimitably, and though there were dotted over it red barns and grey houses ... it did not seem as if it could be a human territory. It could be regarded only as a place for the feet of the clouds which, half as tall as the sky, stood on the far horizon. (*TJ* 228)

The illimitable extent of the sky across the endless plain threatens to depreciate all human activity.

> It *could* be imagined that the people who lived under this immense sky might come to lose the common human sense of their own supreme importance, and to suspect themselves as being of no more account than the fishes which lie at the bottom of the channel; and *might* look up at the great cloud galleons floating above and wonder if these had not for ship's company beings that would be to them as men are to fishes. ... Its breezes were clean enough to nourish strength, but there was something about the proportions of the scene that *would* breed skepticism concerning the value of all activities. (*TJ* 230–1, emphasis added)

Ellen's skepticism and its accompanying terror are continually expressed in the conditional "could" and she finally is able to "dwell contentedly" on the Burkean obscurity of the landscape: "It could not be beautiful. A plain of mud could not be beautiful. Yet the mind could dwell contentedly on this new and curious estate of nature, this substance that was neither earth nor water, this place that was neither land nor sea" (*TJ* 231). Ellen's Romantic sensibility finds inspiration in the threatening mudflats: "This, like the Pentlands, was far more than a place. It was a mental state, a revisitable peace, a country on whose soil the people and passions of imagination lived more intensely than on other earth" (*TJ* 245).

West's gothic rejection of reason and order and Romantic celebration of the spiritual and imaginative potentialities of wild nature are vivid in Ellen's reflections when she and Richard visit Sir Harry's park. Ellen is captivated by the fanciful neoclassical temple—where Marion and Harry used to meet—but then she realizes that divinity and inspiration lie in nature, not in "human offerings":

> A desire to look out towards the sea and the flatlands came on her. This temple set among the woods was a human place. ... But the sea and the flatlands were not made by man. ... Now she perceived that it was the silver circle of trees which was the real temple. ... It was in there, among the ebony paths which ran along the glistening thickets, that one would find the presence of divinity. (*TJ* 409–10)

As I said, a sensitivity to nature's divine potential has been a characteristic of female gothic novels since Ann Radcliffe. That the sensitivity to nature is nurtured by the heroine's mother is not a gothic norm. Ellen's mother's Romantic appreciation of nature and a typical female gothic mother-daughter kinship plot culminate in Ellen's revelations at the book's end.

In spite of Ellen's affection for Mrs Melville, she strives to differentiate from her mother and to create an identity that is not only separate from her mother's but also a rejection of her own conception of her mother. In typical New Woman fashion, Ellen identifies as a "son" and a "boy" rather than as a "daughter" and a "girl" and she longs for "manly" adventures. "Ellen thought herself a wonderful *new* sort of *woman* who was going to be just like a man" (*TJ* 44, emphasis added). Mrs Melville, for example, is domestic and private. Like a New Woman, Ellen launches into the public world through her work as a secretary to support their household and in her campaign for suffrage. Most of all, Ellen pities her mother for her poor choice of an alcoholic husband who abandoned her to leave them destitute. Resolving to avoid the New Woman heroine victimized by marriage, Ellen is determined not to mimic her mother's marital adversity. Ellen clearly defines maturity as autonomous individuation resulting from a separation from and rejection of her mother. Nonetheless, she only finally "matures" when she is able to understand and to connect with her mother. The female gothic plot thwarts a New Woman ending. Ellen's New Woman type proves to be naïve and immature. A female gothic plot intercedes into Ellen's willful manipulation of her own New Woman plot. Our final understanding of the novel lies in this "contact zone" which includes both genres. Within the context of a female gothic exploration of a mother-daughter relationship, West challenges her early twentieth-century's patriarchal, dualistic, hierarchical, rational ideology and its definition of maturity and heroism as individualistic, independent, and domineering. Instead West offers an egalitarian, mutualistic, imaginative ideology and defines maturity and heroism as mutual, connected, and collaborative.

Ellen's rejection of her mother triggers the sequence of tragedies that follow Marion's suicide. Roger and Poppy accuse Richard and Ellen of driving Marion to suicide because of illicit sex in Ellen's bedroom at Yaverland's End. Richard and Ellen are innocent of these claims. Richard does not hear their accusations or see their "look[s] of lewd accusation" (*TJ* 425). Richard's distraction prompts a vision of her mother in Ellen:

> Now she saw the picture. It was her own mother, her own old mother, shuffling about the kitchen ... in the dirty light of the unwarmed morning; poking forward into the grate with hands on which housework had acted like a skin disease; pulling her flannel dressing-gown about a body which poverty and neglect had made as ugly as the time, the place, the task. ... That was what happened to women who allowed themselves to be disregarded; who allow any other than themselves to dwell in their men's attention. (*TJ* 426)

Ellen rouses Richard from his preoccupation with the words, "Hark what your brother's saying to us. ... He says we're bad" (*TJ* 426). Richard turns on Roger, picks up the breadknife, and "drove the knife into Roger's heart" (*TJ* 426).

The closing scene of *The Judge* where Richard and Ellen fly to Kerith Island to consummate their love before Richard is captured and Ellen left an unwed mother is ambiguous and controversial. Is Ellen doomed to Marion's and her mother's fates or will she be able to carve a new path in her similar situation? Read from an oedipal male gothic perspective both Richard and Ellen have been sentenced to tragedy by their mothers' legacies.

Novelistic conventions and sad endings in similarly plotted contemporary novels also lead to tragic interpretations of the conclusion of *The Judge*. A New Woman approach to the novel is more likely to read the ending as bitter or tragic, also. Pykett gives the example of "the boomerang plot" in New Woman novels:

> The novel's extraordinary conclusion owes something to the boomerang plot of the New Woman novel, a melodramatic dénouement which boomerangs the unconventional heroine back into an apparently conventional feminine role. (Pykett 2000: 118)

Ann Norton's emphasis on social scripts and social attitudes that shape women in spite of their best intentions also implicitly reads Ellen's fate tragically, as a failed New Woman heroine:

> Herein lies one of West's techniques in *The Judge*: to present characters who imagine they are defying the black and white gender roles exaggerated in sentimental or Gothic novels while demonstrating how powerfully such sexual images do control and form their ends. (Norton 1991: 300)

Pykett echoes Norton's belief that Ellen has forsaken her feminist ideals and accepts the bitter knowledge often taught in New Woman texts:

> Ellen, the erstwhile suffragette activist, apparently accepts the biological destiny of motherhood, notwithstanding the lessons she has learned ... about "the insane sexual caprices of men [and] the not less mad excessive sexual steadfastness of women," and about "love, which was either ineffectual or dangerous." (Pykett 2000: 119)

Several critics, including Pykett, refer to Elaine Showalter's interpretation of *The Judge*. Showalter sees the "bitterness" and "intense self-hatred" in the portraits of women who "gave in and despised themselves for giving in" (Showalter 1977: 119; qtd Pykett 2000: 245).

Having cited numerous precedents from other novels and other critics that would direct us to read the ending of *The Judge* tragically and having pointed to textual evidence that proves a sad ending, Pykett then turns away from novelistic conventions and textual evidence to Bonnie Kime Scott's argument that both West and James Joyce enact a modernist generative cycle. Using Scott, Pykett suggests that the ending may also be read as Ellen's "ascent rather than descent into motherhood" (Pykett 2000: 119).

> Scott suggests that both *The Judge* and *Ulysses* develop a characteristically modernist cyclical theory of history. ... In West's case "the over-arching figure" in this process of refiguration is the generative cycle, in which the creative or constructive cycle is ... feminine and the destructive or disruptive incident is gendered masculine. (Pykett 2000: 120)[13]

I agree with Pykett's reading of Ellen's journey as an ascent into motherhood which justifies her claim for victory at the novel's end. Scott's generative cycle is implicit in the celebration of nature that Ellen learns from her mother and in the appreciation of nature at the book's close. A female gothic reading endorses and also explains Pykett's suggestion of a positive reading. Pykett struggles to justify an affirmative reading because she—like Ellen—is hampered by New Woman conventions. A. R. Cunningham explains that the New Woman novel's commitment to realism and the reality of women's social position often leads to compromise—if not contradiction. Ellen Melville would fit Cunningham's New Woman heroine of the "purity school": "The New Woman of the purity school rejected the absurdities of an imposed feminine delicacy while retaining much of the traditional structures of sexual relationships" (Cunningham 1973: 181). Cunningham admits that "these novels do not on the whole offer an encouraging picture of what emancipated theories could achieve in practical terms" (Cunningham 1973: 182). John Kucich describes the problem that West avoided by combining her New Woman plot with a female gothic plot. In analyzing scholars' criticisms of the New Woman novelist Sarah Grand, he frames the problem as a problem of the choice of literary conventions: "A woman's choice of form would always involve a belated selection among possibilities that seemed only to aggravate women's lack of cultural authority" (Kucich 1996: 202). Kucich bemoans the authority of male genres which constricts women's choices (in a New Woman novel). But we have seen that the gothic has already been gendered female and therefore liberates a woman writer from male cultural authorities. West's combination of female gothic conventions with New Woman conventions creates a contact zone where different interpretations interplay: what emerges is an ending that subverts a male gothic tragic ending or a New Woman bitter, sad, or contradictory ending.

A female gothic perspective views this final scene on the island as self-realization for Ellen and therefore offers Ellen a fate less tragic than either Mrs Melville's or Marion's. In calling out to get Richard's attention, Ellen was trying to avoid her mother's fate of self-sacrifice and insignificance. This rejection and separation from her mother was a hubristic assertion of self—an action more characteristic of Marion Yaverland than of Mrs Melville. As Ellen contemplates the [male gothic] "*horror* of all that had happened to her," she also realizes the folly of her self-important exclamations and gains an understanding of herself and her common humanity:

> But the *horror* of all that had happened to her, and its refusal to be anything but *horror*, viewed from whatever aspect, had begun to be agony when there broke on her that which is the reward of tragedy. She perceived the miraculous beauty of the common lot. Men and women taking children home in trams ... people on summer afternoons going into the country in brakes ... that wedding-party she and her mother had seen long ago. (*TJ* 428, emphasis added)

Her memory of her mother reminds her of the "miraculous beauty of the common lot" and she understands that her mother's failure to insist on herself was modesty and an allegiance to her shared humanity with the "common lot" and not self-sacrifice. The inspiration of the island landscape reminds Ellen of nature's divinity, peace, and proportion: "The call of the redshanks, the cloud shadows that moved over the marshes like the footprints of invisible presences, made her feel calm" (*TJ* 430).

At this closure, Ellen has reconnected with her mother and defines her own identity in terms of her mother's love of nature and her affirmation of a common humanity. This is Ellen's victory and the conclusion to the mother-daughter plot of this multipronged story.

> Though the night should engulf Richard and Marion, the triumph was not with the night. In throwing in her lot with them and with the human race which is perpetually defeated, she was nevertheless on the side of victory. (*TJ* 430)

In Ellen's final reconciliation with both Marion and her mother, West offers a new view of the heroic and rejects oedipal violence to argue for a mutualistic, egalitarian world where people live not in contention or domination, but in mutual support and connectedness.

4

"A Mystical Confusion of Substance": Satire and Fantasy Fuse in Rebecca West's *Harriet Hume*

West was able to solve the challenges posed by writing a New Woman novel by combining New Woman novel conventions with gothic novel conventions in *The Judge*. *The Judge*'s reach is broad: it addresses troubling social, political, and economic issues—such as women's suffrage, workplace harassment, poverty, classism, industrial capitalism, and single motherhood—while foregrounding personal issues such as family relationships, heterosexual love, spirituality, and the imagination. West's use of the gothic—and especially its recurrent references to the Burkean (i.e. gothic) sublime in nature—and her development of a transcendent imaginative connection with nature based on nineteenth-century British Romantic poetry's celebration of nature and the imagination draw attention to art's transformative abilities in this novel.

Many of the preoccupations of *The Judge* will continue to figure in West's works. West's next published novel is *Harriet Hume* (1929). It too addresses the New Woman, classism, the "masculinist-capitalist" system, and the transformative potential of the imagination. *Harriet Hume*'s style and tone are strikingly different from *The Judge*'s. Politics—and especially a criticism of imperialism and a "masculinist-capitalist order"—gain much greater prominence in this work.[1]

The Judge fuses two "minor" genres that are often "gendered" and inherently subversive. *Harriet Hume* blends political satire and fantasy. Political satire has a more elevated and a more established generic tradition than the New Woman novel, the gothic novel, or fantasy. West nonetheless combines genres in *Harriet Hume* to subversive ends. *Harriet Hume* uses political satire and fantasy to critique West's society as an invidious and inherently violent patriarchal-capitalist-imperialist system. As Jacques Derrida later critiqued Western logocentrism, West criticizes the dualistic and hierarchical values of her contemporary society because they deny the "other." By combining the conventions of political satire and fantasy, *Harriet Hume* promotes a Derridean celebration of *différance* through a *jouissance* that subverts the ironclad strictures of West's contemporary society.

Harriet Hume was written in the late 1920s and published in 1929. It tells the story of two characters, Harriet Hume and Arnold Condorex, by depicting the events of just five days in their lives: the last day of their young-adult love affair and their four subsequent meetings over the next twenty years. Arnold's butler makes an occasional appearance and two policemen meet up with Arnold and Harriet at the very end, but there are really no significant characters except for Harriet and Arnold. Unless one counts London. The vivid descriptions of London give the city a palpable presence.

Part 1 Political satire

West chooses both conservative and revolutionary genres for her transformative goals throughout her career. *Harriet Hume* blends two potentially subversive genres. West explains the inherently subversive nature of satire and "wit" in "The Strange Necessity": "The Anglo-Irish ... were revolutionary by temperament and wanted to create exactly what their environment said should remain uncreated. They were therefore bound to be witty, since wit is in its essence revolutionary, a readiness to show that the foundations on which our assumptions stand are rotten and might as well be kicked out of the way with a phrase" (*SN* 152).

The novel's portrait of Arnold Condorex and his career are at the heart of its political satire. *Harriet Hume* is an indirect satire in the Menippean tradition whose portrait of Arnold Condorex indicts the British class system and more specifically British imperialism and the exploitative values that inform it. Arnold is infected with a drive for power that has been imposed upon him by his culture: "'But a man must rise in the world!' ... [This] intention was unalterably a part of himself. He could no more remove it than he could uproot his own breath. ... It dominated him, he was its instrument" (*HH* 56–7). West suggests early in the novel that Arnold's ambition is deadly and violent when she compares it to "lead": "For he felt his intention to rise in the world like lead in his bosom" (*HH* 60). Arnold sometimes fleetingly regrets the cost of his rise, but he rationalizes, "I could never have suffered obscurity. ... I shall not rest until all men have admitted that I am their peer" (*HH* 113). In describing Arnold's mania, West chooses the word "peer"—which can mean "a person of the same rank" *or* a "nobleman"—deliberately. She blames British society's hierarchical nature for the system's emphasis on power.

Arnold is devoted to self-aggrandizement through power. He forsakes Harriet in the first chapter in order to court women whose connections can help his political career. The novel traces the rise of his career and the deceptions and betrayals that enable it. West employs predictable satiric strategies including exaggeration and ridicule to underline the folly of Arnold's ways. Arnold's social rank and power are both fatuous. His social standing comes from his marriage to a woman of title and status whom he does not love or respect (he compares her to a limp anchovy [*HH* 177]). His political achievement received its first boost through a speech about a place in Asia (Mondh) which does not exist. His possessions—including the "vast Chimborazi-Mecklenburgh" car (*HH* 112)—are all obtained through enormous debt and the credit of his fraudulent social standing and name. His political career advances through betraying his friends and patrons and making foreign alliances based on false premises.

Though they are appalling, the typically Menippean exaggerated depictions of Arnold's failings risk seeming comic rather than malign. The similarities between West's portraits of Arnold Condorex and the Archduke Franz Ferdinand in *Black Lamb and Grey Falcon* emphasize the gravity of Arnold's political betrayals and wrongdoings and also the seriousness of West's satiric intentions. Arnold's faults are not to be taken lightly. In *Black Lamb and Grey Falcon,* West blames centuries of imperialism by many foreign powers for the strife in the former Yugoslavia and views this imperialism as the cause of the First World War. West deplores the assassination of Franz Ferdinand, but she also criticizes his imperialist role as Archduke of the vast Austrian-Hungarian Empire which suppressed the national culture in countries it occupied. Arnold Condorex and Franz Ferdinand are remarkably similar. West unsympathetically portrays the Archduke as an arrogant imperialist (like Arnold who was stationed in India for a time) who imposed himself and his power on others and thus incurred his own death. According to West, Ferdinand—like Arnold—is driven by his obsession for power. His acts—like Arnold's—are greedy and self-serving. Some—like Arnold's—are also fatuous. West describes a "rumour that ... the Kaiser laid before Franz Ferdinand a plan for remaking the map of Europe" that is reminiscent of Arnold's invention of new places on the map of Asia (*BLGF* 340). Arnold is paranoid and obsessed because he was not "born with family and fortune" (*HH* 189). According to West, Ferdinand was also embittered with a "sense of being betrayed by life" (*BLGF* 334). Both Ferdinand and Arnold advance themselves by betraying others who are therefore ready for revenge and by making alliances with scoundrels who then turn on them.[2]

Arnold's suicide inevitably results from a chain-reaction of self-centered and devious decisions. Ferdinand's death—and thus the Great War—is also pictured as the result of suicidal decisions. West says of Ferdinand's assassination in Sarajevo:

> The character of the event is not stamped with murder, but with suicide. Nobody worked to ensure the murder ... so hard as the people who were murdered. ... Long ago he himself ... had placed at their posts the beaters who should drive him down through a narrowing world to the spot where Princip's bullet would find him. (*BLGF* 336, 350)

At the end of *Black Lamb and Grey Falcon*'s account of Ferdinand's death in Sarajevo, West invokes the Archduke and says to him, "So was your life and my life mortally wounded" (*BLGF* 350). The close parallels between Arnold and Ferdinand suggest that the Great War was just one link in a long chain of events caused by the imperialist actions of a "masculinist and capitalist" system that in West's mind originated before the war and continued during the time *Harriet Hume* was being written (West 1933b: 484).

Reprehensible as both Ferdinand and Arnold are, West does not entirely blame them for their actions. Her comments on Ferdinand and his wife could also be applied to Arnold: "Yet they were of their time. They could not be blamed for morbidity in a society which adored death, which found joy in contemplating the death of beasts, the death of souls in a rigid social system, the death of peoples under an oppressive empire" (*BLGF* 350). Arnold and Ferdinand are both perpetrators and victims of the "masculinist and capitalist" system that West decries.

Black Lamb and Grey Falcon is not ironic or satiric. *Harriet Hume* is. The exaggeration of Arnold's faults make him ridiculous compared to Ferdinand, but no less dangerous. As Leon Guilhamet says of satire: "If comedy presents its ridiculous objects as things of no importance, the harmlessly ugly or base, satire interprets the ridiculous as harmful or destructive" (Guilhamet 1987: 7).

The irony of characters' names in *Harriet Hume* contribute to the political satire. Typical of many satires, the names are often exaggerated or pretentious. Arnold's last name is Condorex (condor = a vulture; rex = king); his fatuous title is Lord of Mondh (*monde* = world, which—typical of satires—is ironic and pretentious because it does not actually exist); his profiteering political allies are named Faycequonpeut (*fait ce qu'on peut* = do whatever you please), Scorchington (scorch = to devastate completely before abandoning to the enemy), Grindlay (grind = to crush, oppress, or harass), Filiaepandarus (*filiae* = children, pander = a person who caters to or profits from the weaknesses or vices of others; pimp), Tarnishwing (tarnish = to diminish or destroy, stain, sully) and Camaralzaman of Mangostan. Arnold belongs to an elite club named Senile Abercorn; he visits a club named Boodles for "English gentleman" who possess an "ineradicable loyalty to Venus, Mars, and Bacchus" (*HH* 113). Arnold and Filiaepandarus create a company called "London Hills Exploitation Company, Ltd" (*HH* 169). All of the names reflect the corrupt, exploitative, rapacious nature of the politics behind imperialism. Some of the old guard politicians have more integrity than Arnold and his cohort, but these aristocrats are at best weak and ineffectual. Their effete names such as Derrydown and Ladydady suggest that the decadent aristocratic system is degenerate and deteriorating.

Harriet's lack of ambition underlines the faults of Arnold's drive for power. If she has any ambition, it is to advance music for its own sake. Because of her small hands, she is better suited for chamber music than for solo performances. Her comparisons between different forms of music and different forms of government underline her differences from Arnold. Arnold thinks of her chamber music as failure or defeat:

> This is surely much less glorious than to have concerts dedicated to her solo performance, or to have whole orchestras dedicated to her accompaniment, as she used to do. ... He scanned her face for marks of failure. ... But the creature held herself as confidently as an heiress. (*HH* 139–40)

To Harriet, however, "To sit alone at one's instrument is to be like an unlimited monarch," which she does not desire (*HH* 143). She compares "orchestral performance" that depends on the authority of the conductor to an unruly democracy of many parts that risks instability. "Chamber music," which requires the agreement, harmony, and self-effacement of its individual players, is "the ideal form of government." She wants not power, but to be kind (*HH* 143–4). And she wants the universe to be like music. "If I have been no service to you," she says to Arnold when she warns him of a trap to ensnare him in his schemes, "then the world is not good music" (*HH* 206).

Through its portrait of Arnold Condorex, *Harriet Hume* defines the faults of this deadly "masculinist and capitalist" system and suggests remedies for it. West criticizes this system for its materialism, its elevation of power, its hierarchy, its logical positivism, and its persecution of the other. With our proleptic advantage, we can use Jacques Derrida's critique of Western culture's "Philosophy of the

Same" to frame West's theories in contemporary terms. The similarities between West's and Derrida's theories highlight the violence inherent in even Arnold's seemingly trivial actions. A comparison between West and Derrida can also lay a foundation for an analysis of West's esthetic in this novel. The subversive aims of West's artistic practice help us understand West's place in modernism.

West condemns the masculinist-capitalist-imperialist system most emphatically because of its intolerance—its inability to accept what might proleptically be called Derridean *différance.* Harriet and Arnold become increasingly estranged during the course of the book. Harriet's character and values contrast with Arnold's. Their differences alienate Arnold and he comes to detest Harriet as his "opposite." The last chapter depicts his mad chase across London in order to murder his "opposite," Harriet. Arnold's monomaniacal pursuit of his "opposite" is a brilliant premonition of the violence inherent in what Derrida calls the "Philosophy of the Same." Through her depiction of Arnold in *Harriet Hume,* West argues that a sort of Derridean Philosophy of the Same underpins imperialism.

Arnold's goal is to insist on unity and identity and exclude difference. Having unquestioningly accepted the edicts of British society, he has completely convinced himself that "a man must rise in the world" and that he must do so according to the criteria imposed on him by that twentieth-century patriarchal-capitalist-imperialist world. He is famous for his talents for "negotiation" which resemble Derrida's description of Western metaphysics in their totalizing power. Arnold can make almost anything conform to the scheme of things he has inherited. This ability to compel facts to conform to his system resembles Western metaphysics' ability to negate "the other" through rationalization:

> For all of Arnold Condorex's advancement had been earned by his talent for negotiation, and with none could he negotiate more successfully than with himself. He had dealt with his own soul most ably on this matter, begging himself to forget that and to remember this, to let that go because it had a sharp edge and would draw blood whenever it was picked up, but to keep that because it dovetailed with this or that to make a profitable whole. (*HH* 72)

His powers of negotiation assail the "confusion of substance" that seems, to Arnold, to be the world's natural state (*HH* 253, 255, 261). Arnold's logocentrism would like to "fix" things stably into categories: "Why what a universe this is! One cannot mention any of its details without being shocked by its confusion! ... I would transport you to a purer world where things sit more stably in their categories. I would clang an iron gate on you and shut you in" (*HH* 209).

These same powers of negotiation compel Arnold to see difference as alien and Harriet as an intolerable "other." Arnold sees Harriet as his "opposite." Because she is his "opposite" and he is committed to his Philosophy of the Same, he often cannot understand her. He says to her in their penultimate encounter, "But what you have said to me to-night has for the most part been so peculiar to your world, which is not mine, that I have had the greatest difficulty in finding any answers. ... And why was it so? ... It is because you are my opposite" (*HH* 212). With Derridean logic, this recognition of difference leads to exclusion: "He made motions with his hands as if to beat her away from his home, stepped backwards over the threshold, and slammed the door ... and he claimed jauntily, 'Well, I have excluded her!'" (*HH* 212–13). Understanding necessarily leads to hatred because Harriet's point of view contradicts Arnold's and threatens his own philosophy: "She had come between him and every human being's right not to know quite what he is doing" (*HH* 110).

The steps in Arnold's assault of his "opposite" closely resemble Derrida's description of Western metaphysics' suppression of the other. At first he tries to assimilate Harriet—through kind words and charm. West sees the threat in this kind of assimilation. Harriet "knew his praise of her was not without its viciousness" (*HH* 100). When he cannot assimilate her, he resorts to hierarchy and judges her as trivial and insignificant. He dismisses "Harriet's infernal witchcraft" (*HH* 109) as "outside the field of reason, and nothing that he had ever intended to occupy his time with further" (*HH* 94). This hierarchical judgment belittles her as a "fool," a "silly slut," a "wench," a "trollop," and a "goose." Arnold's objectification of Harriet is most obvious in this denigration through epithets which subordinates Harriet according to the values of his patriarchal and rationalist world. Nonetheless, all of these maneuvers deny Harriet's subject position.

In his discussion of Levinas, Derrida recognizes the isolating and unethical nature of the denial of the "other": "To renounce the other is to enclose oneself within solitude (and the bad solitude of solidity and self-identity) and to repress ethical transcendence" (Derrida 1978: 91). This denial results in "parricide" and violence, according to Derrida:

> Incapable of respecting the Being and meaning of the other, phenomenology and ontology would be philosophies of violence. Through them, the entire philosophical tradition, in its meaning and at bottom, would make common cause with oppression and with the totalitarianism of the same. (Derrida 1978: 91)

West illustrates the danger and violence behind such an intolerance of difference through the extremity of Arnold's final reaction. When Harriet insists on her difference from him and refuses to interpret the world and his actions according to his rationalizations, he feels that the only way he can survive is to murder her: "There is no room in the world of spirits for opposites ... it has room for only one will. There is not a particle of accommodation for opposites. ... To concede to one's opposite, in the most infinitesimal degree, is to die" (*HH* 204–5).

In the end, Arnold understands the violence inherent in his insistence that they are opposites and in his attempts to dismiss difference through negotiation:

> Do not forget that I found it impossible to work without surrendering to the principle of negotiation; and that it led to murder, and logically so. For that principle forbids one ever to let the simple essences of things react on each other and so produce a real and inevitable event; it prefers that one should perpetually tamper with the materials of life, picking this way with the finger-nail, flattening that with the thumb, and scraping that off with one's knife and stamping it on the ground at one's feet; and the most ambitious performance in that line, ay and the most effective, and ... the most horrible is murder. (*HH* 268)

Arnold's explanation of the murderous potential of his insistence on his ideology reveals West's attitudes toward imperialism, an invidious, masculinist, and capitalist system whose ethos inevitably leads to violence.

According to the logic of satire, if the novel condemns Arnold, then Arnold's "opposite" must be celebrated. W. O. S. Sutherland contends that "satire's traditional purpose is to reform" (Sutherland 1965: 9) and he claims, "The [satiric] poet indicates an unfavorable attitude towards the values which are the subject of the satire and a favorable attitude toward the values which act as criterion" (Sutherland 1965: 11). As we shall see, Harriet acts as a satiric "criterion" in many ways. Nevertheless, to obey the logic of satire and to elevate Harriet over Arnold would be to succumb to the dualism that West deplores. West subverts this satiric convention of dualistic hierarchy. Many critics fall victim to this logic. For example, Jane Marcus contends that "the dualism she damns in her critical writing informs her own fiction" (Marcus 1984: 147).

West avoids the dualistic satiric trap by fusing her political satire with a fantasy. A Derridean play of *différance* enlivens the "contact zone" where fantasy and satire meet and allows West's novel to embody the esthetic and the politics it promotes.

Harriet's contrasts with Arnold suggest the possibility of another worldview. Arnold is ruled by the prevailing ideology, but West insists that there are alternatives. The alternative worldviews need not be constructed dualistically. West has been called Manichean, but *Harriet Hume* reveals that—like

Derrida—she believes that dualistic binaries (Reason/Irrationality, Male/Female, Civilization/Nature, Spirituality/Sensuality) are *constructs*, ways of denying the "other." Harriet recognizes that she and Arnold are different, but she does not see difference as problematic. Arnold calls their "confusion ... [of] opposites" "an unseemly chaos" and asks, "You would agree, would you not, my dear, that we are opposites?" Harriet replies, "Ay, we are opposites. ... But surely that is no great harm. There is the North, and there is the South, and there is no *war* between them" (*HH* 203, emphasis added). She sees her "difference" as a "supplement" to Arnold rather than as a "negation" of his values. Arnold, too, finally sees that the hatred stemming from difference is not inherent in difference, but rather is "of [his] own making": "I clean forgot your pretty image about the North and the South, which would have kept me from identifying difference with enmity, and I most maliciously pretended that the spiritual world had been infected by you with a condition of hatred that was entirely of my own making" (*HH* 271).

Harriet's celebration of *différance* demonstrates West's objection to the dualism that has dominated modern thought. West believes that life is complicated and puzzling and that the "truth" exceeds our intellectual comprehension. The limited human intellect cannot truly divine the complexity of the world, so we falsely reduce things to easy antitheses. She explains in an essay,

> This refusal leaves man to indulge in some of his characteristically false logic. His mind, which is inadequate for the purpose of mastering his environment and therefore always oversimplifies, sees the universe in antitheses, in dichotomies. He says, foolishly enough, for one cannot cut into clean halves two substances that pass into each other by insensible gradation, that there is light and darkness, life and death, pleasure and pain. (West 1940: 337)

The danger of our intellects' falling into simplistic dualisms leads West to criticize modern society's elevation of science, the intellect, and reason. Harriet's playful imagination, her commitment to art, and her fairy tales promote the imagination to help to undermine the authoritative, logocentric system Arnold relies upon. Life refuses to reduce itself to the easy binaries that the human mind creates. Arnold himself suggests that he and Harriet together form a "mystical confusion of substance" (*HH* 203). Ann Norton recognizes that *Harriet Hume* demonstrates our human tendency to fall into habits of dualism while at the same time critiquing dualism:

> *Harriet Hume* is about the way people see the world in pairs of opposites—male/female, artist/politician, private life/public life—and Arnold thinks of men and

> women in broad, dualistic stereotypes. But it is to mock just such thinking that West grants Harriet the power to read Arnold's mind. (Norton 2000: 52)

West celebrates Harriet's spirit and imagination because they refuse to submit to phallogocentrism. Arnold recognizes her spirituality early in their relationship. He reflects, "Of all the women he had ever known she was the most ethereal. Loving her was like swathing oneself with a long scarf of spirit" (*HH* 11). He later remarks that "her spirit was so marvellously transcending all ordinary human limitations" (*HH* 32). She is frequently called spritelike names, including a "nymph" (*HH* 83), a "witch" (*HH* 22), a "sylph," and a "Maenad" (*HH* 102). Harriet's ethereal spirituality is closely linked with her active imagination. When Arnold sees her in the park in their second encounter, he thinks, "If I catch her while she is still there [by the pond] ... she may tell me a fairy-tale about those quacking fellows. She is full of fancy" (*HH* 84–5).

Harriet's spirituality and imagination account for her artistic talents. They also ironically (according to Western dualism that opposes spirit and matter as well as art and nature) connect her with nature whereas Arnold's heavy and objectifying materialism alienates him from nature. West insists on Harriet's sensuality and physical strength which seems to emanate from her spirituality, rather than contradict it. Several critics acknowledge West's challenge to dualism in her portrait of Harriet. In an article about Harriet as a musician Francesca Frigerio comments on the power of Harriet's body in controlling her massive piano: "The idea that the body is controlled by the instrument is here turned upside down: the instrument becomes a prolongation of the body and yields meekly to its solicitations" (Frigerio 2006: 135). Bonnie Kime Scott argues that West "refigures the modernist binary" by giving Harriet qualities that are usually figured in dualistic ways: "Harriet positions herself in the stereotypically masculine domain of culture, as performer, critic, and owner. She does this, however, without relinquishing what is usually placed in opposition to masculine/culture" (Scott 1991: 182). As Frigerio recognizes, Harriet "embodies a model of femininity that powerfully resists some of the cultural and social stereotypes traditionally associated with women artists" (Frigerio 2006: 125). Margaret D. Stetz also recognizes West's "desire to embrace contradictions" in her analysis of West's connections with Oscar Wilde and estheticism (Stetz 2006: 161–2).[3]

This inclusive fecundity differs from Arnold's blind sterility that stems from his singular gift for "negotiation." West's comments on Saint Augustine suggest that Arnold's lack of morals result from his rejection of the imagination. "He [Augustine] was indifferent to the effects of the persecutions he was thus initiating, not because he was cruel, but because his imagination had completely disappeared, as it sometimes does in men of action" (*SA* 140).

Harriet's ability to contain what we conventionally think of as opposites (e.g. art and nature; spirituality and sensuality) is part of what West calls Harriet's "prodigiousness." If a talent for negotiation distinguishes Arnold, an oxymoronic "prodigiousness" distinguishes Harriet. It is Harriet's prodigiousness that both spurs Arnold to and prevents him from excluding her: "When, once across his threshold, he vehemently slammed the door, the vehemence was because he imagined himself slamming it on the prodigiousness of Harriet Hume" (*HH* 67). Her "prodigiousness" suggests the extraordinary and marvelous potential of her variety. It is always mentioned in conjunction with her ability to encompass difference. Arnold feels

> as if they were being swept off the solid earth by a tide of prodigiousness. There was an added marvel in feeling under his hand her heart-beat which showed that though her spirit was so marvellously transcending all ordinary human limitations, she nevertheless kept as faithful a bond with fact as the tick of a clock. (*HH* 32)

The policemen at the novel's end recognize the same ability to encompass transcendent spirit and everyday fact: "'An excellent lady', said the elder policeman, 'and manysided, for I can see that she is full of poetry and fancy and whatnot, and yet not unmindful of the consequences which may follow if the poor weak sons of Adam sit themselves down on cold stone'" (*HH* 273). The epigraph of the book, which comes from Dryden, captures this same oxymoronic quality: "And like white witches, mischievously good." Like Harriet, the word "prodigious" contains contradictory meanings. It can mean "extraordinary in size, amount, extent, degree, force etc" or "wonderful or marvelous," but also "abnormal" or "monstrous" or "ominous." Harriet and the word itself challenge our normal dualistic mindset: things do not have to be "either/or"; rather they can be "both."

Part 2 Fantasy

Harriet's prodigiousness insists on multiplicity and openness. The novel itself is as multiplicitous as Harriet. West achieves this multiplicity which embodies her esthetic by combining her political satire with a fantasy. Although it is clearly a political satire, West does not call her novel a satire; she calls it a "London

Fantasy." It is almost a catalog of the variety of forms which fantasy can take. It contains several interpolated fairy tales which Harriet spins to delight Arnold. Harriet has occult powers including the ability to read Arnold's mind. Harriet's magical powers transform her garden and its spring flowers into a sort of synesthetic symphony at the end of the novel. By the conclusion, Harriet and Arnold may both have entered a world of fantasy or they may both be ghosts. A mannered, fey language lends an unreal aura to the whole. These fantastic, imaginative effects affront conventional notions of "normality" or the "real" and subvert logic and reason in favor of the irrational and spiritual.

West has her own particular definition of "fantasy" which figures into the poetics she articulates in the essay "The Strange Necessity." "The Strange Necessity" uses the word "fantasy" to describe an artist's "hypothesis covering the whole of existence" (*SN* 61). Both Harriet and Arnold are determined through the novel to "test" the perameters and the reliability of their individual worldviews, or "fantasies." According to "The Strange Necessity," "Throughout the whole of his life the individual does nothing but match his fantasy with reality and try to establish either by affirmation or alteration, an exact correspondence" (*SN* 62). Arnold's mad dash across London in pursuit of his "opposite" is his last desperate attempt to make his "fantasy" accord with reality.[4] Part of Arnold's frustration is Harriet's unflagging devotion to her own "fantasy."

Fantasy—in its traditional sense of the make believe or the marvelous—is not foreign to satire. One thinks most immediately of Jonathan Swift's *Gulliver's Travels.* Mikhail Bakhtin argues that modern fantasies are "the direct descendants of ... the *menippea*" (qtd Jackson 1981: 14). Fantasy is an ideal genre for West's transformative and subversive aims. Defined by W. R. Irwin as "a story based on and controlled by an overt violation of what is generally accepted as possibility" (Irwin 1976: xxiii), a fantasy flouts Arnold's logical positivism and his elevation of reason and "categories."

In spite of fantasy's obvious affront to "reality" and "reason," it has not always been used for subversive ends. Renaissance and Enlightenment fairy tales were often popular, oral folk tales rewritten in order to inculcate aristocratic and conservative values.[5] According to Jack Zipes, "The educated writers purposely appropriated the oral folk tale and converted it into a type of literary discourse about mores, values, and manners so that children would become civilized according to the social code of the time" (Zipes 1983: 3). By the nineteenth and early twentieth century, however, writers had begun to perceive the subversive potential of fairy tales. Zipes mentions George McDonald, Oscar Wilde, and L. Frank Baum as particularly influential practitioners of fairy tales. West was familiar with their works and belongs in their company.[6] "They were the ones who used the fairy tale as a radical mirror to reflect what was wrong with the general discourse on manners, mores, and norms in society, and they commented on this by altering the specific discourse on civilization in the fairy-tale genre" (Zipes 1983: 99).

Harriet Hume presents a whimsical world that elevates imagination, creativity and art to promote equality, non-utilitarianism, tolerance, and diversity, but it does not reject reason, politics, or the public life. Harriet recognizes Arnold's important accomplishments:

> You must admit that when you [Arnold] were not pursuing the chimera of greatness, you performed many very worthy achievements that enabled our species to establish itself on this globe more firmly. Did you not see to the building of bridges, the teaching of children, the suppression of riot and bloodshed? (*HH* 267)

West does not want to expunge the public world. She wants to transform politics through a dynamic play between values that allow variety and difference to prevail. West's portraits of Arnold and Harriet, their careers, and their romance clearly demonstrate these values. Her deployment of many different "kinds" of fantasy allow her novel to embody its esthetic. The dialogue between satire and fantasy creates a "contact zone" that West hopes will lead to the transformation of real world politics.

Harriet Hume's use of Tzvetan Todorov's "fantastic" particularly helps West achieve her transgressive goals. Todorov's ideas about and definitions of the kinds of fantasy offer a useful frame for interpreting West's manipulation of the conventions of fantasy. *The Fantastic: A Structural Approach to a Literary Genre* defines three genres along a fantasy continuum: the uncanny, the fantastic, and the marvelous. Todorov's definition of the "marvelous" is close to Irwin's definition of fantasy: the marvelous occurs when "the reader decides that new laws of nature must be entertained to account for the [apparently supernatural] phenomenon" (Todorov 1975: 41). As our discussion has illustrated, many of the features of West's "London Fantasy" conform to Todorov's genre, the marvelous.[7] At the other end of Todorov's continuum is the uncanny where "the reader decides that the laws of reality remain intact and permit an explanation of the phenomenon described" (Todorov 1975: 41). If the policemen in Chapter 5, for example, are real and not ghosts, *Harriet Hume* may have elements of the uncanny where things seem "marvelous" but have a real world explanation. Marion's perceptive powers in *The Judge*, for example, are not "marvelous." They are so unusual, however, that they border on the "uncanny." Many features of Arnold's final pursuit of Harriet could also be uncanny.

The middle term in Todorov's continuum is the fantastic which is defined by the readers' uncertainty. This uncertainty leads them to "hesitate" between a "natural and a supernatural explanation of the events described" (Todorov 1975: 33).[8] The fantastic exists in the transformative "contact zone" that we have analyzed in all of West's works. Harriet's occult powers are one example of the fantastic. Her ability to read Arnold's mind appears to be "supernatural" and thus places the novel in the realm of the marvelous. Harriet, however, explains that her psychic abilities are "natural" extensions of her artistic abilities (*HH* 35). West's esthetic theories corroborate Harriet's interpretation of her powers. According to "The Strange Necessity," Harriet's psychic skills could be extreme versions of "empathy":

> Art ... deals with man's experience of uncontrollable material that can tell lies to the observers and has to be circumvented in the exercise of this gift before one can get the truth. This circumvention is contrived by the use of empathy, which is our power of projecting ourselves into the destiny of others by fantasy, and which we employ in different ways to suit the different arts. (*SN* 176)

Peter Wolfe interprets Harriet's powers as a "natural" celebration of love: "The ability to join in the reality of another person is the fullest expression of love" (Wolfe 1971: 43). Arnold and the reader, however, hesitate and find themselves hovering in the fantastic where they cannot decide if her abilities have a "natural or a supernatural explanation" (Todorov 1975: 33). The reader's and Arnold's hesitation between realms intensifies as the story develops in the account of Arnold's political and personal downfall. The marvelous increasingly invades the real world and Arnold's grasp on reality becomes questionable. As his butler contradicts Arnold in Chapter 4, the reader wonders if the butler is in the "real" world and Arnold is either in a "dream" or if his ordeals have driven him "crazy." If Arnold is in a dreamworld, the novel has entered the marvelous. If Arnold is crazy, we are in the uncanny.

In Chapter 5, after rushing madly across London in order to kill his "opposite," Arnold aims his pistol at Harriet through the window of her house, but two policemen stop him. After a desultory conversation between Harriet, Arnold, and the policemen, Harriet and Arnold are reconciled. The book closes with Arnold at the threshold of Harriet's house and the policemen wishing them "A Very Happy Eternity."

By the time we reach this conclusion which seems to usher us from the uncertainty of the fantastic into the marvelous, many questions about the "natural or supernatural" nature of "the events described" have arisen. Harriet, for example, has just returned from a visit to her family where she was "obliged to go ... to assist at a religious ceremony ... [that] they could not well have ... without me" (*HH* 272). Could this be her funeral? How could she be dead if the policemen just stopped Arnold from shooting her? It also seems possible that the policemen are already dead. One of the policemen talks of catching pneumonia twenty years ago and the other mentions diving into the water to rescue a boy five years ago. The policemen's faces also seem ghostlike; Arnold looks "from the face of one to another and see[s] nothing but patches of white dimness between a helmet and a chin-strap" (*HH* 264). If the policemen's faces are different from Arnold's and Harriet's faces and the policemen are ghosts, then can Arnold and Harriet be ghosts? Uncertainty abounds.

If we are in the realm of the marvelous at the end of story, questions about the "real" status of earlier seemingly realistic details emerge. As early as Chapter 1, we witness Arnold's triumphant thoughts about his "rising in the world," when

> a misgiving came on him. It was as if one, sitting in a fine room he had lately furnished and preening himself because all was well and all was paid for, should see between two of the floor boards a dark pool trickling. Where had he been infected with this monstrous doubt that rising in the world was not the supreme good? (*HH* 63)[9]

One wonders if this is a premonition of his suicide? Or had the suicide already occurred before the beginning of the novel? In Chapter 2 and Chapter 3, Harriet's gown has red stains first from cherries and then from "a drop of wine" (*HH* 128, 204). Could these be blood stains from wounds from Arnold's pistol? Is Harriet already dead? In Chapter 3, Arnold and Harriet debate whether or not imaginary beings can have ghosts which leads to Harriet's conjecture, "Though, indeed, it is hard enough to distinguish which of the multitudinous forms of the universe are ghosts" (*HH* 156). Are Harriet and Arnold already ghosts during this early conversation? Harriet regrets the fact that she and Arnold still love each other in Chapter 3 in terms that could imply that they are dead:

> And to-day is terrible because it has shown we are still concerned with one another. Each of us has always hoped that a stranger would come who would scatter holy water on the image of the other and lay it for ever, but time goes on, and that stranger does not come.

> He murmured, "Ay, so it is, so it is," and the darkness round him became as absolute as if it were the womb, the grave. (*HH* 167)

Are they scattering holy water on their dead bodies? Is the darkness really the darkness of the grave?[10]

Another proof of the fantastic nature of the novel is the lack of consensus among critics about the novel's conclusion. Jane Marcus believes that Arnold's suicide "is a fantasy" (Marcus 1984: 145). However, she does not believe that Arnold has killed Harriet at the novel's end. Peter Wolfe concludes that both Harriet and Arnold are dead at the end of the novel, but Arnold's death is only "possibly a suicide" (*HH* 45). He does not question the reality of the policemen. Carl Rollyson, like Wolfe, believes that Arnold is dead, but is not sure if it is suicide. He, however, believes that the policemen are dead, but asserts that Harriet "refuses to die" (Rollyson 1998: 71). Ann Norton captures the fantastic potential of the novel in questioning whether we are supposed to read the ending "literally or symbolically": "It is hard to know whether Arnold's suicide and murder of Harriet are fantasy or reality" (Norton 2000: 55). Bonnie Kime Scott also insists on the indeterminacy of the novel: "The action of *Harriet Hume* is difficult to represent in realistic terms ... Arnold Condorex wishes to shoot Harriet, and may actually do so before killing himself" (Scott 1987: 279).

Todorov believes that very few works sustain "the fantastic in its pure state" through their conclusions. Henry James's "The Turn of the Screw" is one of the only books in which "the ambiguity [persists] to the very end, i.e. even beyond the narrative itself" (Todorov 1975: 43). *Harriet Hume* may be another rare case of the "pure fantastic."

The uncertainty and indeterminacy of the fantastic serve West's transformative goals well. Todorov is a formalist and does not delve deeply into social, cultural, or political dimensions of genre analysis, but even this Russian formalist recognizes the disruptive, subversive potential in the fantastic which breaks "fixed law[s]" and "established rule[s]": "For the transgression of the law to provoke a rapid modification, supernatural forces must intervene" (Todorov 1975: 165). He also acknowledges the social and political possibilities of literary transgressions:

> We see, finally, how the social and the literary functions coincide: in both cases, we are concerned with a transgression of the law. Whether it is in social life or in narrative, the intervention of the supernatural element always constitutes a break in the system of pre-established rules, and in doing so finds its justification. (Todorov 1975: 166)

Rosemary Jackson, who draws from Todorov's work, also stresses the transgressive power of the fantastic: "Fantastic literature ... opens up, for a brief moment, on to disorder, on to illegality, on to that which lies outside the law, that which is outside dominant value systems" (Jackson 1981: 4). She stresses the necessary dialogue between fantasy and the real in the fantastic. Like my model of hybrid genres, the interaction between the real and the marvelous give the fantastic its transformative powers according to Jackson. Because Todorov's marvelous can exist on its own, it has the potential to disrupt "the real world," but it can also exist outside of, and therefore, not affect the real world. In its requisite interaction between the supernatural and the real, the fantastic transforms the real world. Jackson, too, sees the "prodigious" potential of the fantastic. Just as Harriet encompasses contradictions, the "basic trope of fantasy," according to Jackson, "is the oxymoron, a figure of speech which holds together contradictions and sustains them in an impossible unity, without progressing toward synthesis" (Jackson 1981: 21).

Normally associated with Harriet, the words "prodigious" and "prodigy" return in the novel when Arnold commits suicide, which is the definitive act that initiates serious questions—on the part of the readers and Arnold—about whether the novel is "real," "marvelous," "uncanny," or "fantastic." Arnold's butler tells him that his servants are awake in the middle of the night. "Why, since an hour ago they have none of them been able to sleep in their beds for a feeling that something *prodigious* was about to happen in the house" (*HH* 215, emphasis added). Soon after this the butler informs Arnold that "the *prodigy* they expected is happening. ... There are three strange ladies descending the staircase, with a rope of flowers in their hands." These are the three Graces from a painting by Joshua Reynolds who are the subjects of Harriet's most sustained fairy tale—and who have supposedly been transformed into trees in Harriet's garden. As beautiful and fanciful figures who possibly mark Arnold's presumable suicide, they conform to several definitions of the word "prodigy," including "wonderful," "marvelous," "prophetic," and "monstrous." As fairy-tale figures who cross the boundary from fairy tale into the real world, they usher the novel into the fantastic.

Scenes which cause one to hesitate between a "real," "marvelous," or "uncanny" interpretation of the story increase in number after Arnold's possible suicide. One of the most striking of the fantastic scenes occurs in Harriet's garden at the end of the novel. Harriet's magic produces a sort of synaesthesia—a combining of sensory spheres which flouts rationalist thinking that would sort the world into stable categories. All of nature seems "confused" or inverted in her garden at the end of the book as her magic ushers in the creative wonder of spring. Stars drip sweetness; grass and flowers "pressing up through the earth" like "rain hissing upwards"; snowdrop flowers appear like a "pattering [of] ... an inverted hailstorm"; and "like slow lightning the cherry-blossom drew its white design" (*HH* 279, 281). So complete is the transfiguration of the senses that "a phrase in a sonata by Mozart" becomes a "pretty blue flower"; "almond trees" become "second violins"; "daffodils," "brasses"; and "hawthorn trees," "wood-winds" (*HH* 282). Just as Harriet's prodigiousness has transformed her garden into a fantastic sphere, West hopes that her novel can transform her contemporaries' lives and their world.

If Harriet as a person upsets Arnold's logocentric, patriarchal, and dualistic worldview, *Harriet Hume*, as a novel, uses its combination of satire and the fantastic (a generic celebration of Derridean *différance* and excess) to overturn West's contemporary world and its masculinist-capitalistic-dualistic system. The indeterminacy of the fantastic underlines the novel's lack of closure or definition which embody the openness and multiplicity that the text celebrates. There is no one truth. All these devices undermine power and authority in favor of free play and variety. West does not want to "fix" anything—nor to rule or to dominate. Just as Harriet's house has no door, this novel has no central gateway to truth.[11] We must approach truth indirectly and unconventionally.

West's generic hybrid of satire and fantasy moves the text beyond Derrida's theories. In fact, her ambition in *Harriet Hume* to overturn a constraining and authoritative social system corresponds remarkably with her own definition of a mystic:

> A mystic distrusts all institutions. ... He fears lest the thickness of their walls shall prevent man from hearing when God speaks to him. ... We see why the institution has so often cried out ... in accusation against the mystic. (qtd Rainer 1965: 260)

As frequently happens, West's detractors are her most telling interpreters. They misunderstand West because they are firmly entrenched in the logocentric, authoritative system that she would subvert and because they are committed to this system's conventions. Peter Wolfe, for example, criticizes *Harriet Hume* as the "most artificial and the most arbitrary" of West's works and decries its excess: "The dreariest conglomerate in the book, however, is a sentence that extends to 224 words, refreshed by only three semicolons" (Wolfe 1971: 42). He also casts aspersions on the fairy tales and the long, lyrical descriptions of London: "She weakens dramatic impact by inserting several long set passages which neither advance the plot nor extend it" (Wolfe 1971: 43). Wolfe fails to see that arbitrariness, excessiveness, and playfulness are precisely the effects West *wants* to achieve. A linear, logical plot written in concise language would undo the esthetic which inspires the novel. West's own description of Virginia Woolf's *Orlando* could apply to *Harriet Hume*:

> There does not seem any reason at all to doubt that in this book has been issued a poetic masterpiece of the first rank; that is, a work which illuminates an important part of human experience by using words to do more than describe the logical behavior of matter, by letting language by its music and its power to evoke images convey meanings too subtle and too profound to be formulated in intellectual statements. (West 1928b "Genius": 1)

West's work itself is "prodigious." She has used a dualistic portrait of men and women to highlight *différance* in order to refute dualism. She celebrates difference to dissolve duality into a "mystical confusion of substance." She also insists on indeterminacy and openness in her fusion of satire and fantasy. West offers a solution to the many forms of dualism—the dissociation of sensibility and the loss of a unity of being—that beset the modern consciousness. Many modernists solved this regrettable dualism through a reconciliation of opposites or through a synthesis. West offers another solution through her Derridean celebration of heterogeneity and excess—what could be called "*jouissance.*"

5

Art's "Blazing Jewel" in *The Strange Necessity*

The Judge was published in 1922 and *Harriet Hume* in 1929. West also worked on her unfinished novel *Sunflower* throughout the 1920s. During this time she was traveling, lecturing, writing for British and American journals, and also composing her collection of essays *The Strange Necessity* (1928). The book contains the title essay and several of West's pieces written for American and British journals during the 1920s. *The Strange Necessity* is the most unabashedly hybrid of West's works. The eponymous essay contains 198 pages arranged into six sections which blend several genres in order to analyze and to explain the "strange necessity" of art for a meaningful life and for a moral society. Generic hybridity is inherently subversive insofar as it mixes "fixed categories" (and thus, undermines their "fixity"). Nonetheless one certainly can imagine a work that combines two hidebound genres which might inhibit artistic possibilities. An examination of "The Strange Necessity" can afford us a test case for the transformative potential inherent in hybridity. The critical assessment (by West's contemporaries and also by subsequent West scholars) of West's interdisciplinary essay can also measure the potential or the threat of hybridity. Following are the genres contained in this work:

- A novella in the tradition of James Joyce's *Ulysses* (1922) and Virginia Woolf's *Mrs Dalloway* (1925). The essay recounts the reflections of a twentieth-century narrator-*flâneuse* as she strolls through the streets of Paris on a brisk fall day.
- A scientific treatise that popularizes the discoveries made by Ivan Pavlov (1849–1936) in his experiments that resulted in *Conditioned Reflexes.*[1]
- West's "poetics," an explanation of the meaning and function of art.
- A book review of James Joyce's *Ulysses*, typical of the many reviews that West was publishing at this time.
- Twelve essays from the 1920s (mostly book reviews) from *The New York Herald-Tribune*, *The Bookman*, and *The New Statesman.*

Part 1 Novella

The story-like frame for West's essay announces its hybrid nature. West's biographer and critic, Carl Rollyson, has called "The Strange Necessity" "a work of criticism and esthetics in the form of a novel" (Rollyson 2007: 57). West describes her narrative method in a letter to Richard Ellmann as "criticism in a personal and almost fictional framework" (*SL* 327). West pays tribute to *Ulysses* by imitating Joyce's narrative mode. Joyce's novel follows the peregrinations of Leopold Bloom and Stephen Dedalus as they wander the streets of Dublin on June 16, 1904. By treating everyday people following mundane lives, Joyce draws upon and expands a realist esthetic practiced by his predecessors such as Henrik Ibsen, Anton Chekhov, and George Bernard Shaw. By naming his novel *Ulysses,* Joyce suggests that Bloom is a heroic figure and that the sublunary lives of middle- and lower-middle-class people deserve heroic stature. Woolf's *Mrs Dalloway* likewise gives heroic status to upper-middle-class Clarissa Dalloway, her family, and her associates as they navigate the streets of London on a June day. West pays homage to the realist esthetic that informs these other profane adventures by rendering one day in the life of her heroine as she strolls through the streets of Paris. Like Joyce's and Woolf's narratives, West narrator's adventures are distinguished by their apparent triviality. The narrator buys a book of poems and a black lace dress, retrieves letters from the post office, visits a lawyer about investments, detours to the Louvre in order to glance at an Ingres painting, and stops at a milliners to try on some hats. This elevation of the middle class and their preoccupations subverts British elitism. West's readers were familiar with her attention to class issues in *The Return of the Soldier* and *The Judge.*

Part 2 Scientific analysis

The crux of "The Strange Necessity" is West's analysis of Pavlov's *Conditioned Reflexes.* Pavlov's experiments with dogs and his discoveries about the physiology of the brain and the central nervous system provide the methods and concepts essential to West's poetics. She dwells, in particular, on Pavlov's description of the "investigatory reflex," which she calls the "What-is-it" reflex (*SN* 74): the part of the mind or central nervous system that surveys the flood of sensory stimuli that bombard us and then ferrets out the relevant stimuli that will lead to an "excitatory complex." This excitatory complex instructs the nervous system how to react to the stimuli. All this takes place in the cerebral cortex. The more analytical the investigatory reflex, the better the synthesis which results in the excitatory complex: "The healthy human being automatically rejects excitatory complexes which are the results of statements about the experience instead of being the products of analysis and synthesis" (*SN* 183).

Although science and art may appear dissimilar, an examination of their similar operations reveals many commonalities: "In fact, art is out to collect information about the phenomena of the universe, just as science is" (*SN* 118). Art, like science, creates a pattern that interprets reality.

Part 3 Poetics

Part 3A Similarities between scientists and artists

West's analogy between the cerebral cortex and its analyses and syntheses by means of an investigatory reflex that results in an excitatory complex are central to her poetics, which explains the necessity of art. "The Strange Necessity" stakes out West's place in a long line of artists and philosophers who have reflected upon the meaning and the function of art including Plato and Aristotle. The British tradition includes Sir Phillip Sidney, William Wordsworth, Percy Bysshe Shelley, and Matthew Arnold. Several of West's fellow modernists developed poetics particularly suited to the modernist world. "The Strange Necessity" belongs among modernist manifestoes and poetics by William Butler Yeats, Virginia Woolf, Mina Loy, Ezra Pound, and T. S. Eliot.[2]

According to West, artists turn to the world's phenomena, collect the salient stimuli (using their investigatory reflex), and organize these stimuli into an excitatory complex. This excitatory complex produces a pattern, which is an artist's personal interpretation of reality. West christens an artist's pattern, a "fantasy." Some artists' fantasies approach the true pattern of the universe more successfully than others. In addition, some fantasies are relevant to a wider range of people than others.[3] Jane Austen, Thomas Hardy, and Marcel Proust all have fantasies that have particular relevance to a great number of people. West esteems Proust because "to establish this argument about life, to coerce events into this pattern, was his passion whether he were living or writing" (*SN* 111). "Good art" is "the product of a powerful nature that has been able to form an interesting and intricate fantasy or which is able to prosecute with spectacular vigour the effort to make the fantasy and reality match" (*SN* 65). Talented artists use their highly developed "empathy" which enables them "to penetrate imaginatively into the experiences of others" (*SN* 100). West describes the intensity of her appreciation of art as "a blazing jewel" (*SN* 195). Inferior art is produced by artists whose idiosyncratic temperaments create fantasies which are not relevant to most people *or* whose fantasies make statements about the world which lack the "analysis" and "synthesis" of fine art.[4]

Part 3B A national culture as an external cerebral cortex

An artist's genius and the range of an artist's experiences affect the quality and the influence of a work of art. Even more important than an individual author's innate talents is the artist's geographic and historic location. West argues that individual artists draw on a "common fund" of accumulated experience (*SN* 167). This common fund of experience and art create a sort of super-cortex that supports individual artists. True to the democratic and inclusive impulses that inform all her works, these nationally shared experiences can be trivial. What is important is that they be shared among individuals with a common culture. West explains,

> What the artist needs is to live in a world unified by common experience and common art. Then he can serve himself by noting the postman's morning greeting, the first sentence in the newspaper leader, the type used for an advertisement on the hoardings, the way the flowers are planted in the cottage gardens—for all these phenomena are determined by the experiences of the human agents responsible for them and the effect on those agents of the analysis and synthesis of similar experiences of the artists and scientists who have operated within the same zone of civilization. (*SN* 172)

West invokes Fyodor Dostoevsky to explain the importance of a shared culture to artists: Dostoevsky believes "that man must maintain all his connections with his native country if he is to establish a connection with God" (*SN* 147). Authors who are exiled from their countries are at an immense disadvantage because they have to start from scratch so to speak. In the meantime, artists at home in a cultural tradition draw upon patterns of fantasies that have the potency and wealth of centuries of analyses and syntheses.

West provides numerous examples of artists who profit from the "common fund of ascertained reality" (*SN* 167) and artists whose works suffer because they are alienated or exiled. Goethe, for example, profits from a tradition: "The real impressiveness of a Genius like Goethe lies not in the perfection of any individual piece of work he performed, but in the ubiquity which he displayed scouting on every frontier of the collective intelligence" (*SN* 65). Alienated writers who are deprived access to the collective intelligence suffer a real disadvantage: "Wild, wild, is the *émigré*, the *déraciné*. ... Consider the increasing complication, the titanic efforts to spin cocoons out of themselves that would account for everything, which marked the works of those great exiles" (*SN* 172–3). Rudyard Kipling, who spent most of his life in exile, is an example: "Here is some one who knows nothing of life except what he had found out for himself" (*SN* 157).

A comparison between William Butler Yeats and William Blake demonstrates the importance of an inherited national culture. West argues that both George Moore and Yeats suffer because they are Anglo-Protestants in an Irish-Catholic country; they

> are great artists ... under a handicap which does not seem to press on native-born writers of the same sort. ... It seems as if they know nothing of life except what they have found out for themselves. Their power of analyzing and synthesizing their own experience is unequaled, but they seem to be cloistered from the knowledge of anybody else's analyses and syntheses. (*SN* 154)

West believes that Yeats is more intelligent and more "sane" than his fellow-mystic, William Blake. Nonetheless, Blake's mystical works are superior to Yeats's.[5]

Is West's poetics that stresses a coherent culture subversive? The risk of "nationalism" which can result in a knee-jerk xenophobia and which will result in Nazis in Germany and Fascists in Italy suggest the conservative threat of West's poetics. A political journalist as well as a literary critic and a creative writer, West recognizes the risks implicit in her position. She will deal more thoroughly with the differences between her cultural nationalism and Germany's and Italy's politics in *Black Lamb and Grey Falcon* (1941). She does, nonetheless, address this problem in "The Strange Necessity." People benefit from a rich cultural tradition, but the advantages of a national culture does not excuse any sort of racial, ethnic, or national prejudice. After quoting Dostoevsky's validation of cultural coherence, West emphatically condemns any sort of "social prejudice."

> Dostoevsky may not have seen an elderly English Colonel alluding to "those damned Frenchies" or a New York banker announcing that he has withdrawn his child from the Newfoundland School because it has accepted among its pupils the son of a Jewish millionaire, but we have, and we are perfectly certain that at no moment are such persons further from their god. (*SN* 147)

Her cultural nationalism undermines the prevailing social, political, and economic attitudes of her times because of its inclusive, nonhierarchical emphasis.[6] Poetics since Aristotle have been inclined to rank literary genres. Aristotle viewed tragedy as the highest form of art. Epic also was among the elite genres for Aristotle. The impulse to hierarchize genres endured so long that both Joyce and Pound fell under its sway. West resists all efforts to give one genre priority over another. As we saw in the list of trivial events that can create a cultural and national tradition, she opposed any form of elitism in literature. She topples traditional hierarchies such as social class, wealth, career, and position as she ponders the features of "good" art. In *A Letter to a Grandfather* and in *Black Lamb and Grey Falcon* the lowly are the most high. (A Negro carnival worker is divine and the Yugoslavian peasants have great nobility.)

Artists who profit from a national tradition also create works of art that are more likely to be unified. West argues, "I do not think we can exaggerate the fundamental unity of all art and all experience" (*SN* 189). This elevation of a cultural tradition which can encourage art's coherence is typical of many modernists.[7] Yeats's effort to regain a "unity of being" in the modern world was his lifelong endeavor. One thinks obviously of T. S. Eliot, whose *The Waste Land* (1922) draws on many different traditions, and also his essay "Tradition and the Individual Talent" (1919). A regret for the loss of a national cultural tradition is also linked with a desire for a unity of experience by many modernists. Eliot's essay "The Metaphysical Poets" decries a modern "dissociation of sensibility" and hence also promotes a kind of unity or synthesis which existed in the past, but is no longer viable in the modern world.[8] Douglas Mao compares West to Eliot, but to the "later" Eliot and cogently captures their differences: "West's invocation of Europe and tradition ... bears comparison to T. S. Eliot's use of these terms. ... But where Eliot treats a common culture as both the foundation and the ambition of a ecclesiastical Europe, West's ultimate term is not culture but survival in a hostile universe" (Mao 2008: 206).

T. S. Eliot's ideas about tradition in the late 1920s were influencing and in turn being influenced by the Humanists, especially Paul Elmer More and Irving Babbitt. West would take issue with the Humanists' elevation of tradition and took pains to distinguish her arguments in favor of cultural nationalism from their worship of tradition—especially in several articles in the early 1930s (after *The Strange Necessity* was published). West would like her contemporary literature to create its own sort of "contact zone" where literature from the past and contemporary literature converse with each other. She fears that Humanists revere the past at the expense of modern writers:

> It is true that acceptance of Professor Babbitt's main thesis will do nobody any harm. To prefer Aristotle to Rousseau is certainly the way of grace ... it illumines argument to have Professor Babbitt state the case again with his unrivalled power of allusion. ... But to accept his attitude towards the moderns seems to me a pity. (West 1930: 516)

West repeatedly defends the relevance and the importance of modernist literature against the Humanists: "I do not find however that humanism is likely to maintain tradition as satisfactorily as the modern writers—Proust, Joyce, Lawrence, Virginia Woolf, Aldous Huxley to name but a few whom it sweepingly repudiates" (West 1930: 515). Always aware of elitism, she also faults the Humanists' elitism:

> We have strayed into a world, not high in the intellectual cosmogony, where it is held that certain beliefs are in themselves a certificate of mental gentility. Those who hold them are entitled to look at persons of equal gifts and attainments who do not hold them as, in another world ... persons in the Social Register look at persons not in the Social Register. (West 1930: 514)

In discussing West's choice of the word "nationalism" or "national traditions" in "The Strange Necessity" and its corollary discussion, Mao finds, "Perhaps more interestingly problematic, however, is her use of 'nationalism' to name something that we would more usually call 'culture'" (Mao 2008: 208). I believe that West uses "nationalism" because her condemnation of imperialism underlies all her works and all her theories. To West "nationalism" is the opposite of "imperialism." The very word condemns one's country's exertion of its political, economic, or cultural power on another country. In recognizing a country's moral right to its own culture, "nationalism" is more emphatic than "cultural tradition," for example. I also think that West wanted to distance her insistence on the necessity of a connection to one's national culture from the [New] Humanists' promotion of "tradition." She also would want to separate herself from the Humanists because of her interdisciplinary approach and her firm desire for art and science to cooperate toward understanding. West regretted the Humanists' rejection of science and especially theories of evolution. Finally, the word "nationalism" in the 1920s had much less resonance than it has today. *The Strange Necessity* was published in 1928, but West wrote many of the articles and parts of its title essay in the mid-1920s. At this time, imperialism was as great a threat as fascism. With the rise of fascism, West's term "nationalism" gained connotations that she could not have fully predicted in the mid-twenties.

Part 3C The hybrid advantage

"The Strange Necessity" proves the value of hybridity. West's insistence on the relevance of science in understanding art and the parallels she makes between the two fields invite her readers into an interdisciplinary "contact zone" where they must maneuver in order to gain one or several generic perspectives. The instability of this zone encourages openness and transformation. We have witnessed the transgressive potential of this space "between" genres where different genres parley and interact in an open, inclusive space rather than confront each other in a dominant and subordinate relation or a dualistic dynamic.

A corollary of West's works' commitment to a transformative hybrid dynamic is an awareness of British class systems. "The Strange Necessity" delves into West's subversive poetics to locate art's transformative potential in the middle class. Change often brought growth or prosperity to members of the British middle class in the nineteenth century and the early twentieth century. They, therefore, encourage or permit change. The aristocracy, on the other hand, are content with their place in a hierarchical society and thus resist change.[9]

West's poetics in "The Strange Necessity" is inspired by her desire to understand why she instinctively ranks her encounters with Joyce's works as more significant than the many other activities she engaged in on her Paris promenade. She asks,

> Why could I not give the whole of my psychic energy to Paris ... to dresses and hats ... to love and money? Yet the soul knows best. There must have been something in *Ulysses*, something about James Joyce, the understanding of which was more essential to me than anything of these things. (*SN* 52)

This essential importance of *Ulysses* leads West to esteem art and literature above her other preoccupations on this autumn day.

Part 4 Book review of James Joyce's *Ulysses*

West considers *Ulysses* a masterpiece. She particularly admires the characters Leopold and Molly Bloom. Comparing Leopold to a "court jester" and "the

Shakespearean fool," she praises him because he lends nobility to a simple, earthy soul. Bloom is a reminder to all Joyce's readers not to forget their material, physical aspects and not to aspire too high.

> I do most solemnly maintain that Leopold Bloom is one of the greatest creations of all time; that in him something true is said about man. ... Simply he stands before us, convincing us that man wishes to fall back from humanity into the earth, and that in that wish is power, as the façade of Notre Dame stands above us, convincing us that man wishes to rise from humanity into the sky, and that in that wish is power. (*SN* 43–4)

West also praises Molly's monologue, the grand finale of the novel: "In the last forty two pages [Molly Bloom] becomes one of the most tremendous summations of life that have ever been caught in the net of art" (*SN* 47).

West's praise of *Ulysses*, however, is not unalloyed. She takes issue with Joyce on several counts. Moreover, some of the features that give her qualms were the features that other modernists celebrated—and which gave Joyce eminence in the ranks of the experimental avant-garde. West, no doubt, realizes that her comments will *épater l'avant-garde* just as her contemporaries also deliberately *épater le bourgeois.* For example, West did not champion the parallels between Joyce's novel and Homer's *Odyssey.* She felt that the dualistic—essentially Manichean—structure of *Ulysses* was incompatible with a classical structure: "For Mr Joyce to write his Manichean epic with a dove-tailing fidelity to a Greek pattern is as sensible as it would be to write a novel about Middle Western farm life in French alexandrines" (*SN* 29).

She also took issue with Joyce's stream-of-consciousness technique. Joyce's method, she argues, assumes that words are language's essential units. She believes that sentences are more fundamental to language than words.[10] Some of Joyce's attempts to be "revolutionary" actually violate the organic unity of his art: "Seduced by his use of heterodox technique into believing himself to be a wholly emancipated writer, James Joyce is not at all ahead of his times in his enslavement to the sentimental" (*SN* 20).

West groups her most serious criticisms of *Ulysses* under the rubric of sentimentalism and sentimentality. Sentimentality violates the essential unity of all art and all experience. When an author violates the organic unity of a work either for the sake of his personal emotions or in order to manipulate his audience's emotions, he is guilty of sentimentality. A work of art should have the organic unity of a tree (*SN* 16). When an artist is successful "there is no part which rebels against the whole, there is the peace of unity" (*SN* 17).

A minor example of Joyce's sentimentalism—his desire to gratify himself and to shock his readers—is his use of obscenities. West is not offended by the obscenities and she recognizes that "some artist may ... find it necessary to use these Anglo-Saxon monosyllables ... for the completion of some artistic pattern" (*SN* 21). Nevertheless, West believes that Joyce's obscenities do not fulfill an artistic pattern but rather serve Joyce's personal ego—an atavistic adolescent desire to "protest against the adult order of things" (*SN* 21). Readers can recognize the sentimentality "by that spurt of satisfaction, more actual but also more feeble than authentic artistic emotion which marks the pages whenever he uses them" (*SN* 21). Joyce's impulse to gratify adolescent emotions reveals his narcissism. Authorial narcissism is fatal to the organic unity of a work of art. West connects authorial narcissism with sentimentality in Joyce's narcissistic impulse to manipulate his readers' reactions. Joyce's narcissism is also evident in the character Stephen Dedalus—who is a self-absorbed self-portrait of the young Joyce.

> These too are familiar, and as features in fiction of a not at all revolutionary sort. They are, in fact, the constant ingredient in almost every novel in which an Oxford or a Cambridge graduate looks back on the Oxford or Cambridge undergraduate that he was five minutes previously and reverently commemorates the chrysalis ... the same narcissistic inspiration, which inevitably deforms all its products with sentimentality, since the self-image which it is the aim of narcissism to create is made not out of material that has been imaginatively experienced but out of material that has been selected as likely to please others. ... Again the values have been externally adjusted. (*SN* 22)

In spite of these shortcomings, West insists that Joyce is a man of genius and that *Ulysses* is a masterpiece.

> But I claim that the interweaving rhythms of Leopold Bloom and Stephen Dedalus and Marion Bloom make beauty, beauty of the sort whose recognition is an experience as real as the most intense personal experiences we can have, which gives a sense of reassurance, of exultant confidence in the universe, which no personal experience can give. (*SN* 50)

Part 5 *Pater familias*

West's poetics establishes a place for her among the important modernist writers and critics. The features of art that she promotes and the language she uses directly recall several other modernists' poetics and establish affiliation for her works. Margaret D. Stetz contrasts West's attitudes toward her predecessors with the male modernist "anxiety of influence." Stetz claims that West's "published criticism was dominated by the concept of alliance" (Stetz 1994: 48). In writing about West's relation to the visual artists, Stetz invokes Sandra Gilbert's and Susan Gubar's "female affiliation complex" which they believe was a "preoccupation of all the women writers in our century" (Stetz 1994: 44). Stetz describes West's "efforts to discover and to use models—parent-texts, parent-figures" (Stetz 1994: 43). Inherent in its Freudian constructs, "affiliation" can be conscious or unconscious. Although West is clearly a descendant of Pater, she never claimed him as progenitor. She did, nonetheless, write favorably of the British Decadents' ideals if not their works. In *Henry James,* West criticizes the British Decadents for their "lack of worldly success," but praises them for their "moral mission" (*HJ* 80).[11] Anticipating her use of the word "jewel" in "The Strange Necessity," she praises these descendants of Pater: "It was of inestimable value that it should be cried, no matter in how pert a voice, that words are jewels which, wisely set, make by their shining mental light" (*HJ* 81–2).

Several essays in *The Strange Necessity* consider the work of writers whom West dubs the "literary uncles" to her generation. She lists the "Big Four": "All our youth they hung about the houses of our minds like Uncles, the Big Four: H. G. Wells, George Bernard Shaw, John Galsworthy, and Arnold Bennett" (*SN* 199). West is grateful to these literary uncles for their benign influences and describes each uncle's particular gifts to their descendants. She also enumerates their faults. The choice to make these literary predecessors "uncles" is telling. It suggests "affiliation" with this previous generation of writers, but not direct descent. Choosing "uncles" is perhaps a way to avoid the "anxiety of influence" more common in filiation of direct descent. It can also be a way for a woman author to acknowledge her debt to tradition (often male) without threatening her separate identity. Chronologically these writers are the correct age to be uncles to West's generation. West, for example, was born in 1892 when Shaw, Wells, Bennett, and Galsworthy would have been respectively thirty-six, twenty-six, twenty-five, and twenty-five years old.[12]

If one were to give "The Strange Necessity" a genealogy, one could create a line of direct descent starting with Walter Pater (1839–91) and especially his work *The Renaissance* (1873, 1888). Pater, who would have been fifty-three years old when West was born, is recognized as the progenitor of several generations of writers in diverse traditions, including estheticism, symbolism, and modernism. The similarities between Pater and West give us a clearer sense of West's essay and also help situate West among her modernist cousins—who are also descendants of Pater. Stetz has demonstrated the filiations between West and the Decadents and Symbolists, especially Oscar Wilde (2006). Wilde (1854–1900) would number among West's uncles (on the other side of the family from the Big Four).

This chapter examines Pater as "*pater familias*" and his influence upon West and her literary cousins in the same line of descent, James Joyce and Virginia Woolf. West's language and ideas in "The Strange Necessity" bear testament to her affiliation with Pater. Her descriptions of the apprehension of art's pattern (a "blazing jewel") recall Joyce's epiphanies and Woolf's "moments of being." Pater, Joyce, Woolf, and West claim that art, the appreciation of art, or an artistic apprehension of reality are crucial to vital living.

Moreover, all of these artists' esthetics are interdisciplinary. Pater and Woolf rely on science's improved understanding of our physical lives to conjecture about our spiritual lives. Joyce's works are replete with scientific details. His epiphanies also draw on the Roman Catholic Church and especially Saint Thomas Aquinas.

The urgency behind these artists' esthetics stems from the spiritual crisis of modernity that influences many of West's works. According to Pater, "We are all *condamnés*, as Victor Hugo says: we are all under sentence of death but with a sort of indefinite reprieve" (Pater 1910: 238). Joyce echoes Pater's sentiment in the expression he coined: "the incertitude of the void" (Joyce 1986: 572). Woolf captures this same human vulnerability in numerous images in her works such as the following description of Mr Ramsay in *To the Lighthouse*:

> It was his fate, his peculiarity whether he wished it or not, to come out thus on a spit of land which the sea is slowly eating away, and there to stand like a desolate sea-bird alone. (Woolf 1927: 43–4)

Mr Ramsay—like many modernist figures—is alone, isolated, and precariously perched on deteriorating land "with a sort of indefinite reprieve," as Pater would say. Clarissa Dalloway's comment in hearing of Septimus Smith's suicide echoes Mr Ramsay's sense of human vulnerability: "In the middle of my party, here is death" (Woolf 1925a: 279). West too registers human frailty in her comment, "My personal happiness is staggeringly insecure" (*SN* 193).

Typically, humans combat the "incertitude of the void" and the fleeting nature of life through religion or—in a secular world—by achieving a sort of immortality through achievements such as political power, personal fame, or material possessions. Pater and his modernist descendants do not measure their lives by the items "found in our obituaries/Or under seals broken by the lean solicitor/In our empty rooms" (T. S. Eliot, *The Waste Land*) *or* through Love, Politics, and Religion (Dr Bradshaw's tripartite gods in Woolf's *Mrs Dalloway*). Pater, Joyce, Woolf, and West (and many other modernist authors) reject traditional secular attempts to challenge the fleeting insignificance of our lives as hierarchical, materialistic, and dualistic. They affirm intense moments of life or experience which can provide significance to our lives.

Life, for Pater, is composed of a multitude of sense impressions which our consciousness seizes and analyzes. He declares, "The service of philosophy, of speculative culture, towards the human spirit, is to rouse, to startle it to a life of constant and eager observation" (Pater 1910: 236). Marshaling these observations together, the goal is "not the fruit of experience, but experience itself. ... To burn always with this hard, gemlike flame, to maintain this ecstasy, is success in life" (Pater 1910: 236).

Woolf, like Pater, chooses scientific language to frame her promotion of "gemlike" experiences which she calls "moments of being." She enjoins her readers of "Modern Fiction" to

> examine for a moment an ordinary mind on an ordinary day. The mind receives a myriad impressions—trivial, fantastic, evanescent, or engraved with the sharpness of steel. From all sides they come, an incessant shower of innumerable atoms. (Woolf 1925b: 154)

Woolf discovers "moments of being" which give significance to life. Woolf's "moments of being" intervene in her life with "a sudden violent shock; something happens so violently that I have remembered it all my life" (Woolf 1976: 71). Woolf celebrates these seemingly trivial "moments of being" as glimpses of truth—that are, according to the very nature of reality, necessarily fleeting and irrational (unintellectual). They seem utterly unimportant, but to Woolf they confront the void. Clarissa Dalloway's following "moments" are typical:

> Looking at the flowers, at the trees with the smoke winding off them and the rooks rising; falling. ... Heaven only knows why one loves it so, how one sees it so, making it up, building it round one, tumbling it, creating it every moment afresh ... In people's eyes, in the swing, tramp, and trudge; in the bellow and the uproar ... what she loves; life; London; this moment of June. (Woolf 1925a: 3)

Woolf's moments of being resemble West's appreciation of art by revealing "a pattern" and also in their organic unity: "Behind the cotton wool is hidden a pattern; that we ... are connected with this; that the whole world is a work of art; that we are parts of this world of art" (Woolf 1976: 72). Pater decries habits which make our lives monotonous and dull. Habits inhibit flame-like, intense moments. Woolf also contrasts boring, senseless living with her intense "moments of being." She contrasts the intensity of her "moments of being" with moments "imbedded in cotton wool" which she also calls "moments of nonbeing." Woolf's moments of nonbeing resemble the unimportant errands in "The Strange Necessity" which pale in the memory in contrast with West's "blazing jewel," the moments of appreciation of art.

Joyce's "epiphanies" also share many qualities with Pater's gem-like moments and Woolf's "moments of being." Stephen Dedalus reflects on epiphanies in *Ulysses* and defines them in the earlier work *Stephen Hero*: "a sudden spiritual manifestation, whether in the vulgarity of speech or a gesture or in a memorable phase of the mind itself" (Joyce 1963: 210). Joyce's epiphanies share a unity or integrity with Woolf's moments of being and with West's blazing jewels: "The three things requisite for beauty are, integrity, a wholeness, symmetry and radiance" (Joyce 1963: 212). These qualities, which are borrowed from Thomas Aquinas's theology, serve Joyce's secular and esthetic goals well. Joyce's account of an epiphany's dynamics recalls West's investigatory reflex which asks "what-is-it" and the pattern and structure of West's concomitant excitatory complex. The spiritual is present and transcendent in the incarnate physicality of an epiphany: "Its soul; its whatness, leaps to us from the vestment of its appearance. The soul of the commonest object, the structure of which is so adjusted, seems to us radiant" (Joyce 1963: 213).

West's description of the "blazing jewel" of art in "The Strange Necessity" echoes Pater.[13] She compares her appreciation of art to a "blazing jewel" five times in "The Strange Necessity." She also describes her experience in terms of illumination. West's reaction to *Ulysses* is a case in point: "This blazing jewel that I have at the bottom of my pocket, this crystalline concentration of glory, this deep and serene and intense emotion that I feel before the greatest work of art" (*SN* 195). Pater and West both choose the metaphor of fire to stress the intensity of an artistic experience. Woolf also chooses metaphors of light and illumination to portray art's ability to order life's chaos. The dinner party at the Ramsay's in *To the Lighthouse* is chaotic and the guests are hostile, isolated, and bitter. Then the candles on the table are lit and harmony results: "Now all the candles were lit up, and the faces on both side of the table were brought nearer by the candlelight, and composed, as they had not been in the twilight, into a party round a table, for the night was now shut off by panes of glass, which ... inside the room, seemed to be order and dry land" (Woolf 1927: 97). Mrs Ramsay asserts that "of such moments ... the thing is made that endures" the flux and the disorder of moments of nonbeing (Woolf 1927: 105).

Fires also have the paradoxical quality that William Shakespeare's Sonnet 73 describes: "The glowing of such fire/That on the ashes of his youth doth lie/As the deathbed whereon it must expire,/Consumed with that which it was nourished by." The more intense a fire is, the more quickly it destroys itself. West consistently develops and celebrates paradoxes in order to defy the dualism that underpins Western metaphysics. A "gem" appeals to Pater because of its concentration and its precision. It is Pater's goal to increase the quality of life by increasing the intensity of the moments which fill up our appointed "intervals": "For our chance lies in expanding that interval, in getting as many pulsations as possible into the given time" (Pater 1910: 238). The importance that West attaches to "pattern" and "design" gives special resonance to her literary jewels and their "crystalline concentration" (*SN* 198). "Crystalline" can mean "transparent," "clear," or "like a crystal." A crystal is a solid material whose constituent atoms, molecules, or ions are arranged in an *ordered pattern* extending in all three spatial dimensions. The metaphor of a crystal suits West's hybrid, interdisciplinary goals because of its scientific associations. Art's jewel has an intricate structure which is transparent to the beholder—and therefore reveals a "pattern" intrinsic to all good art.

These modernist intense moments—which provide significance to our lives—are often "private" and subjective. Pater captures this inherent subjectivity:

> Experience, already reduced to a group of impressions, is ringed round for each one of us by that thick wall of personality through which no real voice has ever pierced on its way to us, or from us to that which we can only conjecture to be without. Every one of those impressions is the impression of the individual in his isolation, each mind keeping as a solitary prisoner its own dream of a world. (Pater 1910: 235)

Deplorable as the values which underpin them are, the traditional challenges to human vulnerability and transience—such as Colonel Bradshaw's Politics, Love, and Religion (in Woolf's *Mrs Dalloway*)—do have virtues. These beliefs and the institutions that support them create "society" in the pure as well as institutional sense.[14] They can unite isolated personalities and therefore avoid the inevitable subjectivity of "that thick wall of personality" which keeps "the individual in his isolation ... as a solitary prisoner."

Woolf and West address the threat of isolation implicit in subjectivity more directly than many modernists. Woolf does not completely accept Pater's "thick wall of personality." She chooses metaphors that acknowledge the potential isolation of her "moments of being," but also gesture toward a solution: "Life is not a series of gig lamps symmetrically arranged; life is a luminous halo, *a semi-transparent* envelope surrounding us from the beginning of consciousness to the end" (Woolf 1925b: 154, emphasis added). Although we are doomed to subjectivity because of our isolation, Woolf's "envelopes" of personality are "semi-transparent." She believes that one individual's moments of being can intuitively connect with another's. The similarities between Septimus's and Clarissa's moments of being mean that they intuitively connect.[15] They make their own party, so to speak. In *To the Lighthouse* Mr Carmichael and Mrs Ramsay look at a basket of fruit. They both explore the fruit creatively and imaginatively. Their visions are different and their personalities are inimical, but they nonetheless "connect" through their simultaneous visions.[16]

West solves the threat of isolation implicit in the inherent subjectivity of her blazing jewel with her "super-cortex": the shared national cultural tradition that kinsmen possess and that an artist can draw upon. Every authentic work of art adds to the super-cortex. Thus, in spite of the isolation and subjectivity of individual experiences, humans can have a common fund of art. West declares, "What the artist needs is to live in a world unified by common experience and common art" (*SN* 172). "When man made art make itself half-inside and half-outside him, that making became an essential part of him" (*SN* 173).

Pater, Joyce, Woolf, and West would foster a richer life through heightened perception of and participation in the impressions of the world around them. Art plays an essential role in a meaningful life for all of them. Joyce's epiphanies are spiritual moments grounded in mundane existence; one can create and appreciate them in our sublunary lives. Or an artist can convey the *quidditas* of a thing through his epiphanies in his work of art. Woolf's moments of being contribute to a life worth living; like Joyce's epiphanies, they can be the building blocks of a timeless work of art. Pater and West agree with Woolf's assertion that "the whole world is a work of art; that we are parts of this work of art" (Woolf 1925b: 72). Pater closes his encomium to passionate living—in "expanding that interval, in getting as many pulsations as possible into the given time"—with the assertion that art is the most direct avenue to the ecstasy in living: "Of such wisdom, the poetic passion, the desire of beauty, the love of art for art's sake, has most. For art comes to you proposing frankly to give nothing but the highest quality to your moments as they pass, and simply for these moments' sake" (Pater 1910: 238). All these artists revere art and its potential to enrich life or to animate the life instinct within the conceptual frameworks that they create.

Under the aegis of Walter Pater as "*pater familias*" these several authors—and many of their cousins—justify and affirm art's "strange necessity." Of them all, West is perhaps the most adamant about art's mandate and its necessity: "It is possible for a man to carry on a sort of existence without art, of course, just as a decorticated dog need not die immediately" (*SN* 174). She elaborates by comparing a decorticated dog to a human being without art:

> A man to whom Henry Ford is a greater man than Shakespeare need not die of it. He can get along in the lap of a lucky economic dispensation exactly as a decorticated dog can get along in the shelter of a laboratory. But when he goes forth into the world he will be without a guide to see that he lives, instead of performing those disordered fantasies of conduct that in no way arrest death. (*SN* 174)

Part 6 Critical reception of *The Strange Necessity*

In spite of the commonalities between West and her contemporaries and of her praise of Joyce and many other artists, the reception of *The Strange Necessity* among West's contemporary artists and critics was mixed, often hostile, certainly controversial—at times wrongheaded. Its reception did not fall into predictable factions. George Bernard Shaw, for example, whom West portrayed as a genial, but limited literary uncle, seemed amused. Whereas other literary uncles received her portraits of them with indignation.[17] Because many of West's critics condemned the volume's hybrid nature, an examination of their critiques can enhance our understanding of West's hybrid ambitions. The contemporary reviews and the subsequent scholarship treat many aspects of *The Strange Necessity.* Many reviews praise West for her analysis of *Ulysses.* In spite of the actual range of opinions about West's analysis of Joyce's work, Joyce's champions (who included William Carlos Williams and Samuel Beckett) resented West's analysis. The cultural myths that modernist scholars inherit from their scholarly predecessors tell a tale of West's misguided opinions of *Ulysses.*

West was roundly attacked for her reservations about aspects of *Ulysses*. In spite of the hostility against West in 1928, twenty-first century Joyce scholar Austin Briggs has read all the pertinent documents and concludes, "In fact, for all its reservations 'The Strange Necessity' is unequivocal in the question of Joyce's genius and importance. ... 'The Strange Necessity' simply cannot be read as an attack of Joyce" (Briggs 1996: 88). It *was* nevertheless read as an attack of Joyce. An examination of critics' resistance to West's essay reveals the cultural context for West's subversive, transformative hybrid goals.

The critiques of *The Strange Necessity* fall into three main categories:

- Hybridity of genres is denounced.
- Unappreciated qualities are "gendered."
- The essay is dismissed because it falls into a "lowbrow" genre such as journalism or political polemics.[18]

Many features of "The Strange Necessity" make it an unstable text for its readers. For example, West pays tribute to Joyce in using her own sort of stream-of-consciousness—which Carl Rollyson describes as a "new form of writing for her that is not easy to follow" (Rollyson 2007: 53). Nevertheless, it is the text's generic variety and its insistent transgression of conventional borders or boundaries that decisively flout reader expectations to create a subversive and transformative text. The text shifts unpredictably from one genre to another. The essay is broken into six sections which have different topics, but no topic is "contained" in one section. Signposts fail to give readers clear directions. This leaves the readers floundering in this erratic contact zone searching for direction and stability. Edward Garnett captures a reader's experience of the text in his 1928 review. The review is for the most part eloquent in its praise of West. It begins, "If the main function of criticism be to render just judgments, a lesser one is to stimulate the reader, to excite him to think. ... For her stimulating qualities when Miss West mounts the platform she bears off many prizes" (Garnett 1928: 135). Garnett continues in this commendatory vein over several paragraphs. He describes the readers' pleasure in "the flow of Miss West's critical observation [which] is agreeably diversified by her retrospections, descriptions, and perceptions of Paris" when suddenly the tone changes with the mention of West's analyses of Pavlov: "We are getting on famously till in an unfortunate hour she plunges knee-deep into a quagmire of pseudo-scientific theorizing" (Garnett 1928: 135). West does not adequately prepare Garnett-as-reader for the many shifts between genres and Garnett—like many readers—finds himself disoriented. The reader needs guidance for the "uptake" that will place him in a known generic world with conventions that give him bearings and that position him to understand West's text. Garnett finds himself figuratively "stuck in the mud" and unable to gain a secure footing. Other critics and reviews express the same generic quandary that leaves readers "grasping at straws" in a literal way in order to locate themselves in a familiar, comfortable space. "Contact zones"—because of their inclusive and open respect for the variety of genres within them—are often difficult spaces. They are especially difficult for readers who depend upon fixity, defined categories, hierarchy, or ranking to help find their bearings.

William Carlos Williams also disparages the generic hybridity of "The Strange Necessity": "A descent to Freudian expedients of classification is in a literary discussion a mark of defeat. Here is a mixing of categories, a fault in logic—that is unimaginable in a person of orderly mind" (Williams 1929: 83). Williams reminds one of Arnold Condorex in his desire to fix things securely into categories. West's esthetic enterprise is to question categories and to move her texts and her readers across borders and boundaries in order to challenge their preconceptions and to move them toward transformation.

Williams ascribes the uncomfortable instability to West, not to her readers: "I saw Rebecca West straining toward some insistence she could not quite achieve so that she appeared wholly off balance ... evidences of exaggeration and nervousness." Williams's approach to West's subversive method is implicitly a "gendered" reading: "off balance," "exaggeration," and "nervousness" are all traits more commonly applied to women than men.

As Williams's disparagement demonstrates, the condemnations of "The Strange Necessity" were often gendered. Victoria Glendinning and Austin Briggs both claim that Joyce took offense because his sacred, highbrow epic was treated on a par with West's lace dress and hats.[19] This protest against lace dresses and hats seems surprising since Joyce's middle-class hero sells ads for newspapers and is described in base and earthy terms. Leopold Bloom is preoccupied throughout *Ulysses* by mundane pursuits and cloacal subjects. The condemnation of West's feminine interests is even more surprising given the fact that she ultimately decides that "art"—and specifically Joyce's *Ulysses*—is superior to her other interests. The particular vehemence against hats and dresses leads one to conclude that West's detractors are sexist as well as hierarchical. They might not have been so insulted had West chosen more masculine pursuits in her perambulatory reflections on Joyce. Conrad Aiken betrays a sexist dualism when he blames "The Strange Necessity" for being "highly personal" (a predictable reproach against women) and requests, "If she could somehow treat her audience a little less as if it were gathered for tea" (Aiken 1929: 211).

Critic Kathryn Laing defends West's attention to dresses and hats—West's "clothes complex"—as a deliberate challenge to her culture's unexamined hierarchies: "It is through this [clothes] complex that they both [Woolf and West] examine the conventionally established equation between femininity, associated with the popular and the vulgar, and masculinized high culture" (Laing 1997: 66). Quoting Laing, Francesco Frigerio also calls attention to the subversive nature of West's contradiction of traditional gendered binaries since "The Strange Necessity"'s narrator is both "a fashion-conscious *flâneur* and a scientific commentator and art critic ... under the banner of border-crossing" (Frigerio 2002: 68).

In addition to subverting traditional gender binaries, West also contradicts the literary binaries, highbrow and lowbrow. For example, Conrad Aiken justifies his contempt for West on the grounds that she is a popular journalist: "One suspects that Miss West belongs rather with the type of journalist-critic than with that soberer and perhaps duller company ... [who] give themselves up to a pure passion for exploration or analysis. There is a good deal of the show woman in Miss West" (Aiken 1929: 212). She refuses to guard pure esthetics from the taint of politics and social issues. Such irreverence earned her criticism from her contemporaries, but is viewed in a different light by twenty-first century scholar Patrick Collier: "She [West] remains the rare critic of the 1920s and 1930s who insisted on both social and political relevance of art and the value of high modernism" (Collier 2006: 173). Collier argues for the merit of West's hybridity. As we have witnessed she refused to entertain the hierarchical constructions that dominated literary criticism in the 1920s and 1930s. For Collier her "commitment to journalism as a force for social advancement and reform provides a perspective through which to measure other modernists' political engagement—including Eliot's, Woolf's, Joyce's and MacCauley's" (Collier 2006: 173).

It is difficult to define West's contemporaries' view of generic hybridity in general and West's hybridity in particular. Although many critics commented on her generic *variety*, this often implied that individual works were in different genres, not that individual works contained more than one genre. *The Strange Necessity* provides an important instance where West's contemporaries recognized that it contains several genres in one work. As a case in point to measure West's fellow modernists' attitudes toward generic hybridity, the critical reception of *The Strange Necessity* suggests that even modernist authors who prided themselves on their own literary experiments and on their esteem for others' experiments found generic hybridity disturbing and threatening. As the most unabashedly hybrid of her works, *The Strange Necessity* proves the importance of West's generic hybridity in all of her works.

6

"The Tragic Spirit has Come Back into Life": West's Works of the 1930s, *A Letter to a Grandfather, St Augustine, The Thinking Reed,* and *The Harsh Voice*

The Strange Necessity (1928) and *Harriet Hume* (1929) are both influenced by the politics, economics, and culture of the "interwar period": a period so distinct that Kristen Bluemel has dubbed it "intermodernism." They escaped the Great Depression, however. The works discussed in this chapter were published in the early and mid-1930s; they respond to an era of trauma and dread which witnessed the stock market crash, the Depression, unrest in Spain which would lead to the Spanish Civil War (1936), strife between Japan and China,[1] and the rise of the Third Reich. Politics and economics overshadowed even the most private lives during this period and they assume a prominence in West's works also.

One of the most original works of this period, *A Letter to a Grandfather* (1933) is an ingenious amalgam of several genres (including an epistolary novella, literary criticism, burlesque, political journalism, and a mystical vision). *St Augustine* (1933) is a biography combined with history and psychoanalysis. *The Thinking Reed* (1936), which fuses tragedy and farce, is the hallmark work of this period. *The Harsh Voice* (1935) is a collection of short stories very much in the vein of *The Thinking Reed.*

A Letter to a Grandfather (1933)

A Letter to a Grandfather is a monograph in the Hogarth Letters Series, which was comprised of twelve letters written by prominent people, including E. M. Forster, Louis Golding, Viscount Cecil, Virginia Woolf, and Hugh Walpole. The other letters were addressed to diverse figures such as W. B. Yeats, "a Young Poet," Adolf Hitler, and "an M. P. on Disarmament." *A Letter to a Grandfather* is from "C. B.," a contemporary member of the fictional Beauchamp family. A member of each generation of the Beauchamp family has a religious vision—"one moment when life was presented ... as a unity"—that is shaped by its contemporary history (*LG* 33). West's choice for her letter reflects her desire for filiation evinced in *The Strange Necessity* and also a skittishness about direct filiation. The first vision by Philippe de Beauchamp was commemorated by an abbey in 1230. Sir John Beauchamp's vision in 1453 resulted in a religious painting of the Trinity, the Virgin Mary, and a legion of saints. Richard Beauchamp expressed his 1670 vision in a poem, "Ode to St Catherine." Since science dominated the end of the nineteenth century, C. B.'s grandfather's vision is scientific. Her grandfather's vision is regrettably unfathomable to her because he has "insulated your articulateness within a screen of pure mathematics" (*LG* 33). C. B.'s vision takes place on a June afternoon in Paris, at the Fête de Neuilly, a sort of carnival on the outskirts of the city.[2] Apparently undaunted by the critical excoriation she received for reviewing Joyce's *Ulysses* while describing her errands for dresses and hats in "The Strange Necessity," C. B.'s letter to her grandfather begins with her description of her dash through Paris to buy clothes. The vision descends upon C. B. as she watches the rhythmical movements of a black carnival worker who ushers patrons onto a merry-go-round. A tawdry carnival and an aged, impoverished carnival worker do not seem propitious subjects for a vision of eternity, but C. B. comes to understand their aptness.

The urgency of contemporary politics stirred the Woolfs to sponsor the Hogarth Letter Series. West's interpretation of their request might seem eccentric, but it allows her to celebrate spirituality and art, to highlight the role of tradition in culture and politics, and to define the nature of her contemporary world in a hybrid work that embodies her ambitions. The letter also gives a historical frame to her contemporary critique. C. B., for example, repeatedly remarks upon a general disintegration of culture since the Reformation. "Of course, it's obvious that something's gone wrong in the last few centuries," she says when discussing her "hereditary faculty of vision" (*LG* 8). She reminds her grandfather, "You said something about it having been the great fault of the Reformation that it broke so many eggs which could not go into that particular omelette" (*LG* 9–10).

In spite of its radically different circumstances, certain aspects of C. B.'s vision echo other Beauchamp visions to underline the importance of tradition. This repetition of aspects of other visions also lends C. B.'s vision universality—a central feature of religion to West. The vision's location in a particular moment gives it a specificity that grows out of her descriptions of art. She contrasts these features of art and religion in her biography of Saint Augustine: "A work of art is the analysis of an experience, an expression of the consciousness of the universe at a particular moment. Religion aims at the analysis of experience, at an expression of the consciousness of the universe through all time" (*SA* 52).

One of her vision's most remarkable features, which links it to other Beauchamp visions, is a dove which "shot forth" from the black man's magician-like gestures:

> With the first finger and thumb of his left hand he described a circle, and into this circle shot the first finger of his right hand. His teeth shone, his rolling eyeballs exhibited the whites of his eyes; it was as if a gleaming bird, a dove, shot forth from his face and in its flight became his finger. (*LG* 41)

Doves figure in the thirteenth-century abbey of Philippe de Beauchamp, in the fifteenth-century painting commissioned by John Beauchamp, and in the counsel of Geoffrey Beauchamp in the eighteenth century. (In "The Strange Necessity," West's narrator sees a dove at the moment she buys a book of Joyce poems.) Doves symbolize the spirit—its purity and its indomitability.

As the characters Margaret and Kitty in *The Return of the Soldier* demonstrate, West pictures the spiritual life and the material life in dire conflict throughout history. Both spirit and matter are fierce in their efforts to prevail. West describes the doves who live in the dovecote of Philippe de Beauchamp's medieval abbey: "The dove, the thing that flies forth, the *logos*, the symbol of the spirit ... that flew down from its tower and pecked the seedcorn and ravaged the crops, while the peasants cursed" (*LG* 12). Material forces do their best to extinguish the spirit, but "there is nothing more evident in history than the persistence of the life of the spirit, and its power to raise up defenders" (*LG* 25). West's works of the 1930s stress the intensity and severity of this battle between the material (as manifested in money, sex, power, and politics) and the spiritual.

Another feature common to several visions is more opaque. C. B. describes it as a "stretched consciousness." When a consciousness stretches through space, it also extends through time beyond the limitations of its fixed position to attain infinity or eternity. According to West's formulation in *St Augustine*, art becomes religion. The quality of this extended consciousness changes according to its time period. In John Beauchamp's 1453 vision, it was beneficent: "So doubtless it has seemed in the moment of his vision; his consciousness stretched up and down through time and out through space ... it grew easily, reaching out from ordinary limited knowledge into experience of infinity and eternity, like a branch of may reaching out into the early summer air" (*LG* 14). Philippe de Beauchamp's stretched consciousness was more severe. His 1230 abbey was

> the kind of architecture, worked in blackish stone, that would have put into the mind the idea of a man stretch on a cross. The arches and doorways and sanctuaries give such a sense of breadth that the consciousness strains itself to follow right and left as far as it can, like outstretched arms; the vaults rise to such a height that the consciousness strains up and down, like a torso stretched so that the muscles are gnarled in the recess under the ribs. (*LG* 11)

C. B. sees the carnival worker as a "gaunt figure extended on a cross" and likens him to Philippe's vision:

> I also saw a gaunt figure extended on a cross, and if the cross was mere existence the pattern was the glorious same, there was the same tension, there was the same heroic attempt to cover all, to know all, to feel all, although fixed to one point in the universe, and thereby pinned to ignorance. (*LG* 44)

The heroic attempt to fathom all in spite of the inevitability of failure is key to all of West's works in the 1930s. It is fundamental to the tragic vision that inspires all these works.

This tragic vision is determined by West's sense of her "fixed point" in time. The Great War made manifest the tragic spirit of our modern age in C. B.'s youth. To C. B.'s disappointment, "I have been still further shocked and enraged by my slow discovery that peace is not much better" (*LG* 34). C. B. regrets materialism and the consequent corruptibility of the body, but "I find still worse ... the more precocious rottenness of the mind. ... People are tired and disoriented, they do not follow any road to truth" (*LG* 34–5). Sadism and masochism infect both the conservatives and the liberals who "have not got out of the fateful ring-fence of primitive ideas where every good must be paid for by pain and sacrifice" (*LG* 36). This "ring-fence" reappears to account for our modern tragedies in *St Augustine* and in *Black Lamb and Grey Falcon.*

Although she accepts that "life is a different thing in different times," C. B. is at first disappointed with the seeming triviality and grimness of her vision. Her acknowledgment of her hereditary gift turns to "uptake" and she expects the glory and the dignity of earlier mystical visions. In one of many allusions to T. S. Eliot in the works of 1930s, West mocks C. B. and Eliot in C. B.'s initial disappointment:

> I feel that in my spiritual apotheosis the nice thing would have been for me to be like the clergyman's mournful widow, muttering about my Waste Lands, moaning

> because it is Ash Wednesday, or to be a Romantic, melting and guttering with my own heat like a candle, or to be a simmering-pot of ethical activity. But that is cowardice. I am a fool to be ashamed of what I saw. It was almost intolerably without comfort or benignity. (*LG* 43)

West's allusions imply that *A Letter to a Grandfather* (and implicitly, as we shall see, *The Thinking Reed*) is a better response to our modernist condition than Eliot's *The Waste Land* (1922) or "Ash Wednesday" (1930). Instead of *The Waste Land* or the glory and dignity of her relatives' visions, C. B.'s vision is a burlesque typical of West's hybrids. In *A Letter to a Grandfather*, high mixes with low and grim reality crosses with imaginative wonder. The genres meet equally and C. B. and West's readers are transformed and reconciled to this vision and to their contemporary world. As C. B.'s consciousness stretches through time, she is able to face the true nature of her historic position and affirm it. The Fête de Neuilly is ugly, dirty, and cheap. C. B. describes it as

> the Utrillo-like face of meaner Neuilly: the houses painted violet-grey like a healing bruise, their shutters waiting with a patient look for that hour when they should be shut and each room might be the ciborium of some dreary copulation, some murderous assault; a quarter set aside for consummations of the cancerous human need to be cruel and to suffer. (*LG* 38)

The worker is pale, ragged, and exhausted. Nevertheless, the Holy Spirit emanates from him: "That I see the spirit not as holy or independent, but as the white product of dark gestures, the refined descendant of man's primitive play, does not matter; I still revere the dove and its flight" (*LG* 44). C. B. compares her age to winter and accepts its tragic necessity: "The tragic spirit has come back into life. We feel under no necessity to sentimentalize it and pretend it is pleasanter than it is. We can embrace it in its completeness, we can accept the truth" (*LG* 44).

All of West's works of the 1930s are shaped by this frank reconciliation with the tragic realities of her time and the determination to "exult" nonetheless. This acceptance and resilience are captured in the "heroic attempt to cover all, to know all, to feel all" (*LG* 43–4) and to celebrate the spirit—embodied in the images of the carnival worker as a "gaunt figure extended on a cross" and the dove that shoots forth from his hands.

West will further develop her interpretation of the "tragic sense of life" in *St Augustine*. Although the spirit of these works is tragic, their structures conform less conventionally to a classic or a modern sense of tragedy. C. B. does seem to experience catharsis—a cleansing of emotions through pity or fear: the letter opens with her description of the fear she has felt for three weeks since her vision. C. B. and the audience experience both fear and pity for the carnival worker. Nonetheless, these emotions do not drive the work as they would in a traditional tragedy. Nor is the carnival worker a traditional tragic protagonist. His essential nature is ironic. His ironic nature is epitomized in the disparity between his humble, worn vestments and his exalted achievements. The carnival worker is reminiscent of the court jester or the Shakespearean fool whom West describes in "The Strange Necessity." The court jester reins in human aspirations and hubris to remind us of our essentially limited and material condition. The carnival worker reminds us that the holy spirit emanates from the lowly and base or as the Yeats's character Crazy Jane reminds us, "fair and foul are near of kin,/ And fair needs foul" ("Crazy Jane Talks with the Bishop").

The carnival worker is also a burlesque of a noble gentleman: "On the platform in front of this merry-go-round stood a negro, a very tall negro, no longer young, dressed in evening clothes made of faded scarlet cloth, wearing a top-hat, and carrying a cane with a gold crook for a handle" (*LG* 39–40). According to Leo Hughes, burlesque is "imitation with the intent to ridicule" (Hughes 1956: 18). The lowly carnival worker ushering his patrons onto a merry-go-round is dressed in the regalia of upper-class evening wear. The fact that he is a Negro gives an added twist to the subversive parody. West has made her carnival worker black to call attention to her critique of imperialism—which pervades the works of this time. In his tattered aristocratic evening garb, calling his customers to ride, the worker mimics and parodies the values that have subordinated him. This critique is all the more pointed because the merry-go-round is not the traditional carousel of horses, but rather a spinning circle of "little motor-cars" (*LG* 39). West uses automobiles as icons for an industrial, capitalist system in both *A Letter to a Grandfather* and *The Thinking Reed*. These carousel cars go around in circles to suggest that capitalist industrialism is not getting anywhere. The worker's chant has satiric potential also. He calls "out in a hoarse voice that was like the ghost of thunder, 'Aux voitures! aux voitures!'" (*LG* 40). "Aux voitures" could be a pun on the rapacity of commercialism in its near homonym "To the vultures!" or "Oh! Vultures!" Once the patrons board the carousel, the worker does not restrain his disdain and derision of his betters:

> As he bent over his customers, driving them on with his cane, it seemed absurd to think of them as people voluntarily patronizing an amusement. When he had them all in their seats he turned his face to the crowd below, and threw up his cane in the air and caught it. ... He smiled at the crowd, jerking his head back at his customers as if in derision. ... Then he shot back his thumb over his shoulder, contorting his face in a leer. (*LG* 40–1)

The carnival worker mocks the culture and values that he has appropriated. A burlesque mimics as well as derides. One is reminded that though she is living in England, West was the daughter of a Scottish mother and an Irish father raised in Scotland. C. B. also appears to be of "mixed" heritage: the de Beauchamp family was originally French, but at some point migrated to England. (Perhaps eventually to become West's family, the Fairfields?[3]) The carnival worker conforms to Homi Bhabha's figure of a colonist's mimic appropriation. According to Bhabha, some subjects of colonial oppression "put on" their oppressors' manners in order to mock and finally incapacitate their oppressors: "The effect of mimicry on the authority of colonial discourse is profound and disturbing. ... For in 'normalizing' the colonial state or subject, the dream of post-Enlightenment civility alienates its own language of liberty and produces another knowledge of its norms" (Bhabha 1987: 318). The carnival worker mocks the forces that oppress him and, in his own way, triumphs over them. The worker's triumph is essential to C. B.'s vision. The essential irony in the depiction of this worker is also an important trait in West's most important work of the 1930s, *The Thinking Reed*, which combines tragedy with farce. The interplay between a tragic spirit and an ironic form accounts for the special brilliance and depth that informs these works.

St Augustine (1933)

West's nonfiction work of this period spell out many of the concerns that would stamp her 1930s fiction and would color her writing for the rest of her life. Her biography of Saint Augustine is another commissioned work. D. Appleton and Company issued a series of biographies on famous figures including Socrates, Mozart, Voltaire, Mark Twain, and Queen Elizabeth (Orel 1986: 70). Samuel Hynes views *St Augustine* as the turning point in West's career because the assignment liberated her to write generically hybrid works:

> She had taken a step that was to free her from restraining literary convention: she had agreed to write a short life of Saint Augustine. The assignment was an odd one for a literary journalist to take on, but it was a wise one: it led Dame Rebecca to history, religion and psychology and it engaged her mind ... and shaped her thinking for the rest of her career. (Hynes 1977: xiii)

As Hynes acknowledges, *St Augustine* joins biography, history, theology, and psychology. From a generic point of view, critics were most interested in West's use of Freudian psychology to analyze her subject—and especially Augustine's relationship with his mother Monnica.[4]

St Augustine shares tragic and ironic tendencies with the other works of this period. The irony in part inheres in West's insistence on her own particular blend of genres in her biography of this fourth century patriarch and in her original view of him as "the first modern man" (*SA* 159). The rise of fascism as well as the worldwide economic depression and the threat of global war influence West's account of Augustine's tragic vision. Even though West is writing a personal biography of a religious and spiritual leader, she begins her story with a preamble about the political, economic, and historical events which preceded Augustine's birth. The dissolute, fragmented Roman Empire of this time bears a striking resemblance to Europe in the 1930s. Some of West's favorite targets suffer the inevitable blow. She takes a stab at imperialism, for example, in comparing Rome's suppression of African culture in their educational system to England's suppression of Indian traditions (*SA* 31). She also singles out as distinctive of the wisdom in Augustine's *The City of God*, "a sudden magnificent attack on Imperialism. He sees and presents in perfectly ordered paragraphs—though these are scattered far apart in irrelevancies—the psychological advantages that small States enjoy compared with great Empires" (*SA* 126–7). She also condemns Augustine's conservative will-for-power as a statesman at the end of his life. The elder Augustine resembles Arnold Condorex in *Harriet Hume*—and also Marc Sallafranque in *The Thinking Reed*—in his lack of imagination and his narrow vision: "He was indifferent to the effects of the persecution he was thus initiating, not because he was cruel, but because his imagination had completely disappeared, as it sometimes does in men of action" (*SA* 140).[5]

Augustine's theology with its emphasis on suffering and atonement is essentially a tragic vision:

> The idea that matter, and especially matter related to sex, is evil; that man has acquired guilt through his enmeshment in matter; that he must atone for guilt to an angry God; and that this atonement must take the form of suffering, and the renunciation of easy pleasure. (*SA* 159–60)

Just as in *A Letter to a Grandfather* a tragic spirit is defined as peculiarly modern. West calls Augustine the "first modern man" (*SA* 159) and credits him with ideas which have influenced modern thinkers since him. She dubs the "Augustinian complex. … the ring-fence in which the modern mind is prisoner" (*SA* 161).

This tragic "ring-fence" that we have inherited arises in part from Augustine's Manichaeism. Although he officially rejected his early Manichaeism, its dualities shaped every contour of his theories. A preoccupation with dualism also informs West's works and ideas—such as her theories that all humans have a life instinct and a death instinct. As we saw in our discussion of *Harriet Hume*, West objects to the dualism that has prevailed in modern thought and in Augustine. Manichaeism is false to reality, but it captures humans' limited "sense" of the world. Because our deficient intellects cannot divine the complexity of the world, we falsely reduce things to easy antitheses.

Other tragic features of the biography are the frequent discussions of free will. Many modern definitions of tragedy argue that a tragic protagonist must have free will in order to understand his own role in his fate and to choose to face it heroically. Some critics believe that West denies that we have free will (Orel 76). It would be more appropriate to say that West in *St Augustine* suggests that we have "limited will." We cannot choose our personal place in history, our environment, or our families. We, therefore, cannot automatically "will" our lives or our identities. Nonetheless, we can heroically face our destinies; we can turn to art and tradition—something bigger than ourselves—for understanding and support. The concept of free will takes on urgency in the 1930s because of the rise of fascism.

If *St Augustine*'s blend of biography, psychology, and history dwells on politics, it also glorifies art. Political and historical conditions bring us to a spiritual impasse which can be solved by art. West's description of art and tradition in *St Augustine* grows out of her discussions in "The Strange Necessity": "It [art] is bound to incur the disapproval of the death-wish we all have in varying degrees, since by analyzing experience it makes us able to handle experience and increase our hold on life" (*SA* 39).

Drawing on the importance of national cultural traditions and the negative consequences of exile, West claims that Augustine was at nature an artist who was unable to develop his true genius because he was exiled from his native culture. "His vocation was obviously for imaginative writing" (*SA* 39), she states; yet "he never essayed the imaginative work for which he had such an unsurpassed endowment" (*SA* 42). Her comparisons between Augustine and Tolstoy echo her comments about the frustrated geniuses of Yeats, Kipling, and Al Capone in "The Strange Necessity":

> Each of them [Tolstoy and Augustine] is a man living on the fringe of a great civilisation which, by conquering or ignoring the culture of his native land, has imposed its culture on him. Consequently it forces him and his people to apply its standards to their art; but as no people can create according to any standards other than those they find in their own breast, this means that they are prevented from full artistic achievement. (*SA* 41)

Frustrated from his true vocation, according to West, Augustine finally turned to religion.

West focuses on Augustine's family relationships and posits that his close relationship to his devout mother was responsible for his early rejection of and later rapprochement with religion. In West's description, Augustine and Monnica's relationship resembles that of Richard Yaverland and Marion's in *The Judge.* West psychologizes and secularizes Augustine's religiosity and spirituality while still revering them. As she maintains when she suggests that Augustine's religious vision—which he shared with Monnica—may in part have been due to the intensity of the love between mother and son: "To suspect a human basis for the experience is not to belittle it or to deny that the ultimate significance for Augustine was religious" (*SA* 89).

The Thinking Reed (1936)

The Thinking Reed is, according to Peter Wolfe, "the best of the [West's] early novels" (Wolfe 1971: 47). As the story opens, the protagonist Isabelle Terry is in a position not unlike Isabelle Archer in Henry James's *Portrait of a Lady.* She is an attractive, wealthy, twenty-six-year-old, American expatriate pursued by a variety of eligible men.[6] Like James, West makes evident the limitations of women's circumscribed fates that depend not on their education, their accomplishments, or their careers, but upon the men they marry. One of Isabelle's suitors reminds her of her youth and she replies, "Oh, not so young. … No younger than most of the women in the world who have had to make great decisions. That is the special handicap of our sex, the important part of our lives comes before we have acquired any experience" (*TR* 56). Isabelle is a moral young woman with a "competent, steely mind [that] never rested … she was for ever running her faculty of analysis over in her mind with … preposterous zeal" in order to achieve order and calm—qualities she values above all others (*TR* 4).

Part 1 Tragedy

While all of West's other works of the 1930s were informed by a tragic spirit, they did not altogether have traditional tragic features. *The Thinking Reed* is tragic in spirit and also in many of its forms. Isabelle's life is full of tragedies in the everyday sense. She was orphaned while still a child and her first husband Roy, an airplane pilot, was killed in a crash. Another tragedy takes place in the first chapter of the novel. Having moved to France in order to start anew after Roy's death, Isabelle takes up with dashing André de Verviers, who is not an appropriate match. She tries to break from him, but he will not release her. She is driven to a deliberate act that looks impulsive in order to rid herself of André so that she can marry Laurence Vernon, a southern aristocrat, who embodies all the principles of tradition, equanimity, and reason that she treasures. Vernon, however, unwittingly witnesses the scene Isabelle makes to break from Verviers; he is repulsed and therefore rejects Isabelle. In order to save face with Vernon, she literally stumbles into an engagement with Marc Sallafranque, a bumbling, stocky French industrialist who manufactures cheap cars.

Isabelle finds marriage to Marc surprisingly agreeable. We witness their vibrant social life in Paris and especially their frenzied holidays at the watering holes of the rich-and-famous on French coasts during the height of the Roaring Twenties—or *les Années Folles.*

The tragedies in *A Thinking Reed* do not depend entirely upon the leading characters' "fatal flaws." Unlike many modern tragedies, the tragic "faults" do indeed lie in "the stars" and not entirely in "themselves."[7] As West explains in *St Augustine*, our historical situation determines our fates as well as our individual characters.[8] Isabelle and Marc find themselves in a decadent society with deplorable morals. West implies that all of Western society is infected. The rich are depicted as vain and self-centered votaries of sin and self-indulgence. One is reminded of West's criticism of the Côte d'Azur in "The Strange Necessity." The narrator complains of her vacation in the south of France that was full of "direct experience that had not been digested," analyzed, and synthesized into art:

> Now, that something has to be done with all these experiences, that they cannot be carried about by the individual in the form in which they were ingested, is proven by the deplorable condition of all colonies of expatriates who settle down in beautiful surroundings with nothing to do from year's end to year's end but enjoy their sensations. Invariably such attempt to mitigate the stream of experience that is constantly flowing towards them by clouds of alcohol, and to organize life into some sort of pattern by the invention of scandal. (*SN* 187–8)

The Thinking Reed's descriptions of the lives of sport, sun, drinking, and gambling echo the condemnation of these rich expatriates in "The Strange

Necessity": "They had refused all succour offered to them by the mind, and there is simply not enough for the body to do unassisted during the whole twenty-four hours" (*TR* 92). Because of their monomaniacal pursuit of pleasure and their obsessive devotion to decadence, West frequently ironically describes these cosmopolitans as monks or nuns. They suffer because of their self-imposed deprivation from all occupations most people find rewarding and they become petty, bitter, and trivial: "The invisible scourgings in this convent without walls had power to draw blood" (*TR* 93).

The immediate source of society's malady is money. Ann Norton says that *The Thinking Reed* is "almost a study of money's corrupting influence on both sexes" (Norton 2000: 56). Many of Marc's and Isabelle's acquaintances are aristocrats with inherited wealth. Some of them are aristocrats without inherited wealth—which makes them on the whole worse rather than better than their peers. There are also the predictable millionaire Americans whose capitalistic wealth is multiplying in the stock market. Isabelle's deceased parents left her an income which her American Uncle Honoré invests for her. Marc and others are upper-middle-class industrialists who have earned their money through industry. Gangsters and criminals also dwell in their midst. Isabelle recognizes wealth's corrupting powers: "I tell you, money is a poison. … Only wealth or some toxic condition like alcoholism could degenerate the brain to that degree" (*TR* 393).

The votaries of the Côte d'Azur are reprehensible in the extreme. Other characters offer alternatives to their decadence, but all of the alternatives have their limitations. West uses the different men in Isabelle's life to delineate some of these alternatives. Laurence Vernon, the southern aristocrat, offers one option. Isabelle admires him because "he was fighting … every attempt to enslave the people by the same conscienceless industrialism as has made the Yankees the drab men-machines they were" (*TR* 17). His values contrast with the prevailing Jazz Age attitudes. Dissipation, disorder, and violence are foreign to him. He lives in an antebellum, classical mansion in Virginia—that deliberately recalls Thomas Jefferson's Mount Vernon—and he leads a tranquil, measured life, immersed in tradition. Isabelle reflects on the classical authors Laurence reads and his respect for tradition:

> Those books [Plato, Lucretius, Plotinus] had made her wonder if she might not work out some spiritual equivalent of the Einstein theory regarding the re-entrant nature of time, for it was plainly through reading these writers of the remote past that Laurence owed his serene command over the present. (*TR* 16)

One is reminded of West's theory in "The Strange Necessity" that one needs a sense of tradition in order to deal with the challenges of the present. Isabelle articulates West's theories in her comparisons between Roy and Laurence:

> Perhaps we are all of us born with one foot on the present, and can grip it with the other only if we swing it far enough back into the past. Her husband, dear Roy, had never made the experiment, and he seemed as if he had to hop about, whirling his arms and legs, to keep his balance on the moment. (*TR* 16)

This description aptly describes both Roy's and Laurence's deficiencies. Roy lacks a foot swinging back into the past. Laurence, on the other hand, has both feet cemented in the past which saps his engagement in the present. Laurence's reverence for tradition resembles the elevation of past culture by West's contemporaries, the Humanists. West questioned Irving Babbitt's and Paul Elmer More's ability "to act as guide to tradition through this age" (West 1930: 515). Laurence—like More and Babbitt—may be "among the most learned men now living. Their learning does not however prevent them from laboring under certain disqualifications which forbid them to understand contemporary life" (West 1930: 515). In spite of his serenity, Laurence's lack of vitality and lack of engagement in the present give him what Isabelle later describes as a "pithlessness." He lacks vigor or force and is without a center because he is so detached from life. He resembles the well-meaning English aristocrats whom Alan Fielding disparages: "They are complete parasites, who can't earn their keep. … His mind's amoebic, because the world's never demanded that he organize it into efficiency. He's an old dear ... but they haven't put anything into life" (*TR* 396). Just as West recommends that Babbitt and More read her modernist contemporaries, we might say of Laurence that he is less "likely to maintain traditions as satisfactorily as the modern writers—Proust, Joyce, Lawrence, Virginia Woolf, Aldous Huxley, to name but a few" (West 1930: 515).

Alan Fielding offers a sort of pastoral alternative (last names are telling for West). Repulsed by the aristocratic values and ways of life of his family in England, he has left England and bought a seventeenth-century cottage in the Parisian countryside. He lives modestly on a small income and on his work as a painter and designer. Alan's fastidious values and desire for a life of order and "pattern" are almost identical to Isabelle's. Isabelle is attracted to him because they are so much alike. His home is "an exact correspondence to her ideal" (*TR* 383). Nevertheless, although he has left England "to get away from all the Pootses [the superficial aristocrats]" (*TR* 398), he does not really escape. They follow him. He no longer fully participates in the world he has rejected, but he still depends on it and he has not really constructed a viable alternative. Nor does he do anything to help the nurses or the mineworkers whom his deplorable relatives persecute. Alan's "gentleness" is not equipped to battle the forces he rejects. Marc's vitality—which all the other men lack—makes him the appropriate mate for Isabelle in spite of his many faults which make him seem an inappropriate match.

Part 2 Farce

With Marc's entrance into the novel, West announces the hybrid impulse that combines tragedy and farce to shape *The Thinking Reed.* He is an awkward, boorish man whose impulsive actions often lead to the chaos and violence that Isabelle abhors. He utterly lacks the restraint, sophistication, and refinement that distinguish Isabelle. In contemplating why she could not marry him, Isabelle reflects, "He was too grossly, too comically successful as an industrialist … his wide mouth made a muzzle like a terrier's, expressing a purely sensuous gaiety and melancholy. … He was *comically violent*" (*TR* 29, 30, emphasis added). Soon after Isabelle accepts Marc's marriage proposal in order to save face for having disgraced herself in front of Laurence Vernon, Marc makes a classic "comically violent" move: out of sheer delight he kicks a waiter carrying two glasses of brandy on a tray.

> A waiter passed them, carrying two glasses of brandy on a tray. Marc's left foot clothed in a yellow shoe shot out and caught him on the behind. The tray clattered on the floor underneath the caisse, a wall was streaked by two brown stains and shivers of glass, the waiter howled, the cassière bent forward a Roman eyebrow and a fortress bosom, the vestiaire ran out holding one grey and two brown hats, chasseurs swarmed … the maîtres d'hôtel of the inside and outside restaurants ran in and stood like stars in conjunction. (*TR* 63–4)

Farce has crossed the threshold. And Isabelle recognizes the two genres that will shape her life (and this novel). She reflects, "She had contrived that violence should not make her life a tragedy. It might yet make her life a farce, which she would find hardly more tolerable" (*TR* 64). The scene would not be a farce if the waiter were really injured or if the cassière's insult was serious or if the maîtres d'hôtel might lose their jobs. According to Irving Howe, "Farce brings pleasure through humiliation. … And then, a sort of magical cancellation ... the world is restored" (Howe 1990: 6). In this case, the order is restored through Marc's good humor, his familiar relationships with the restaurant staff, his good will, and his reparations money. Order is momentarily restored, but it is the nature of farce to repeatedly return to "the danger, destruction, and torment of farce, an ancient form of merrymaking" (Bermel 1990: 13).

Farce and tragedy will alternate and also interact throughout *The Thinking Reed*. West uses hybrid genres to subvert and to transform the ideologies that shape her world. The crises of the 1930s demand radical transformation. By depicting these crises as modern tragedies, West defines many of the fatal flaws of her contemporary society. "The danger, destruction, and torment of farce" provide tactics for the revolution necessary to create a more humane, inclusive, life-giving world.[9]

West's contemporary readers would have appreciated the farce in *The Thinking Reed* because of its popularity in the theater and in film during the 1920s and the 1930s. The novel takes place during the Roaring Twenties and Albert Bermel reminds us that farce was in the ascendant precisely during the period that the novel portrays: "The decade from 1919 to 1929, roughly what Scott Fitzgerald called the Jazz Age, saw a richer gush of farce than any comparable period in history" (Bermel 1990: 167). Farce continued to thrive in the 1930s when film actors and directors were able to refine methods and to develop new techniques. Bermel claims that "Chaplin's *City Lights* (1931) and *Modern Times* (1935) represent his farce at its most exquisitely sustained" (Bermel 1990: 206). West admired Noël Coward's farces of this period. *The Thinking Reed* shares Coward's pieces' "didactic" aims to improve their audience's manners and morals through exposing their characters' moral deficiencies. In defending Coward against T. S. Eliot's remark that "Mr Coward's drama is one of 'pure amusement' without any ethical motive" (West 1932: rpt Scott 1990: 590), West insists,

> There is possibly no other playwright, and few writers except Jeremiah and the author of Ecclesiastes, who are more inveterately didactic than Mr Coward. His farces are tense with rage at the ill-mannered wastrels that enact them; he has never written a revue which is not interlarded with songs against the world, the flesh, and the devil as directly stated as any of Dr Watts's hymns. (Scott 1990: 590)

As is often the case, West comments on herself as she comments on Coward. *The Thinking Reed* is "tense with rage at the ill-mannered wastrels that enact" it. Many of the characters that West satirizes—especially the cosmopolitan friends at the French playgrounds for the rich—are predictable farcical characters. West satirizes them by giving them preposterous names such as "Poots" and "Lady Barnaclouth" and homes like the "Villa Sans Souci." Marc has worked tirelessly to create his successful automobile factory, but his name "Sallafranque," which suggests "dirty money," does not exempt him from the stain of his society. As Bermel remarks, "All characters are their creators' puppets, but the ones in farce seem especially impersonal. Many of them have descended from stock characters or types" (Bermel 1990: 24). Poots, for example, is a young British aristocrat, Lady Virginia Sandways, who has recently married a friend of Marc's from his school days. Poots keeps Isabelle, Marc, and their friends waiting for dinner on the first night of their Easter vacation. She is described entirely as a "type":

> Isabelle [who is pregnant and needs to eat] felt it extremely annoying that they had had to wait so long for somebody so little individual as Poots. They surely could have gone in to dinner with any of those replicas of her which had surrounded them when they first sat down in the bar. (*TR* 177)

Exaggerated, stock characters occur frequently in farce in order to give the readers or the audience enough "distance" to laugh at their absurdities without empathy for their susceptibilities.

A similar dynamic informs an interchange between Marc and his acquaintance Annette. Laura and Annette's feuds disrupt and spoil their coteries' holidays numerous times during Marc and Isabelle's different vacations:

> "Did you hear what I said to Laura at the Golf House this morning?" … Annette bent lower and continued in this solemn, self-impressed voice. … She was taking breath, in order to start on some proliferating story, when Marc interrupted her. "But are you not Laura?" he asked, sleepily but not stupidly. Annette drew back her head sharply. "What are you talking about, Marc?" she asked. … "I'm Annette Lexington. You know me!" Her expression became charged with an infantile meanness. "You've been to my house often enough. At Antibes." "Was it your house?" asked Marc. … "I thought it was Laura's." "Well, you have been to Laura's house as well." … "That is what I am complaining about," Marc continued. "You both have houses at Antibes, you both have the same colour of hair, you have both had several husbands. There are really not sufficient points of difference between you. Naturally I cannot tell you apart." … "If you disagree with her, you should be silent about it. It is in the nature of a personal business within yourself, like the engenderment of gas in one's intestines, which should not be shared with the rest of the world." (*TR* 257–9)

This scene borders on farce because of its ridiculousness. Annette believes that her trivial spat with Laura bears the gravity of affairs of state. Marc cannot take her seriously as an individual. Their lack of individuality means that we laugh *at* them as character types.[10] Marc's offensive remark seals the scene with a farcical *touché*. Why are bodily functions funny? Because they remind us of our common humanity. No matter what our pretenses to dignity or importance, we are all mortal animals with the same physiology. We are all susceptible to slipping on bananas or in Marc's words, we all experience "the engenderment of gas in one's intestines." Marc's comment "levels" Annette's (or is it Laura's?) pretentions and we readers laugh at her as we are reminded of the similarities that she denies.[11]

Many of the most pretentious characters are also the most farcical. They are farcical to the readers (their audience) because the readers have the advantage of distance and knowledge of the characters' shortcomings. But even the characters *in* the story treat Marc as farcical, as the clown who pricks the balloons on the world's pretentions and watches them burst to bring us all down to the same level. The best—such as two of his employees—understand that he is both "farcical" and "noble": "One or two spectacled, high-shouldered intellectuals, whose genuinely amused yet tender smiles showed that they had perfectly grasped Marc's farcical and noble character" (*TR* 74). He is a farce magnet who can implicate even Isabelle in a farcical situation such as a visit from French priests who need to nullify Isabelle's first marriage. The priests assume that Isabelle is divorced and are "incredulous," but pleased to discover that Roy "had been killed in an aeroplane" (*TR* 67). Their response is comical in their pleasure with Roy's early demise: "*Ah, mais parfaitment, mais naturellement*." Nothing is immune from farce: neither religion nor death. Nor Isabelle. She *needs* farce to shatter her hope for order and control and her belief that rationality and intellect can organize life. Farce reminds us that "all attempts to rationalize life are irrational" (Howe 1990: 5).

Many of Isabelle's scenes have the ingredients for farce, but not its spirit. The scene in the courtyard where Isabelle violently breaks the stems of the roses André had given her, tears off the petals, and grinds the petals into the mud has the impulsive violence characteristic of farce. It also has the impossible coincidences of farce: who could have predicted that Laurence Vernon's ancient *instructrice* would live above the same courtyard and that Laurence would be visiting her for the first time in many years at the moment Isabelle appears at André's doorstep?

The subsequent scene at the restaurant where Marc appears conveniently just in time to save Isabelle from the disgrace of presuming Laurence's proposal also has farcical timing. Nonetheless, the scenes are somber and heartbreaking. They reveal the fine line that balances between tragedy and farce. Isabelle is everything that farce is not: serious, self-important, and controlling. As the restaurant scene unfolds and Marc's appearance approaches, there is, nonetheless, a sparkle of farcical glitter. Laurence reveals that he witnessed Isabelle's atrocity and Isabelle explains the predicament that drove her to it. Having learned that the woman-he-supposedly-loves has been exploited by a callous cad and that she was forced into a deliberately impolite act that was neither "mad" or heedless, he cannot find it in his heart to forgive Isabelle her indiscretion. Laurence reveals his unsympathetic (dare one say "cruel"?) nature. Isabelle suddenly realizes that "inside [Marc] has a lot of the goodness and sweetness of Roy" (*TR* 61). Laurence is left exposed—and actually ridiculous (if he would only admit it). "She [Isabelle] stood up, but he did not say the word, or do anything but regard her with the queer mask, as of a stricken hyena, that people wear who are making haste laughing at themselves before other people can start laughing at them. Her plan [to save face] had evidently succeeded perfectly. Its only defect was that it left her in possession of Sallafranque, which was a responsibility that she might as well assume fully at once." Oh, how the mighty have fallen: the clown-like industrialist has leveled the haughty aristocrat through sheer "goodness and sweetness."

Isabelle comes to realize that her life has had many of the qualities of a farce, in spite of her efforts to cultivate peace and civility. She describes the pace and the course of her life in erratic, frantic terms typical of farces.[12]

> She had progressed erratically, dizzily, often losing sight of her goal, by repercussion after repercussion with men travelling at violent rates of speed on paths chosen for no other motive than the opportunities they gave for violence. … Then she had ricocheted from that shock [Roy's crash] to the arms of André de Verviers … his violent frivolity sent her staggering to the violent act of destroying the roses at his door, which sent her into collision with the violent coldness of Laurence, which sent her into the orbit of the violent heat of Marc. (*TR* 419)

The climactic scene of Isabelle and Marc's personal tragedy also has many predictable features of a farce, especially coincidence. In the crisis of the novel, a radiantly pregnant Isabelle and an overworked Marc escape to the French coast for an Easter holiday. They inadvertently find themselves compelled to entertain a group of corrupt and pretentious people they despise. "Courtesy"—the social rules to create civil, humane society—forces Isabelle and Marc to entertain a collection of "ill-mannered wastrels" (reminiscent of a Noël Coward play) and then the same "courtesy" propels them from one unlikely miserable situation to another.

Isabelle and Marc have come to Le Touquet with their friend, Luba, an exiled Russian princess who has recently been deserted by her long-standing partner. Isabelle and Marc plan a *bon voyage* dinner for an American, Mr Pillans, who they would like as a partner for Luba. Poots finagles an invitation for herself, her husband, and a gangster Benny d'Alperoussa. Marc's morals are outraged at the prospect of hosting Monsieur and Madame d'Alperoussa. The evening takes on the qualities of a nightmare "snow-ball farce." French playwright Feydeau—a master of the snowball farce—claimed that the "rule was to throw together as soon as possible the very characters who must under no circumstances meet each other" (Davis 1978: 75). According to formula, things get worse and worse. A British earl who also happens to write a gossip column for a British Sunday paper somehow ends up in a table near theirs. The restaurant is full of people of questionable morals whom the d'Alperoussas self-righteously spurn. A family who own land near Marc's factory and despise him because he does not share their right-wing politics see Marc hosting the d'Alperoussas, so they now have the perfect device to ruin Marc's influence in the government.

The Casino—where they proceed after dinner—takes on the aspect of a minotaur's maze where each turn leads to greater danger. The overbearing Lady Barnaclouth surfaces from the horde of vile luminaries. Isabelle wants to spare Madame d'Alperoussa from Lady Barnaclouth's egotism and offensive pretenses. Madame d'Alperoussa takes this as a social slight from Isabelle who must rectify things while in the throes of illness. Tensions mount. Marc gets drunk and is on the verge of gambling a copious amount of chips which will ruin his reputation and his business. So, again with her signature brilliant calculation, Isabelle screams, slaps Luba's cheek, and accuses Marc of adultery with Luba in order to prevent him from gambling. The ruse succeeds but at great cost to Isabelle: "The brutality she was doing to her own nature amounted to torture" (*TR* 306). Isabelle collapses in the first stages of her miscarriage.

In spite of the tragic nature of this climactic scene, West reminds her readers of its farcical features and potential in its rapid pace and in its impossible coincidences of people and events who converge in one place. The chapter closes with Madame d'Alperoussa in a classic farcical "fall from dignity." Marc turns to

Madame d'Alperoussa for help with Isabelle, but "she turned her back and fled, recognizing the approach of her implacable enemy, scandal" (*TR* 308).

> As she ran, she caught her heel in the hem of her dress and fell full-length on the ground. She sat up immediately, but her jewels were awry, her sinewy legs stuck out in front of her at an obtuse angle, covered only at the vertex by her crumpled dress and the rose-coloured chiffon frills of her drawers, which looked as incongruous as if they had been decorating a mule or a pylon; and an unspoken oath was clearly visible between her firm, fluted lips. The people round her broke into nervous laughter, which spread all through the crowd behind, becoming fainter and yet more harsh and spiteful as it travelled. (*TR* 308)

Madame d'Alperoussa has spent the evening in pretentious avowals of her unimpeachable moral character and her irreproachable dignity. Yet at this climactic moment when she could have turned to help Isabelle (her morally impeccable hostess) and offer succor to the sick and the downtrodden, she flees. But the intractability of the universe catches her and exposes her to the people she has scorned all evening.

The scene is a *tour de force* which deftly places farce on "the ludicrous fringe of tragedy" (Bermel 1990: 52). Readers simultaneously feel heart-wrenching sympathy for Isabelle and disdainful scorn for Madame d'Alperoussa. Bermel explains the contrasting effects: "What counts here is the *disparity* between the character and his surroundings. In farce, that disparity is laughable; in tragedy, heartrending. We don't laugh at the tragic protagonist; he lacks the protective shell of his farcical counterpart, the indestructibility" (Bermel 1990: 56).

In spite of the events in her life which could conventionally be labeled "tragic," Isabelle does not think of herself as a victim of either fate or circumstances until the catastrophe of her miscarriage. The last third of the novel charts the course of Isabelle's convalescence—from hospital to nursing homes and to her home in Paris. Hospitals, spas, sanatoriums, psychologists, Marc's contrition: nothing can reconcile her to the misery or the injustice of her fate nor to the plight of being married to a man who has brought such disaster upon her.

Having finally decided to divorce, Isabelle suddenly sees that she values Marc and their marriage and they reconcile. She accepts her loss and her life and faces them with dignity in a classically tragic fashion when she understands her own failings and the limitations of her perspectives. Isabelle's *hamartia* is her super-rationality and her desire for control. She comes to realize that her interpretation of her marriage and the circumstances that led up to her marriage relied too much on superficial facts and not enough on her intuitive (emotional?) understanding of her marriage. The reconciliation scene with Marc acknowledges the impossibility or futility of knowledge:

> She said weeping, "I did not know," and he answered,
> "Neither did I."
> "One knows nothing," she said.
> "Nothing," he repeated. (*TR* 412)

Isabelle realizes that her approach to life and to relationships has been too rational and controlling. Her desire for control has led her to a "rage for order" and reason that has been the last thing she needs. She admits this as she tries to explain to Alan Fielding why she cannot marry him, "It is an extraordinary thing, and I do not approve of it, that I am much more excited than I usually let myself be, and yet I believe I am talking much more sensibly than I usually do" (*TR* 407).

Marc's farcical nature gives him vitality and undermines the "inflated" and iniquitous world they find themselves in. Whereas Alan and Isabelle, for example, are incredibly perceptive, the Sallafranques "had no humour except good humour and were wholly deficient in irony" (*TR* 72). This naiveté results in social blunders and miscalculations with workers. Marc's energy leads to the kind of excesses which result in Isabelle's miscarriage. Nonetheless, all these shortcomings also result in the vigor which fuels Marc's passion for Isabelle and his genuine love for his fellow humans. This vigor gives him the strength to create an industrial empire. Marc has other virtues as well. He is good-natured, extraordinarily kind, generous, honest, and incredibly hard-working. Isabelle comes to recognize that "the violence and disorder that she hated … could only be worsted by a force greater than itself, such as made Marc so strong a man" (*TR* 404) and that she had been incorrect in believing that Laurence's serenity or Alan's fastidiousness could defeat the forces that corrupt society. This is also because Marc is so immersed in the real world. The ultimate sin in this book is to lose touch with "the draught of truth" (that Jenny affirms in *The Return of the Soldier*). Marc, more than any other character, because he actually makes something, is redeemed by his "communion with reality" (*RS* 182). Isabelle says to him, "Your work … keeps you in touch with reality, when you do wrong you fail, when you do right you succeed" (*TR* 421).

Marc is the correct match for Isabelle because she longs to engage with reality and escape from "be[ing] in a vacuum, insulated from life by flattery" and money; she wants her "life … determined by necessity" (*TR* 421; see Norton 2000: 14). His excess of feeling, vitality, and disorder are a healthy complement and correction for Isabelle's rage for order. That their union is an accident is altogether appropriate: it demonstrates the unpredictability of life that will irresistibly defeat our efforts to control or to restrain it. Marriage with Marc leads Isabelle eventually to embrace the opportunities provided by life's abundance and happenstance.[13]

West's readers hope that Marc's connection with the real world will help Isabelle and Marc survive the cosmic tragedy that overshadows the whole novel. The imminent stock market crash provides the irony essential to all of West's works of the 1930s. The readers possess a dramatic irony common in farce: "More often than not, the audience's position of privilege permits it to foretell a downfall that is concealed from the character himself" (Davis 1978: 63).

The Thinking Reed was published in 1936 about a pre-Depression world. However, the readers know the fate of most of the fortunes so blithely dispensed. As Ann Norton reminds us, West tells us on the first page of the novel that the events are unfolding in 1928. The novel closes in August of 1929. West reminds the readers of various "crashes" in order to increase the ironic tension. Roy's obsessive "rejection of all other activities in favour of the pleasures of describing vast trajectories through space, no matter what might happen at the point of impact" (*TR* 419) becomes symbolic of a whole generation's self-seeking pleasures founded on the insubstantial sky-rocketing of the stock exchange.

Roy crashes an airplane. Alan Fielding experiences a different kind of "crash." For him, all of the evils of wealth were epitomized in his aristocratic Aunt Agatha, a termagant who mercilessly used her privilege and money to bully everyone from Prime Ministers to her own family members and servants. Her appalling behavior caused Alan to renounce his aristocratic life in England. As a youth, Alan thought that he was the only one who perceived his aunt's cruelty. After she died, however, everyone who had had anything to do with her flourished in her absence and her "admirers" were proven hypocrites. Alan refers to the aftermath of Agatha's death as "the crash" (*TR* 395). His "crash" is his disillusionment caused by the falsity of wealth and the hypocrisy and cruelty which underpinned his world. This "crash" can also be interpreted metaphorically. In the moral economy of the book, the stock market "crash" proved the superficiality and fragility of the wealth and privilege the rich had staked their lives and identities upon. The Depression threatens to turn all the characters' lives into tragedies. The crash also has farcical potential. Since the prevailing character flaws in the novel are arrogance and pretension—and especially the self-important pretensions of the rich—the readers know just how ridiculous and "insubstantial" all the pretensions are.

Both Roy's "crash" and Alan's "crash" occur because of a lack of "substance." Money's ultimate failing in *The Thinking Reed* is its lack of connection with reality. This is also the cause of the stock market crash in West's eyes. Marc says to Isabelle of her future: "The increase in the capital value of your fortune during the last few years is so enormous that it must be pure fantasy, it can have no correspondence with reality" (*TR* 428).

As *The Thinking Reed* closes, it is August, and Marc and Isabelle have just received a letter from Isabelle's American Uncle Honoré whose apprehension about the stock market has caused him to cancel his September visit to Paris. The reader knows that the stock market will falter in September and plummet in October. Marc discusses the possibility and Isabelle replies, "But I know that it ought to happen. … Is it possible that you do not feel that the mould in which our lives have been cast is horrible, and ought to be broken?" (*TR* 429). Like all of West's works, *The Thinking Reed* calls for a radical reshaping of our world. West uses the same metaphor (breaking the mold) in her essay "Regretfully" that condemns [the New] Humanism and argues for the necessity of romanticism and classicism which she calls "that dual process in art" (*EE* 304). When an artist "exposes his intellect and his emotions to a new stimulus … the effort is disturbing to himself and to others. It *breaks the mould of the universe* as it was before this new experience was added to it." West continues, "It is no use complaining because he has disturbed the universe. Harmony will come later. Art promises this, and it is the high joy of humanity that it has fulfilled its promise" (*EE* 305, emphasis added).

West's discussion of the complex potential of the interaction between the romantic and the classical has implications for the generic hybridity of *The Thinking Reed.* Farce meets tragedy in a generic contact zone and a subtle, complex work emerges. Read as a tragedy, *The Thinking Reed* reveals the inadequacy of Isabelle's elevation of the intellect and her desire for control. A tragic reading also condemns the gross materialism, superficiality, and ostentation of a generation of cosmopolitan wastrels. Seen from the vantage of farce, the novel's Cowardesque satire introduces art's transformational potential into the work. The violence inherent in farce will break the mold of the universe while it also affirms what West calls the "life force."

The Thinking Reed is a work of art which combines tragedy and farce in order to transform the universe and restore harmony to a world traumatized by the Great Depression and political unrest. Isabelle and Marc have survived the tragedy of losing their child and yet they "still revere the dove and its flight" (*LG* 44). As C. B. insists: "The tragic spirit has come back into life. We feel under no necessity to sentimentalize it and pretend it is pleasanter than it is. We can embrace it in its completeness, we can accept the truth" (*LG* 44). Isabelle and Marc affirm life and also recognize the necessity of change. Breaking the mold of the universe requires violence—Marc's life-affirming violence. It also requires that we challenge what society defines as "rational" or "sane." All of West's generic hybrids include at least one genre that interrogates our definitions of the real in order to disrupt the false constructs that oppress and enslave humanity.

The Thinking Reed champions the values that farce affirms. Farce is a supremely popular genre. As the longevity of *Punch and Judy* attests, it appeals to all classes and all ages. Its special appeal to the lower echelons is probably explained by the fact that they are so often victims in life and art. Farce is antiauthoritarian. The audience delights when servants outwit their masters or when a child flails an authoritarian father. Farce mocks all inequity and "what makes the mockery amusing is that it reduces us all to smallness" (Howe 1990: 6). It is irreverent, but it is also celebratory. At its most basic, it is a celebration of the life force that all humanity share. Davis describes "a farcical *tour de force*: that full roar of laughter, tinged with recognition of a common humanity, which marks the high points of the genre" (Davis 1978: 88).

Given the economic and the political situation, *The Thinking Reed* is a daring work to write in 1936. It is also a defiant work. While celebrating modernists and modernist writers in the 1930s, West never meekly subscribes to prevailing orthodoxies. *A Letter to a Grandfather* alludes to T. S. Eliot's *The Waste Land* and "Ash Wednesday" in order to suggest alternative approaches to modernist problems. Although West repeatedly honors T. S. Eliot's poetic genius and praises *The Waste Land* in her essays of this period, she does not choose that course. *The Thinking Reed* shares many qualities of *The Waste Land*: a bleak, tragic vision; a disjointed depiction of the alienation of cosmopolitanism; barren and infertile land and people; spiritually vapid sex; a variety of points of view; and an essential irony. *The Thinking Reed*, nonetheless, affirms the life force and hopes for fertility.[14] Luba marries Mr Pillans and Marc and Isabelle receive news of her pregnancy. Although Roy was [probably] infertile and Isabelle miscarried Marc's child, the novel closes with hope that Marc and Isabelle will have children. Isabelle associates Marc—who loves the rain—with the "rain running abundantly down the skylights" (*TR* 409). His vitality has the fertility as well as the violence of a rainstorm. As West argues in her essay "Regretfully," "It is no use complaining because [the artist] has disturbed the universe. Harmony will come later."

The Harsh Voice (1935)

The Harsh Voice, a collection of short stories, shares many qualities with *The Thinking Reed* and will thus receive short shrift in this study. Although the characters and settings differ, thematic and technical similarities give coherence to the four stories which are all set in the United States during the Depression. The first line of the first story invokes the Depression and the war to strike the tragic and ironic note that dominates this collection and all of West works of the 1930s.

> One evening a year or two before the war, when most people still took it for granted that the overwhelming tragedies of life related to the private affairs of individuals. ... (*HV* 3)

As these lines imply, the Depression is not the only source of suffering in these stories. Most of the stories recall the title of West's early short story "Indissoluble Matrimony."[15] The indissolubility of marital ties is another theme common to all four stories. Another cause of grief is the impossibility of communication.

In spite of the stories' tragic spirit, they are not tragic in mode. There is no catharsis or tragic recognition and the emphasis is often social as well as individual. The stories blend tragedy with other genres we have seen in West's 1930s works, including burlesque, political satire, and farce, but also melodrama. All four stories are narrated in the third person, but from the point of view of one of the characters in the story. This *style indirect libre* accounts for a great deal of dramatic irony. These stories often satirize their characters' circumscribed vision or the social conventions that construct our perceptions and our lives.

The Harsh Voice demands a great deal from its readers. The stories are typical of modern poems and novels: they present the readers with all the ambiguity that the real world presents us. Since there are no longer universal truths dictated by an omnipotent God, these texts deny their readers omniscient narrators or universal morals. The readers must ferret out their own interpretations of events and arrive at their own truths.

This emphasis on the readers' participation in a text is typical of West. West discusses satire in a review of Sinclair Lewis's *Elmer Gantry*: "That is the first necessary condition which the satirist must fulfill. He must fully possess, at least in the world of the imagination, the quality the lack of which he is deriding in others" (*SN* 300). West imagines such a quality in the narrator of "The Strange Necessity." The narrator's animated inquiry into the events of her day and her energetic pursuit of the necessity of art demonstrate precisely the qualities which most of the characters in *The Harsh Voice* lack. West elaborates the necessity to follow the mandates of the soul in her essay "I Believe": "I believe in a process. ... I find an ultimate value in the efforts of human beings to do more than merely exist, to choose and analyze their experiences. ... It also serves the purpose of furnishing each human soul with access to the avenue along which it can advance farthest toward the comprehension and mastery of life" (West 1939: 322–3).

West's readers must often exert themselves in order to analyze and understand these stories. West is definitely taking some risks in this choice of technique. Like Gustav Flaubert or Ford Madox Ford she must make her readers see the shortcomings of a sometimes distasteful person while at the same time maintaining the readers' interest in the stories. The popularity of these short stories suggest that they did succeed in encouraging their readers to furnish their "human soul[s] with access to the avenue along which it can advance farthest toward the comprehension and mastery of life." These stories worked to transform their readers and to transform their readers' world.

7

"To Cast Away All Acquisitions and Certainties": *Black Lamb and Grey Falcon* Combines Travel Genres and the Epic

Section 1 "Fusions that infuriate": The subversion of the travel chronicle and the travel guidebook in *Black Lamb and Grey Falcon*

Part 1 Travel writing in the 1930s

Shortly after *The Thinking Reed* was published, West made a lecture tour to the Balkans—Greece, Bulgaria, and Yugoslavia—on behalf of the Foreign Office's British Council (Glendinning 1987: 163). She made two subsequent trips to Yugoslavia, one with her husband in 1937 and another by herself in 1938. *Black Lamb and Grey Falcon* (1941) was her major work for the rest of the 1930s. It remains in many ways her greatest achievement and a masterpiece of hybridity.

A contemporary *New York Times* review of Rebecca West's *Black Lamb and Grey Falcon* described it as "not only the magnification and intensification of the travel book form, but, one may say, its apotheosis" (Woods 1941: 4). This is an extraordinary—but deserved—claim for a work of travel literature written during what Paul Fussell, Bernard Schweizer, David Farley, and others have depicted as the Golden Age of travel writing.[1] This book joins the throng in staking out the importance of travel writing and in defining West's place in this tradition. Farley's *Modernist Travel Writing* reminds us of travel writing's pivotal role in modernism with the claim: "Travel and travel writing *transformed* literary modernism" (Farley 2010: 1, emphasis added). He examines "the ways in which the dual impulses of mobility and modernism impacted on one another" to redefine modernism (Farley 2010: 194). Fully aware of travel literature as a genre, Farley focuses less on generic strategies and more on "mobility": the physical conditions of travel including borders, passports, and travel regulations. In *Radicals on the Road*, Schweizer argues that West and many of her fellow travelers in the 1930s "pioneered a new tradition" of travel writing which Schweizer defines as "a platform for voicing radical political ideas" (Schweizer 2001: 3). Like Farley and Schweizer, I believe that West's travel writing was "transformative." Like many of West's hybrid works, *Black Lamb and Grey Falcon* subverts and combines several genres in order to achieve her transformational goals. It combines two genres of travel writing with the epic. Her interpretations of these genres manipulate their *existing* conventions to her ends and also frequently subvert these conventions in order to critique the political, cultural, and social orders of her contemporary world. In particular, West combines and interrogates existing conventions of the travel chronicle, the guidebook and the epic in order

- to analyze Western history, politics, and culture;
- to question the cultural mores that shape traditional travel genres;
- and to create a generic counterpoint within a hybrid genre that disrupts West's society's worldview.

Part 2 Imperialist critique: West's criticism of imperialism and her subversion of the colonizing potential of travel genres

Part 2A Travel subgenres: Guidebook and travel chronicle

Two of the most enduring types of travel genres are the guidebook and the travel chronicle. These travel forms have had various permutations and various names.[2] What I call the "travel chronicle" is also frequently called a "travel narrative" or a "travelogue." *Black Lamb and Grey Falcon* is clearly shaped by the conventions of both these forms. The book is a story of West's journey through Yugoslavia accompanied by her husband, her guide Constantine, his wife Gerda, and their driver Dragutin. The drama of the relationships between the members of her group and the personal and psychological growth of these characters form one aspect of the travelogue and thus place it in the "travel chronicle" tradition. Nonetheless, the lion's share of the text is devoted to rapt and meticulous observations of Yugoslavia's landscape, art, architecture, and their historical contexts. This places the book in the "guidebook tradition." West is not the first author who embeds a guidebook in her travel chronicle.

West's work is manifold and her goals are many. In particular, *Black Lamb and Grey Falcon* decries imperialism and the invidious principles that inform it—especially the violence inherent in imperialistic cultures. West's use of the guidebook and the travel chronicle contradicts the "imperialistic" threat of travel literature. As an antidote to imperialism, West promotes political and cultural nationalism, which fosters diversity and cooperation, and which can lead to peace. She advocates an integration of cultures where artistic and historical traditions nurture people who "productively" interact. This book's model of the interface in the contact zone can illustrate the cultural hybridity that West endorses and the subversive use of contradictory genres that promotes her political goals. West's manipulation of genres mimics and cultivates the anti-imperialist politics and the cultural hybridity that she promotes.

Part 2B West's rejection of the tourist's perspective

Both the guidebook and the travel chronicle have often implicitly or explicitly enforced a colonizing agenda. Yugoslavia is not a "colony" of Great Britain. However, "colonizing or objectifying habits" can inform travel literature even if the destination is not part of the narrator's country's empire.[3] Ironically, an adamant *criticism* of imperialism grounds West's alterations of both of these subgenres of travel literature in *Black Lamb and Grey Falcon*. West recognizes the "orientalizing" potential of these forms and she avoids using conventions that reinforce an imperialist ideology.[4]

Both guidebooks and travel chronicles often simplify in order to explain. This simplification results in an objectification of the visited country. Although West's stance risks this sort of mastery, it resists it in many ways.

William W. Stowe describes the guidebook's tendency to "claim positions of dominance": "Tourists are sightseers: their subjugating gaze reduces individuals, institutions, artworks and landscapes to bits of knowledge and elevates the tourists ... to the position of authoritative knower" (Stowe 1994: 48).[5] Stowe describes the guidebook's simplification as a means of domination: "The way of knowing and controlling the world is to reduce complex objects, phenomena, and experiences to sets of graspable facts" (Stowe 1994: 48). The guidebook, according to Stowe, similarly reduces "complex systems of economic and cultural life" (Stowe 1994: 49). For example, Vasi's *New Picture of Rome*'s "description of the Piazza del Popolo takes no notice of the 'popolo' that presumably animates it ... and adds a two-sentence history of the obelisk [erected in Egypt and relocated in 1589]" (Stowe 1994: 49).

West's incredibly dense text strenuously refuses the normal guidebook's diminishment of its object country. She captures the landscape, people, manners, art, and architecture of Yugoslavia in endless detail and with unparalleled appreciation and engagement. For example, she devotes twenty-four pages to a fresco in a church in Grachanitsa—the type of art that would probably be passed over or given one dismissive phrase in most guidebooks. The assassination of Archduke Franz Ferdinand in Sarajevo extends to fifty-two pages over three chapters. Long digressions about minor historical figures or events are frequent. Her book becomes a celebration of Yugoslavia as subject rather than an objectification of the "mastered" object.

Critics rightly disparage West's treatment of the Turks—as more clichéd and more biased than her treatment of especially the Serbs.[6] Nevertheless, even her descriptions of the Turks demonstrate her reluctance to oversimplify. She deplores them as "barbarous" (*BLGF* 897) for their ruthless destruction of Yugoslavia and yet praises their art and opulence. Following are some typical quotations which both criticize and praise the Turkish:

> [Turks] are what a people must become if it suspends all intellectual life and concentrates on the idea of conquest. (*BLGF* 309)
>
> Their whole beings breathed the love of pleasure which is the inspiration of Sarajevo, which was perhaps the great contribution the Turks had to make to culture. (*BLGF* 400)
>
> Turks were in a real sense magnificent. (*BLGF* 907)

Unlike the travel writers who "simplify" their visited country, West repeatedly stresses complexity and recommends that the "tourist" dispossess oneself of knowledge and power rather than appropriate it: "It is not pleasant to be bound to the task of learning all our days. ... To do these things it is necessary to have faith in what is entirely hidden and unknown, to cast away all the acquisitions and certainties" (*BLGF* 380).[7] West wants her readers to understand the "manifold" nature of Yugoslavia: "The thing I wanted to tell him could not be told, however, because it was manifold" (*BLGF* 23).

This refusal to simplify for mastery also refuses to commodify Yugoslavia. Tourists sometimes "master" a visited country in order to turn it into a "commodity" that they possess. Stowe describes this process: "Europe has become for them not so much a ... real place as a commodious signifier ... [which gives them] social and intellectual advantages" (Stowe 1994: 47).

In addition to enhancing a tourist's social position, "guidebooks," according to Stowe, "helped make tourist travel a profoundly empowering activity for individual Americans" (Stowe 1994: 47). Both guidebooks and travel chronicles also master other countries through what Stowe describes as "supercilious judgment on the people and places they visit" (Stowe 1994: 51): buildings are "uncouth," the land "flat," peasantry "depraved in morals," and there is a ubiquitous lack of "cleanliness." Stowe's analysis of American travel writers echoes Mary Louise Pratt and Sara Mill's description of travel chronicles that "master" colonized countries by constructing them as the "other." According to Pratt, "people appear as traces" because of oversimplification. Vast generalizations also dehumanize the other (Pratt 1992: 123).

West portrays her awareness of the risk of "touristic belittlement" through comments on historical and contemporary travelers.

> The nineteenth-century English traveler tended to form an unfavorable opinion of the Christian subjects of the Ottoman empire on the grounds that they were dirty and illiterate and grasping (as poor people, oddly enough, often are) and cringing and inhospitable and ill-mannered (as frightened people, oddly enough, often are). (*BLGF* 1095)

Her fellow travelers "were puzzled and irritated because we had spent so long in Yugoslavia ... 'the people are such barbarians, the life is so savage'" (*BLGF* 1082).

She strenuously insists that a people hold onto their native culture, even if it inconveniences the "tourist":

> Every nation ... has also its unique view of reality, which must contribute to our deliverance, and should therefore be allowed a like encouragement to its consciousness. Let people, then, hold to their own language, their own customs, their own beliefs, *even if this inconveniences the tourist*. (*BLGF* 843, emphasis added)

West counteracts this sort of demeaning construction of the "other" through a tactic that draws on the public/private advantage of travel stories. Edward Said recommends "personalizing" in order to avoid the objectification of the other. West personalizes the people she meets, the historical figures she describes, and the places she visits.[8] Using her own typology, she counters a "lunatic" moonlit vision with an "idiot's" perspective.[9] Minor figures including her driver, monks at historical churches, and Franz Ferdinand's assassin's sister have complex, nuanced personalities. Her detailed accounts of the political acts of historical figures always include stories and specifics of their personal lives and their personal relationships' ramifications. We learn that the Empress Elizabeth of Austria might have "averted the war of 1914" if she "had dealt with the Slavs as she dealt with the Hungarians," but "her work stopped because her marriage ... ceased to be tolerable" (*BLGF* 5). West also dwells on the personal life of Princip, Archduke Franz Ferdinand's assassin, and points out that history books have dehumanized Princip:

> From the court records one would suppose him to be without personal ties, to be perhaps an orphan, at any rate to be wholly absorbed in politics. Yet to the Czech doctor he spoke perpetually of his dear mother, of his brother and their children, and of a girl whom he had loved and whom he had hoped to marry. (*BLGF* 378)

Franz Ferdinand's personal desire for the Serbians to honor his wife—whose lineage excluded her from the Hapsburg dynasty—resulted in insufficient protection in Sarajevo. In other words, a personal act led to political disaster.

Individual subjectivity likewise disproves a potential "Orientalism" in West's portrayal of Militsa and Mehmed, a couple she meets in Skoplje, Macedonia. She has been told not to visit Skoplje: "Worth while going to Skoplje? What an idea! It is just a dreary little provincial town; there's nothing there at all, not an intelligent person" (*BLGF* 809). Militsa, however, disproves this critique: she is a delightful poet and philosopher who knows eight languages. West's portrait of Militsa explicitly contradicts the kind of objectification through superiority that critics like Stowe, Mills, and Pratt find so often characterize travel literature.

> If there are twenty people like this woman scattered between here and China, civilization will not perish. ... Now, when I go through a town of which I know nothing, a town which appears to be a waste land of uniform streets wholly without quality, I look on it in wonder and hope, since it may hold a Mehmed, a Militsa. (*BLGF* 807, 809)

In addition to finding value in "dreary" inconsequential places, West inverts travel literature's tendency to legitimize bourgeois authority by debasing lower-class citizens of the visited countries. West shifts the "center of civilization" from England to Yugoslavia, from urban centers to rural areas, and simultaneously elevates peasants over the bourgeois. She repeatedly stresses Yugoslavia's difference from the West—a difference based on primitive simplicity. West valorizes this apparent crudeness: "Really, we are not so rich in the West as we think we are. Or, rather, there is much we have not got which the people in the Balkans have got in quantity" (*BLGF* 23). While refusing to "sentimentalize" the peasants she sees, she also recognizes the integrity beneath their poverty[10]:

> A gaunt peasant woman with hair light and straight and stiff as hay and a mouth wide as a door had stopped in the roadway at the sight of us. She was so grand,

> so acidulated, so utterly at a disadvantage before almost anyone in the civilized world, and so utterly unaware of being at a disadvantage at all. ... It could be seen that she was a wit, a stoic, a heroine. (*BLGF* 403)

As I said, West is aware of the objectifying risks of being tourists and of writing travel literature.[11] Gerda—the fictional portrait of the wife of her fictional guide Constantine[12]—embodies almost all of the qualities of a tourist who domesticates and denigrates the "other" country. Like Fussell's "tourist," she is obsessed with her personal comfort in this alien land and devotes a great deal of attention to food and fiacres. She feels superior to most people and places. She views gypsies as "dirty and uncivilized savages" (*BLGF* 661) and deplores the variety that West celebrates in Yugoslavia because "there is no order here, no culture, but only a mish-mash of different peoples who are all quite primitive and low" (*BLGF* 662). According to her, decorative folk art (which West reveres) is "not serious art" (*BLGF* 654).

The contrast between Gerda's "Orientalist" view and West's appreciative one is crystallized in the juxtaposition of two cemeteries that they visit. Gerda appreciates a German war memorial because it is massive, monumental, and impersonal. West compares it to a "fortress": "A high circular wall, entered by a slit of a door in a low squat tower ... [inside] a black marble coffin, carved with the names and arms of the German states ... and on the ceiling above it is a mosaic of an eagle with its wings outstretched" (*BLGF* 763). In contrast with Gerda, West's husband captures what could be described as the German monument's "Orientalist" nature: "I don't like it because it pays no sort of respect to the individuals who are buried in it and because it is a tactless reminder of the past to an invaded people" (*BLGF* 763). Gerda's attitude and the German war memorial contrast markedly with the unassuming Slav cemetery that they subsequently visit. Seven thousand "flimsy crosses" recognize the individuality of each soldier. From West's point of view it is "one of the most affecting places in the world. It lies out on the plains among flat fields edged with willows and poplars, and it is a forest of flimsy little wooden crosses painted red, white and blue, each with a name or number, and each with its rose tree" (*BLGF* 766). Gerda's "touristic" perspective sees this cemetery as inferior. "'Think,' said Gerda, as we looked on the wide field of graves, 'think of all these people dying for a lot of Slavs'" (*BLGF* 766).

West's husband explains Gerda's attitude as an emphasis on "product" over "process" which denies others their subjectivity. He explicitly connects her attitude with imperialism: "This is the conqueror's point of view" (*BLGF* 800).

Part 3 Nationalism as a "fusion that infuriates"

Part 3A West's promotion of and definition of a liberal nationalism

As I have demonstrated, West combats this "conqueror's point of view" by giving Yugoslavia the "subject position" that Gerda—and many of the conventions of travel literature—would deny it. West's inversion of travel literature conventions is part of her campaign for a liberal nationalism[13] that would defeat imperialism and its perilous consequences. West's Yugoslavia repeatedly illustrates the importance of maintaining a connection to one's native culture. When other empires imposed their cultures on the Slavic countries, the result was "sterile" (*BLGF* 253), "degrading" (*BLGF* 284), and desiccating. Nationalism to West is feminist and imperialism is patriarchal.[14] An imperialistic education is described as "an education with a male bias" that believes in the "monstrous male rubbish ... that the Roman Empire was a vast civilizing force which spread material and moral well-being all over the ancient world by its rule" (*BLGF* 164). Imperialism oppresses its subjects, but the imperialists are no less fortunate because they are too far from their native cultures. Exile also robs individuals of vitality. Following is a description of "conquerors" who have become "sweet-sour phantoms":

> They looked incredibly fragile ... "they are to human beings what a ship inside a glass bottle is to a real boat." I saw before me what an empire which spreads beyond its legitimate boundaries must do to its subjects. It cannot spread its own life over the conquered areas, for life cannot travel too far from its sources, and it blights the life that is native to those parts. Therefore it imprisons all its subjects in a stale conservatism, in a seedy gentility ... they were sweet-sour phantoms, human wine gone to vinegar. (*BLGF* 903)

As we have seen, "The Strange Necessity" connects James Joyce, W. B. Yeats, Rudyard Kipling, and Scarface Capone because they all lack cultural roots. People who are exiled from their native countries are compelled to create their own interpretations of existence *ex nihilo* without the advantage of accumulated tradition.

Violence and destruction result from citizens' alienation from their own history and culture. West argues that the "violence of the dispossessed" infected Luccheni, who assassinated the Empress Elizabeth of Austria in 1898. Luccheni stabbed the empress apparently without any motive. West blames a modern, urban alienation for his crime:

> He performed his meaningless act out of his consciousness of what is perhaps the most real distress of our age ... he belonged to an urban population for which the

> existing forms of government made no provision, which wandered often workless and always traditionless, without power to control its destiny. (*BLGF* 9)

Luccheni's alienation is similar to Scarface Capone's. It is a specifically modern problem born out of cities whose intricate and complex organizations separate their citizens from their native cultural traditions and from the land. According to West, "Nationalism is simply the determination of a people to cultivate its own soul, to follow the customs bequeathed to it by its ancestors, to develop its traditions according to its own instincts. It is the national equivalent of the individual's determination not to be a slave" (*BLGF* 1101). Accordingly, she repeatedly condemns any force or circumstance that blocks or severs these ties. As we have seen, imperialism is frequently this force. She recognizes the threat inherent in the nationalism of imperialism or any other fanatic, exclusive nationalism. Princip's assassination of Archduke Franz Ferdinand is nationalism gone awry. Nonetheless, Luccheni's irrational violence of the dispossessed who are alienated from their cultural roots results in fascism. "Luccheni," West proclaims, "has got on well in the world. ... But Luccheni [now] is Mussolini" (*BLGF* 17). To West, Mussolini's terrorist camps are the ultimate indictment of fascism and the violence of alienation. She finds no model for them in prewar Europe. ("There could be no more convincing proof of the evil wrought on our civilization by the great cities and their spawn" [*BLGF* 18]).

Fascism is an extreme form of the intolerance of the other that traditional guidebooks and travel chronicles encourage. To West's contemporaries who identify fascism with nationalism rather than alienation, West declares, "There is not the smallest reason for confounding nationalism, which is the desire of a people to be itself, with imperialism which is the desire of a people to prevent other peoples from being themselves" (*BLGF* 843).

Part 3B West's politics of an integrative nationalism: A "fusion that infuriates"

In spite of the importance of remaining connected to one's native traditions, West is not an isolationist or a dualist. Adhering to one's cultural roots does not mean a denial of or an oppression of the other nor does it mean that one should reduce existence to false binaries. Carl Rollyson reports that West chose to tour Yugoslavia for the British Council instead of Finland because it was "a more picturesque and convenient example of the political thesis I wanted to expound" (Rollyson 1995: 148). West hoped that people could maintain ties to their native traditions while "fusing" (*BLGF* 400) or "integrating" (*BLGF* 836) with people with other cultural traditions. The urgency for Yugoslavia of this sort of coalescence made Yugoslavia a "convenient example" of a philosophy she wished all nations would adopt—a philosophy especially urgent in the late 1930s. As Schweizer explains, "West is ultimately fascinated by the fusion of opposites and the ability to overcome antitheses" (Schweizer 2001: 140). This philosophy is most developed in *Black Lamb and Grey Falcon*, but it influences most of her works. Stetz examines this same philosophy of an integrated nationalism in West's essay "The Necessity and Grandeur of the International Idea" which appeared in the collection, *Challenge to Death* (1934):

> Her essay ... was ... a meditation upon the subject of nationalism and upon the relationship between nationhood and internationalism. In her hands, however, the question also evolved into a narrative about the tension between autonomy and the appeal of *merging* oneself with others, as well as about the pull and play ... that surround the act of *uniting*. (Stetz 1994: 49, emphasis added)

Part 3C Examples of a "fusion that infuriates"

West repeatedly meets people who embody her goals for an integrating fusion. The following are three instances of relationships which are strengthened and invigorated when individuals' different nationalities, ethnicities, or cultural traditions connect: (1) a couple from Skoplje: Serbian/Hungarian Militsa and Heregovinian Muslim Mehmed; (2) the parents of West's friend Bulbul ("the Nightingale"): the Jewish mother and Muslim father in Travnik, Bosnia; and (3) the Serbian and Croatian soldiers who guard the mausoleum of the Turkish soldier Gazi Mestan in Kosovo, Serbia. West's Serbian-Jewish guide Constantine and his German wife Gerda embody the vitiated discord of a failed connection.

These hybrid alliances share essential features. Their beauty and fecundity lead to harmony and strength. In spite of their stability, they are unusually active and dynamic. This dynamism animates their transgressive potential which West hopes will transform Western worldviews. West's manipulation of genres propels her book into a similar dynamic, transgressive space that she hopes will galvanize social change.

West dwells on the beauty and the brilliance of the individuals in the integrative couples. Bulbul's Jewish mother is "astonishing in the force of her beauty" (*BLGF* 399). West marvels: "So long as one looked on this woman she seemed lovelier than all other women." In addition, Serbian Militsa "talks with the brilliance of a firefly" (*BLGF* 808). West implies that each individual's beauty is in some ways a result of the couples' harmonious alliances. The benefits of the Serbian and Croatian soldiers' friendship seem reflected in their healthy physiques: "short and sturdy and luminous with health, their skins rose under bronze, their black eyes shining deep and their black hair shining shallow" (*BLGF* 904).

A further testimony to the fertility of their connection, the soldiers' concord also results in a beautiful garden in the desolate plain of Kosovo. The Jewish and Muslim couple in Travnik have produced their outstanding daughter. And Mehmed and Militsa create brilliant scholarship, poetry, and political diplomacy. The fertility of these confederations provides the hope that they will inspire kindred unions.

Their strength and stability promise endurance. West insists that strength comes from fusion in her description of the living room in Travnik:

> But built into this room, and inherent in every word and gesture of its owners, was a tradition ... just as ancient and sure and competent [as those of Western Europe's metropolitan centers]. Whatever event these people met they could outface; the witness to that was their deep serenity. They would meet it with a formula *compounded* of Islam and Judaism. (*BLGF* 400, emphasis added)

Militsa's and Mehmed's strength is also described in architectural terms: "steady as pillars. They are the pillars supporting that invisible house which we must have to shelter us if we are not to be blown away" (*BLGF* 809).

In spite of the strength and stability of these fusions of difference, West insists on their dynamic, active nature. As we have discussed, one of the central tenets of West's philosophy is an elevation of "process" over "product." Peter Wolfe identifies "process" as West's "most encompassing doctrine" (Wolfe 1971: 12). Like me, he aligns "process" with integration. According to Wolfe, "process results in the *meshing* of styles, natural resources, and institutions within a culture" (Wolfe 1971: 13–14, emphasis added). These couples' activity gives them the energy requisite for transgressive change and underlines the importance of "process."

As we saw, Militsa's talk is compared to a "firefly": "She talks with the brilliance of the firefly, but her flight is not wandering, it is a swift passage from one logically determined point to another" (*BLGF* 808). West's description of Militsa and Mehmed's vibrant daily lives is preceded by a description of their motion: "There were Militsa and Mehmed, always in motion, yet always steady. Militsa runs from room to room, from the library to the kitchen, from the kitchen to her bedroom, to ... Mehmed ... rushes downstairs to the garden to play with his gun-dogs" (*BLGF* 809). In spite of their serenity, Bulbul's parents are compared to a boat in motion: "Their household rocked gently on a tide of giving and receiving" (*BLGF* 399).

This energy and vitality inherent in the fusions of cultures contrast starkly with the plains of Kosovo—the field where Constantine claims that Slavic civilization was destroyed because "we were all divided among ourselves" (*BLGF* 902).

> Then we were *stilled* by the *stillness* of Kossovo ... the land lies loosely, like a *sleeper*, in a cradle of featureless hills. Not by any means is the ground level. There a shoulder rises, here a hand supports the *sleeper's* head. But it is obviously prostrate and *passive*, it has *none of the active spirit* that makes mountain and forest and the picturesque valley. (*BLGF* 837, emphasis added)

The distorted syntax of West's awkward phrase "Not by any means is the ground level" in this description of stillness seems to result from the "negative," nullifying nature of the site. Human activity does exist in Kosovo, but the plain "nullifies" all vitality:

> But the plain absorbed them [living and working men and women] and *nullified* them by its own indifference, and there was shown before our eyes the first of all our *disharmonies*, the basis of our later tragedies: the *division* between man and nature. (*BLGF* 838, emphasis added)

Kosovo epitomizes the forces of dualism and division in Yugoslavia and the world that resist the harmonious coalescence West promotes.

The difficulty of the harmonious unions exampled by these three alliances is demonstrated by Constantine and Gerda's failure to coalesce. A Serbian Jew and a Christian German, Constantine and Gerda (like the Slavs at Kosovo) are "divided among ourselves" (*BLGF* 902). Gerda refuses to respect or to value Constantine's nation or religion. Their failed marriage captures in miniature the failed international relationships throughout the world in the late 1930s. Constantine is troubled by his wife's rudeness to his guests and is also vitiated to the point of stagnation by the strain of their relationship: "It was as if in his abandonment to Gerda's *nihilism* he had withdrawn his consent to every *integrating process*, even to the circulation of his own blood" (*BLGF* 836, emphasis added). At the base of Gerda's nihilism—which refuses to "integrate"—is her denial of process. As we discussed in Gerda's objectification of Yugoslavia, West's husband "diagnoses" her problem: "Gerda has no sense of process. ... She wants the result without doing any of the work that goes to make it. ... She wants to enjoy the position of a wife without going to the trouble of making a real marriage" (*BLGF* 799). People who "have lost sight of the importance of process" look at a "product" such as a "loaf of bread" and do "not realize the miracle of endurance and ingenuity [that] had to be performed" before the wheat became a loaf of bread (*BLGF* 801–2). The reader can infer the more global political and philosophical implications of Gerda's attitude in Henry's hyperbolic sense of her threat: "There is no way to be safe from her except to treat her as if she were, finally and exclusively, a threat to existence" (*BLGF* 800). While admitting the threat that "Gerda" presents to the world, West's husband predicts the victory of the Militsas and Mehmeds:

> Let us admit it, for a little while the whole of our world may belong to Gerda. ... She will not be able to keep it. For her contempt for the process makes her unable to conduct any process. ... You cannot administer a country on this principle. (*BLGF* 803)

Since "the whole of our world ... belong[s] to Gerda," West requires that the integrative relationships' energy be transgressive. The Serbian and Croatian soldiers who guard Gazi Mestan's mausoleum remind us of the threat of dualism like Gerda's. They also demonstrate the subversive potential of alliances of difference.West's Serbian driver Dragutin finds the idea of spending the day in the company of a Croat unthinkable because the world exists for him in binaries. But the Serb soldier replies, "It is most surprising how pleasant he is; he is my true friend, and he is a good soldier; I would never have believed it" (*BLGF* 904). Gerda and Dragutin think of Serbs and Croats as "opposites," but where they see difference and opposition, the soldiers see alliance. West describes the improbability and the necessity of their friendship by placing them both literally and figuratively on a precarious ledge where they balance together in defiance of the division of Kosovo:

> On this little ledge they met and clung together, on this cross-wide space from which the dark grasses of Kossovo had been driven back, they who had been born under different flags and had to beat down a wall of lies before they could smile at each other. (*BLGF* 905)

In saying that "the dark grasses of Kossovo had been driven back" from the soldiers' space, West implies that they have defeated the division and stagnation of the philosophy that Kosovo represents for West. The soldiers oppose "a wall of lies," Western morality. The soldiers' victory destabilizes Western society which rests on the principles of division, violence, dualism, and prejudice that inform Kosovo. West portrays the soldiers' final victory against the prejudices that keep them and others like them from thriving in our contemporary world in Serbian Dragutin's final acceptance when he says to the soldiers, "You are what Yugoslavia needs" (*BLGF* 905). Mehmed's political job also succeeds in undoing the prejudice in the society around him:

> Through all the intricacies of post-war Yugoslavian politics, in spite of the temptations they have offered to passion and acquisitiveness, he has urged the importance to the state of fundamental virtue, of honest administration, and of justice towards all races and classes. (*BLGF* 808–9)

West underlines the subversive nature of these alliances when she admits that the Western world's prejudices would probably condemn the qualities that she appreciates in Bulbul's mother. For instance, West says of her gesture of sprinkling West with perfume when she departed, "It was the most gracious farewell imaginable, and the Western world in which I was born would not have approved" (*BLGF* 401). The Western world would be even more outraged because a Muslim and a Jew live together in such extravagant harmony: "It was a *fusion* that would *infuriate* the Western moralist, who not only believes but prefers that one should not be able to eat one's cake and have it. ... So one can have it, as the vulgar say, both ways" (*BLGF* 400, emphasis added). In spite of the fact that these three confederations would outrage Western mores, as Dragutin claims, "you are what Yugoslavia needs."

Part 4 Theorizing a "fusion that infuriates": Genre as politics

West's depictions of these vital confederations can illuminate our discussion of her transgressive manipulation of hybrid genres. All three couples exist and thrive in a literal "contact zone." This book has been using Pratt's colonial idea metaphorically, but it applies literally in *Black Lamb and Grey Falcon*. The contact zone and Freadman's "uptake" work on the narrative level as well as the esthetic level. Pratt specifically addresses the relationships between colonizer and colonized, but Yugoslavia is an apt territory for her theories because of its long history of invasions and shifting boundaries. Relationships in Pratt's contact zone are often unequal or combative because of cultural imbalances of power in colonies. Pratt creates the concept of the "contact zone" in order to redress a simplistic sense of the "encounter" between two cultures as inevitably a relationship of dualistic dominance and subordination: "[The contact zone] foregrounds the interactive, improvisational dimensions of colonial encounters so easily ignored or suppressed by diffusionist accounts of conquest or domination" (Pratt 1992: 7). Admittedly, conventional guidebooks and travel chronicles often do assume a simplistic sense of power relationships in colonized (or uncolonized) countries, but Pratt believes that the reality is more complex, dynamic, and generative—a relationship of influence and exchange rather than purely domination and oppression and of multiplicity instead of stark difference. "A contact perspective emphasizes how subjects are constituted in and or by their relations to each other ... copresence, interaction, interlocking understandings and practices" (Pratt 1992: 7). West is obviously even more optimistic than Pratt about the constitutive power of the contact zone.

Pratt sees travel writing as the scene for a productive encounter in the contact zone. William Stowe shares a similar sense of the transformational potential of cultural interaction in travel writing in *Going Abroad*. Stowe's concept of "liminal space" helps us understand the subversive potential of Freadman's bidirectional uptake between hybrid genres. His analysis stresses travel writing's power to transform the travel writer—and consequently the writer's culture. Stowe borrows from Victor Turner's analysis of ritual and breaks travel into a three-stage structure whose second stage of "social limbo" can be subversive:

> Rituals begin with a "phase of *separation* [which] clearly demarcates sacred space and time from profane." ... The phase of separation is followed by a transitional or marginal state, "a sort of social limbo." ... This state is followed ... by the "reaggregation" of the participant into normal society. (Stowe 1994: 21)

According to Stowe's interpretation of Turner, the writer in most travel literature passes from a sacred or magical phase of separation into the second phase of travel where his experience is "normalized" in order for him to reassimilate into his culture. This "tribal liminal"—which resembles Pratt's contact zone—can be normative, but it can also be "subversive":

> "Tribal liminal" ... is put into the service of normativeness almost as soon as it appears [but the] liminal phase ... can become ... an actually subversive period between a conventional, conservative view of the world and one's place in it as fixed, and a new perception of the world as changeable and the self as capable of effective change. (Stowe 1994: 21)

West, like Stowe, understands the transformational potential in travel literature. West manipulates travel genres in order to create a space where all her readers experience Stowe's "liminal" zone and acquire "a new perception of the world as changeable and the self as capable of effective change."[15]

Stowe's "liminal zone" elaborates on the subversive nature of Freadman's "uptake." When West agrees to use the conventions of travel literature and when her readers sit down to read her book with expectations about the conventions of travel literature, "uptake" occurs. For Freadman and West, "uptake" is productive when "applied to the interaction of, minimally a pair of texts" (Freadman 2002: 40). West manipulates contradictory generic expectations in order to achieve what Freadman calls a "bidirectional relation" (Freadman 2002: 42). Freadman calls "uptake," the "bidirectional relation that holds between the pair; that is ... the text and ... its 'interpretant'" (Freadman 2002: 42). Like Stowe's "liminal" space, "uptake" can be subversive because it crosses a boundary. West describes the principles that underlie her coalescing unions in people whom she meets in her travels. Generically, *Black Lamb and Grey Falcon* embodies the features of her "unholy alliances" by manipulating genres in order to create a subversive text that transforms her readers.

The relationships' dynamic, "integrating process" creates subversive spaces that undermine Western cultural mores. These interactions can be illuminated by Pratt's "contact zone," Stowe's "liminal space," and Freadman's concept of "uptake." These multiplicitous relationships open up the possibility of subversion.

In addition to portraying relationships, West creates shifting spaces of contradictory tendencies in travel conventions in her actual text. This "bidirectional" use of travel conventions makes *Black Lamb and Grey Falcon*, itself, a contact zone or liminal space. As some critics' disparagement of *Black Lamb and Grey Falcon*'s generic variety attests, its combination of many different kinds of genres makes her text itself a "fusion that infuriates."[16] Laura Heffernan captures the dynamic and active nature of West's esthetic in her analysis of "The Strange Necessity." Heffernan also insists on the political nature of this active esthetic. Heffernan highlights the active quality of West's metaphors: "West's metaphors—'system of relations,' 'nexus of forces,' 'recognizable design,' 'collision of Forms' all seem borrowed from the language of esthetic formalism, yet these pieces of literature direct West not inward to their internal forms, but outward to the world" (Heffernan 2008: 317).

Part 5 Contradictory genre expectations create a transformative space in *Black Lamb and Grey Falcon*

West creates transformative spaces in *Black Lamb and Grey Falcon* through contradictory genre expectations. Marina MacKay, also, valorizes the paradox and contradiction in *Black Lamb and Grey Falcon* in her analysis of resurrection: "This book itself, if it aspires to palimpsest-like art, must be paradoxical, inconclusive" (MacKay 2002: 193).[17] For example, a contradictory relationship with authority drives West's manipulation of travel genre conventions. She wants her book to have legitimacy while at the same time she criticizes hierarchies and power structures. West employs travel-writing conventions to gain credibility, but simultaneously upsets travel writing to criticize the values that inform imperialism. These conservative and subversive moves—which are always influenced by West's position as a woman writer—create a shifting, subversive, manifold text: a contact zone or liminal space where uptake can upset fascist, violent, dualistic, or imperialistic attitudes. The readers' "uptakes" shift constantly as West plays with their generic expectations.

In 1941, travel literature was a traditional, popular genre with a wide audience. This turn to more traditional literary forms is typical of many modernist authors in the late 1930s and the 1940s. T. S. Eliot's *Four Quartets*' more intelligible style stems from a desire to promote community. W. H. Auden moved from inscrutable free verse poems to more comprehensible poems in traditional forms. The pressure to reach a larger audience in order to "make action urgent and its nature clear" affected many authors at this time (Auden 1977: 157). Choosing a "popular" genre gives West acceptance and authority. In a way, Schweizer's claims that the 1930s travel writers elevated travel writing into a "literary" form of "high seriousness" also makes West choice of travel literature a "conservative" gesture.

Nonetheless, even though a travel book affords her a large audience and makes this choice a "conservative" move, travel literature is a "marginalized" genre. Fussell calls it a "second-rate" form. Marginalized forms are common for West. West chooses marginalized genres in order to achieve a freedom or license frequently denied to women writers—a liberal move which contradicts what may seem like "conservative" choices.[18] *Black Lamb and Grey Falcon* is cultural history, philosophy, and political journalism in the "guise" of a minor genre.[19]

West's choice of "protagonist" in her travel narrative is also multiple and exploits contradictory expectations toward authority, thus creating a "contact zone" of contradictory "uptakes." In order to give authority to her more ambitious political and philosophical aspirations, West deliberately eschews the established tradition of solitary women travelers as travel writers.[20] Although West's story is based on two trips she took by herself and one that she took with her husband, *Black Lamb and Grey Falcon*'s fictional narrative depicts a trip taken with her husband—and male and female companions. West's husband and her Serbian guide Constantine play prominent parts and give voice to central ideas of her study. As Wolfe argues, "Instead of competing for the reader's admiration she credits most of her best insight to him [her husband]" (Wolfe 1971: 148). West might be criticized for "surrendering" authority to men,[21] but this is a strategic ploy rather than submissive deference. Female narrators of travel narratives were still thought of as eccentric or zany. Lila Marz Harper captures the contradictory stance and the compromising position of women travel writers in her work *Solitary Travelers*:

> My rhetorical focus is on the solitary narrative position, a position which offers an unusual authoritative voice for women but one which at the same time, places her in a personally vulnerable role within her writing ... to present oneself as essentially being alone invites questions about the traveler's morals. (Harper 2001: 17)

Monica Anderson also comments on women travelers' lack of credibility in *Women and the Politics of Travel: 1870–1914:* "Women who transgressed into men's allotted sphere could be labeled both unfeminine and 'unnatural'" (Anderson 2006: 20). Using male props for her ideas protects West's trip (and its insights) from the labels of eccentricity or outlandishness that often brand travelogues by single women.[22]

The patriarchal tendencies in West's move to give "voice" to her male characters is contradicted by her "plural" protagonist. West critiques Western patriarchal values by subverting the tradition of an *individual* male hero.[23] Although West-as-narrator could be called "the protagonist," the story focuses on the *group's* journey and the *group's* passage from innocence to wisdom and understanding. West gives authority to the views expressed in *Black Lamb and Grey Falcon* and also promotes a multiplicity at the core of her project through a dialogic interplay of male and female voices in her story. Moreover, the real "heroes and heroines" of the travel narrative are the three pairs whose integrating fusions outrage the "Western moralist."

Another paradox that animates this text to create a subversive space is the tension between private and public inherent in a woman's travel book. Cultural norms define women's spheres as "private" spheres. We have seen West elevate the private and personal in order to avoid objectification of Yugoslavia, its people and its culture. Nonetheless, *Black Lamb and Grey Falcon*'s historical subjects and West's political agenda make this a very "public" book. West recognizes the "public/private" tension that Sara Mills argues is inherent in *all* women's writing in the most-quoted passage from *Black Lamb and Grey Falcon.* Relying on socially endorsed distinctions West blames women as "idiots" because they are too private and criticizes men as "lunatics" because they are obsessed with public affairs:

> The word "idiot" comes from a Greek root meaning private person. Idiocy is the female defect: intent on their private lives, women follow their fate through a darkness deep as that cast by malformed cells in the brain. It is not worse than the male defect, which is lunacy; they are so obsessed by public affairs that they see the world as by moonlight, which shows the outlines of every object but not the details indicative of their nature. (*BLGF* 3)

While defining these differences, this passage—which falls in a book that validates both the private and the public—clearly condemns either extreme and a dualistic mindset.[24]

West's manipulations of traditional travel narrative stances also create a shifting text whose counterpoint between different points of view results in a subversive liminal space or a contact zone. This manipulation also overturns social hierarchies and furthers her critique of imperialism. William Stowe defines two prevailing narrative stances in the guidebook and the travel chronicle. These were determined by the travel author's native country's relationship to the visited country. In Stowe's analysis, most travel books were written by Americans visiting Europe or by Europeans visiting colonized countries. In the first case, Americans viewed Europe as a repository of their past history and as richer in cultural and artistic traditions than their native land. In the second, the British or the European traveler viewed a third world country (likely a colony) as a place of exoticism and adventure, but inferior in its culture and history.

West's stance toward Yugoslavia is a curious combination of these dominant perspectives. The bulk of the book is devoted to describing Yugoslavia's centuries of rich history, art, and architecture. West sounds like an American visiting Europe when she says, "I had come to Yugoslavia because I knew that the past has made the present and I wanted to see how this process works" (*BLGF* 54). Her veneration for Yugoslavia's cultural history is so profound that she claims, "It is probable that the Battle of Kossovo [1389] deducted as much from civilization as the sum of England after the Tudor age" (*BLGF* 900). She also feels "as if it [Yugoslavia] were my mother country" (*BLGF* 1). On the other hand, its paucity of modern industry or technology and its poverty make Yugoslavia more like a third world country—and make West more like a European visiting a colony than an American in the Old World. She repeatedly stresses Yugoslavia's difference from the West—a difference based on simplicity. The Slavs themselves claim to be "uncivilized." A man in Dalmatia says, "You must make allowances. We are in some respects still barbarous simply because we spent so much of our time defending the West" (*BLGF* 188). West valorizes this apparent crudeness: "Really, we are not so rich in the West as we think we are. Or, rather, there is much we have not got which the people in the Balkans have got in quantity" (*BLGF* 23). West does not go to Yugoslavia as a "colonizer," but one of her central purposes is to observe the effects of the colonization of Yugoslavia by myriad empires.

This complicated stance which shares qualities of both the American in Europe and the European in the colonies suits West's coalescing goals. Like people from different backgrounds who come together in complimentary relationships that "infuriate the Western moralist," West's seemingly contradictory narrative stances create a complex picture of Yugoslavia that defies travelers' or readers' preconceived notions of their relationships to the visited countries.

The readers (and the writer) never rest as they negotiate and try to understand these complex and contradictory manipulations of travel genre expectations. Through the confusion of different narrative stances, both the country, Yugoslavia, and West's book, *Black Lamb and Grey Falcon,* become "contact zones." Pratt describes the unsettling nature of a "contact zone" when she describes the improvised languages that sometimes emerge: "Like societies of the contact zone, such languages are commonly regarded as chaotic, barbarous, lacking in structure" (Pratt 1992: 6).

Like contact zones' societies and languages, *Black Lamb and Grey Falcon* has been deplored for its excesses and criticized for a chaotic use of generic conventions. Pratt finds virtue in chaos and so does West. Life is contradictory and uncertain. It is wrong to deny its disorder or contradictions and it is also our duty to keep on trying to understand. She writes of the Sarajevo *attentat* which at once "left ... civilization disabled" and was "a holy act of liberation" (*BLGF* 381):

> Life ... is loose and purposeless, which weaves a close pattern and doggedly pursues its ends, which is unpredictable and illogical, which follows a straight line from cause to effect, which is bad, which is good. ... The sum will not add up. ... But there is nothing else we can do except try to add up this sum. (*BLGF* 381–2)

Black Lamb and Grey Falcon is West's attempt to "add up the sum." She chooses travel genres to pursue the "unpredictable and illogical." By tracing travel conventions' patterns in *Black Lamb and Grey Falcon* this chapter pays tribute to West's manifold work.

Section 2 "Magnificence and its adoration": The manipulation of epic conventions in *Black Lamb and Grey Falcon*

West's desire to "add up this sum" (literally to comprehend life) leads her to draw on the conventions of the archetypal travel genre, the epic. By fusing an epic with a travel chronicle/guidebook, West is able to enlarge her critique of her contemporary culture and especially to explore (once again) art's imperative role in our personal and public lives.

Bernard Schweizer's *Rebecca West: Heroism, Rebellion, and the Female Epic* and his "Epic Form and (Re)Vision in Rebecca West's *Black Lamb and Grey Falcon*" are the definitive works on West and the epic. His book treats *The Judge, The Fountain Overflows, Cousin Rosamund, This Real Night, Survivors in Mexico,* West's philosophy, and *Black Lamb and Grey Falcon* as epics. The following analysis of *Black Lamb and Grey Falcon* endorses Schweizer's study in many ways and also differs in some ways. For the purposes of this study on hybrid genres, my emphases are quite different from Schweizer's.

Schweizer catalogs many of *Black Lamb and Grey Falcon*'s epic features—including its twelve chapters/books, the poetic quality of her prose, its elevated and ambitious subject, its journey motif, and its quest. He believes that the work lacks a traditional epic invocation. West does, nonetheless, invoke *Ulysses* on the first page of the book. "Then I picked up my book and read that sonnet by Joachim du Bellay, which begins '*Heureux qui, comme Ulysse, a fait un beau voyage*'. I said to myself, 'That is one of the most beautiful poems in the world'" (*BLGF* 1). West also declares her epic ambitions when she tells her readers that she went to Yugoslavia in order to understand Western civilization: "I had to admit that I quite simply and flatly knew nothing at all about the south-eastern corner of Europe; and ... that is to say I know nothing of my own destiny" (*BLGF* 21).

Black Lamb and Grey Falcon, then, is part of a body of modernist epics, many of which evoke the *Odyssey.* These include James Joyce's *Ulysses,* Ezra Pound's *Cantos,* and T. S. Eliot's *The Waste Land.* In this context, searching for the source of modern culture in Yugoslavia is an unusual move. It is part of an internationalism that we have long recognized as an important feature of modernism. Susan Stanford Friedman reminds us of T. S. Eliot's turn to Buddhism, Pound and Stravinsky's appropriation of African primitivism, and Yeats's and Pound's use of Chinese culture and linguistics. It was common of this "internationalism," according to Friedman, to locate modernity in Western capitals such as "London, Paris, New York, Rome and Berlin" (Friedman 2003: 40). Yeats, of course turns to ancient Byzantium for a cultural paradigm, but I can think of no other writer that turns to a contemporary, oppressed, impoverished, mostly rustic Eastern European country in order to define (or disrupt) the Western World and its symbolic systems. West chooses Yugoslavia to criticize the hierarchical and elitist tendencies of modernism and modernity. In her article "Modernism in a Transnational Landscape," Friedman advocates "cultural parataxis" which "decenters" canonical European and American modernisms and approaches modernism as "multiple cultural constructions" with "multiple centers, agencies, and subjectivities" (Friedman 2003: 44–5). This, in many ways, is West's project. Nonetheless, her choice of a country that has been invaded, conquered, and exploited by other countries throughout its history is part of the universalizing tendency of modernism: As I have said, West sees imperialism as the most pervasive and invidious feature of our culture.

As Schweizer recognizes, the epic is patently a "male" genre. West deliberately subverts many of the male features of the epic in order to denounce her contemporary culture and to promote an alternative—feminist—worldview. Starting with Empress Elizabeth of Austria on the third page of her book, women figure importantly in her "public" and her "private" story. World events are also redefined in terms of women and their perspective. Speaking of the far-reaching effect of the First World War, she uses a woman's perspective: "But Danilo's [Prince Danilo of Montenegro in the 19th century] death did not make my great-grandmother cry. ... The *attentat* at Sarajevo had a totally different effect ... I and nearly all women in Europe wept times without number" (*BLGF* 1103).

The epic commonly depicts an individual, powerful male hero who leaves home to have (often violent) adventures that win "glory," power, or property for him and his nation. (The imperialistic qualities of this model are self-evident). West rewrites all these conventions.

She is not powerful and she has no aspirations for power. The book begins with an apology to her husband for the "inconvenience" of the trip. Her subordination and "powerlessness" are emphasized when her second paragraph recounts that "the first time I ever spoke the name 'Yugoslavia'" was after an operation in a London nursing home (*BLGF* 1). She deliberately underlines her unfounded fear before the operation. This is a far cry from the "godlike" or "storm-tossed great" Odysseus, "born for exploits"—or any other traditional warrior or conqueror (1967: Book 1. line 20, 6.1, 10.554). Like Harriet Hume, West-as-narrator does not protest her lack of power, but rather claims "it is life, not power or authority, that gives us joy" (*BLGF* 197). She also uses homely feminine metaphors, rather than heroic terms, to describe the importance of her journey: "Nothing in my life had affected me more deeply than this journey through Yugoslavia ... it was like picking up a strand of wool that would lead me out of a labyrinth in which, to my surprise, I had found myself immured" (*BLGF* 1088–9).

This valorization of weakness and the homely metaphors anticipate her celebration of the oppressed peasants and working class. This elevation is, in turn, part of her subversion of the convention of the individual hero. As we saw, in adopting the conventions of the travel narrative West departed from the established tradition of solitary women travelers as travel writers to create a "plural" protagonist. West also eschews the traditional individual (solitary) epic hero. As we observed West-as-narrator could be called "the protagonist," but the story focuses on the *group's* journey and the group's passage from innocence to wisdom and understanding. As our discussion will prove, the real epic "heroes and heroines" of the story are the Slavic peasants and the European working class. Her description of the Londoners' response to the Second World War's air-raids makes revision of these epic expectations explicit: "There have been heroes on the plains of Troy, on the Elizabethan seas, on the fields of Flanders, in the Albanian mountains ... but none of them was more heroic than these" (*BLGF* 1130).

Other modernists, of course, have interrogated the conventions of the individual, powerful epic hero. West's challenge stems from her feminist revision of cultural values. She took an especially feminist approach to the epic goal of "adventure" or "escape." Fussell describes an overwhelming desire among citizens and writers in the '20s, '30s and '40s to "quit the ... life at home and ... go adventuring" (Fussell 1980: 9). This fervor is fueled, according to Fussell, by a desire for "escape" (Fussell 1980: 13). D. H. Lawrence's Aaron Sisson in *Aaron's Rod* and James Joyce's Stephen Dedalus in *A Portrait of the Artist as a Young Man* are typical of the many figures who have "taken flight to escape something hateful at home" (Fussell 1980: 15). Moreover, the "ad" in "adventure" stresses its inherent movement. Many critics have commented upon the particularly "male" or imperialistic nature of most ideas of adventure. Mills cites Paul Zweig who claims that "adventurers always flee women and reinvent themselves as men in order to find wholly male pleasures" (Mills 1991. 77). According to Martin Green, "To celebrate adventure was to celebrate empire" (Mills 1991: 76).

Constantine's tale of his first lover (whom he regrets having lost) reminds us of the male conventions of "adventure narratives": "All the way to Paris [on the train] I was glad that it looked very well and as it should be, and I the man was leaving her the woman and going to a far place and having new adventures, because I knew that was how it was not and that she was tired of me" (*BLGF* 456).

Countering epic norms, West's epic emphasizes the *return*, not the escape from home or women, or the conquering of other countries. For her, the beauty of Joachim du Bellay's poem *Ulysse* lies in its emphasis on Ulysses' *return home*.

> *Et en quelle saison*
> *Revoiray-je le clos de ma pauvre maison,*
> *Qui m'est une province, et beaucoup d'avantage?* (*BLGF* 1–2)

"Sanity," to West, is defined as being stably in one home: "Only part of us is sane: only part of us loves pleasure and the longer day of happiness, wants to live to our nineties and die in peace, in a house that we built, that shall shelter those who come after us" (*BLGF* 1102). She associates this sane instinct for home with women. She describes a monastery on a desolate island in Dalmatia where "pirates have murdered and looted their altars" for centuries. "Nuns," West claims, "finding themselves as unwholesomely situated, would have gone home" (*BLGF* 225).

This emphasis on the return home is part of West's nationalism that we have discussed in her manipulation of travel chronicle conventions. As our discussion of the tourist demonstrated, nationalism to West is feminist and imperialism is patriarchal. West also gives a feminist aspect to her interpretation of the epic in her condemnation of violence. Violence, of course, is endemic to most epics. Odysseus is described as "sacker of cities," and addressed in the underworld as "mastermind of war" (Homer 1967: 14.447, 11.458). West's analysis of the several types of violence that threaten the Western world unites the many threads which weave her complicated interpretation of several travel genres and the philosophy that informs them.

Black Lamb and Grey Falcon is an anatomy of violence. West admits, "Violence was, indeed, all I knew of the Balkans" (*BLGF* 21). According to West, two types of violence were threatening Europe in the 1930s: (1) the violence of the dispossessed and (2) the violence of the rock. West uses the convergence of these two types of violence to justify British engagement in the Second World War, but her goals are much broader. West hopes to analyze Western culture and to explore the possibility of human change through what she calls the prodigiousness of art.[25] West's manipulation of the conventions of the travel chronicle and the guidebook allows her to denounce the violence of the dispossessed. The violence of the dispossessed is the violence of Luccheni who murdered the Empress

Elizabeth of Austria because of his urban alienation from his native traditions and his native roots in the land.

The violence of the rock is the "violence of sacrifice." West believes that an impulse for self-sacrifice infects all of Western, liberal culture. Her analysis of this violence inspires her book's title: a black lamb is a sacrificial animal and the grey falcon is a symbol of the self-sacrificial impulse that motivated the Serbian Prince Lazar to lose the Battle of Kosovo in 1389.

In attending the ritual sacrifice of lambs for fertility, she deduces her "principle of the rock." West takes pains to communicate the loathsomeness of animal sacrifice. She describes her approach to the rock in gory detail:

> The grass we walked on from the car was trodden and muddied and littered with paper, and as we came nearer the rock we had to pick our way among a number of bleeding cocks' heads. The spectacle was extremely disgusting. The colour of spilt blood is not properly a colour, it is in itself discoloured, it is a visible display of putrescence. ... A great many jars had been thrown down from the rock and lay in shards among the cocks' heads on the trodden grass. Though there was nothing faecal to be seen, the effect was of an ill-kept earth closet. (*BLGF* 823)

She, then, describes the killing of two lambs whose blood is smeared on a baby's forehead. West is repulsed by the "carcasses of the lambs, which were still faintly smoking at the throat" and by the "sickening ... stench" (*BLGF* 824). "What they were doing at the rock was abominable" (*BLGF* 825).[26]

West tries to fathom this abomination. Epic heroes frequently journey to the underworld for wisdom or prophecy. West employs the epic trip to the underworld to dramatize her journey to an understanding of the violence of the rock.[27] Typical of the multiplicity of this text, her heroes and heroines in fact make multiple journeys to the underworld. The text is rife with trips to tombs, memorials, and cemeteries. "Yugoslavia," she remarks, "is always telling me about one death or another" (*BLGF* 917).

Their visit to the Battle of Kosovo memorials constitutes her groups' journey to the underworld and finally unveils the "logic" behind the principle of the rock. To West and to the Slavs, the crucial moment in Yugoslav history is the Battle of Kosovo (1389) where the Slavs were defeated by the Turks. According to legend, the night before the battle a grey falcon turned into Saint Elijah who appeared before the leader of the Serbs, Lazar. Elijah gives Lazar a choice between an earthly kingdom and a heavenly kingdom. If he chooses the earthly kingdom, he will win the battle, but if he chooses the heavenly kingdom he and all his men will be killed. Tsar Lazar chooses a heavenly kingdom and the Slavs are destroyed.

West's underworld journey has two parts. She and her companions first visit Lazar's tomb and they then visit the Plains of Kosovo. The visit to the tomb sets the stage for the understanding that she gains at Kosovo. This first "journey which was astonishing in the directness of its contact with the past" begins with an ominous "strangeness" (*BLGF* 508)—which portends the hell-like nature of the group's journey: "At a point on the plains there was now heaped up a drift of dark cloud; and through this there ran a shaft of lightning. A storm was on us, and it was in alternate blackness and greenish crystal light that we began our journey" (*BLGF* 509). The trip takes place in a storm or with "the black sky ... pressing lower, the cloisters gleamed at us through an untimely dusk" (*BLGF* 510). The group views the corpse of Tsar Lazar dressed in royal garments and West "put out a finger and stroked those hard dry hands" (*BLGF* 516). West recognizes the significance of Lazar's defeat:

> When this man met defeat it was not only he whose will was frustrated, it was a whole people, a whole faith, a wide movement of the human spirit. This is told by the splendid rings on the Tsar Lazar's black and leathery hands; and the refinement of the pomp which presents him in his death, the beauty and gravity of the enfolding ritual, show the worth of what was destroyed with him. (*BLGF* 516)

Nonetheless, the visit is finally inconclusive. It is as if in spite of the tomb's "magic" and the dead's ubiquitous presence, the dead (like the mute ghosts in Dante's *Inferno*) cannot speak.

West gains fuller comprehension during the second stage of her journey, the visit to the Plains of Kosovo. Again, she is explicit about the plains' underworld quality. The sky is described as "a *vault* visible yet of no colour except space" (*BLGF* 838, emphasis added). "It [the plain] is crowded with the dead who died in more than their flesh, whose civilization was cast with them into their graves" (*BLGF* 839). After the fourth Battle of Kosovo, "the night fell for four centuries, limbo became Hell, and manifested the anarchy that is Hell's essential character" (*BLGF* 840).

In her biography of Saint Augustine, West defines loneliness and loss as the essential modern condition. "Kossovo," she says, "more than any other historical site I know, arouses that desolation ... we are alone and terrified" (*BLGF* 838). Nonetheless, West finally refuses to be defeated by the inevitably tragic nature of our existence. After Constantine recounts the legend of the grey falcon and

Lazar, West realizes, "When I had stood by the tomb in the monastery at Vrdnik ... and touched Prince Lazar's mummied hand, I had been well aware that he was one of a pattern familiar to me" (*BLGF* 912). The pattern is the "principle of the rock," the belief in the virtue of sacrifice which West witnessed in the sacrifice of the lamb and which led to self-sacrifice at Kosovo. She declares that the black lamb and the grey falcon were "accomplices" in the Battle of Kosovo and "in nearly all historic crimes and most personal crimes" (*BLGF* 914).

> None of us ... could resist the temptation of accepting this sacrifice as a valid symbol. We believed ... [in] a man cutting the throat of a lamb on a rock to please God and obtain happiness; and when our intelligence told us that the man was performing a disgusting and meaningless act, our response ... [was] to say, "Since it is wrong to be the priest and sacrifice the lamb, I will be the lamb and be sacrificed by the priest." We thereby set up a principle that doom was honourable for innocent things. (*BLGF* 914–15)

West argues that this "power of the rock" has prevailed in the West since the Battle of Kosovo and was affecting liberals in her contemporary England (*BLGF* 915).

Having defined this violence of the rock, she refutes it—and hence rejects the principles that underpin her culture. She argues that the thesis of the legend is false. She will not accept that Lazar had to choose between salvation and damnation. "I do not believe that any man can procure his own salvation by refusing to save millions of people from miserable slavery" (*BLGF* 911).

The pernicious principle of the rock results from many of the values that inform traditional guidebooks, travel chronicles, and epics. West's subversion of the conventions of travel literature contributes to her campaign against the principle of the rock. For example, the utilitarian values that consider visits to foreign places commodities to accumulate in order to increase one's social standing or one's power over another people also make us vulnerable to the principle of the rock. She deduces, "There is a mysterious process at work in the world which has no relation to causality. This process is a penny-in-the-slot-machine of idiot character. If one drops in a piece of suffering, a blessing pops out" (*BLGF* 826). This utilitarian objectification is the denial of process that West's husband locates in Gerda. Ridiculous as this thinking is, West discovers that "I knew this rock well. I had lived under the shadow of it all my life. All our Western thought is founded on this repulsive pretence that pain is the proper *price* of any good *thing*" (*BLGF* 827, emphasis added). West finds the principle that pain and suffering produce goodness in Christianity (especially the Crucifixion), in Christian denominations including Roman Catholicism, Anglicanism, and Methodism, and in most artists, especially Shakespeare.[28]

Individualism supports utilitarianism and has made Westerners particularly susceptible to "the power of the rock." Westerners have been more concerned with individual salvation than with broader social good. West comments on her own egotistic preoccupation with self in order to condemn Western individualism.

> It is possible that we have betrayed life and love for more than five hundred years on a field wider than Kossovo, as wide as Europe. As I perceived it I felt that imbecile anxiety concerning my own behavior in such a crisis, which is a matter of only the slightest importance. What mattered was that I had not served life faithfully, that I had been too anxious for a fictitious personal salvation, and imbecile enough to conceive that I might secure it by hanging round a stinking rock where a man with dirty hands shed blood for no reason. (*BLGF* 915)

West's denunciation of individualism probably accounts for her extreme condemnation of Luther, "who was not even *like* the rock, who *was* the rock, with the sullied grass, the cocks' heads, the grease, the stinking blood. He was the ugliest of the great, a hog magnified and with speech ... [he] strove to muddy life into a sty" (*BLGF* 829, emphasis added).

West accuses herself and her fellow liberals: "We forgot ... the chief moral obligation of humanity, which is to protect works of love" (*BLGF* 915). She urges her fellow liberals to resist fascist violence and not to succumb to the temptation to "exchange the role of priest for the role of lamb" in the Second World War (*BLGF* 915).[29] Individualism's complicity in the "power of the rock" informs her subversion of the traditional elevation of the individual in all forms of travel literature.

According to West's analysis, the Second World War is the result of the convergence of the violence of the dispossessed with the violence of the rock.[30] Nonetheless, the importance of these two theories of violence extends beyond the immediate circumstances of the war. Luccheni, the black lamb, and the grey falcon can be resisted. Art can resist the infection of violence. Her description of art's redemptive power echoes her poetics in "The Strange Necessity": "But there is hope that man may change, for two factors work on him that might disinfect him. One is art ... art gives us hope that history may change its spots and man become honourable. What is art? ... It is the re-living of experience ... so that its true significance is revealed" (*BLGF* 1126–7). West's prodigious work is a homage to the power of art. Her profound and subtle descriptions of art in its many forms manifest art's manifold powers and gifts.

Artifacts demonstrate and interpret Yugoslavia's cultural history as part of West's guidebook. Art is also important to the drama of the travel chronicle. A radio broadcast of Mozart, for example, interrupts a quarrel among the travelers and brings peace:

> We all drew on the comfort which is given out by the major works of Mozart, which is as real and material as the warmth given by a glass of brandy ... it was not merely the indication of a heavenly mode ... an argument too subtle and profound to be put into words ... had been resolved in some true conclusion. (*BLGF* 507–8)

In spite of West's tributes to "high art"—including, frescoes, paintings, ecclesiastical, and civic buildings—Slav peasant embroidery perhaps best epitomizes art for West in *Black Lamb and Grey Falcon.* She makes frequent reference to these "solemn and magnificent embroideries of the Slav peasant woman" throughout the book (*BLGF* 1099). Peasant embroideries in West's prologue's introduction to Yugoslavia share the profound and inexpressible wonder of Mozart's music. West also dwells on the intricate beauty of the embroidery on Lazar's burial garments.

Several features account for the embroideries' quintessence. They call attention to the labor of the individual women who created them and thus are works of "process" that honor the subjectivity of the artist. The embroideries also witness and perpetuate a native, cultural heritage.

> If Europeans have not the virtues of the Macedonian peasant, our life is lost. ... All that we are and do means nothing, all that our ancestors were and did means nothing, unless we are naturally the equals of the peasant women on the Skopska Tserna Gora and in Bitolj, whose fingers never forget the pattern that an ancient culture had created as symbols for what it had discovered regarding life and death. (*BLGF* 805–6)

In addition, the embroideries' decorative, nonrepresentational quality emphasizes "form" which is the essence of art for West (who deplores the "flowers and hearts on the Austrian belts" [*BLGF* 1099]). She asserts, "Art is not a plaything, but a necessity, and its essence, form, is not a decorative adjustment, but a cup into which life can be poured and lifted to the lips and be tasted" (*BLGF* 55). Embroidery defies—and in fact flaunts—utilitarian values. This is especially true of peasant embroidery.

> The splendour of these dresses was more impressive because it was not summer. The brocade of a rajah's costume or the silks of an Ascot crowd are within the

> confines of prudence, because the rajah is going to have a golden umbrella held over him and the Ascot crowd is not far from shelter, but these costumes were made for the winter in a land of unmetalled roads, where snow lay till it melted and mud might be knee-deep, and showed a gorgeous lavishness, for hours and days, and even years had been spent in the stuffs and skins and embroideries which were thus put at the mercy of the bad weather. (*BLGF* 64)

Such an extravagance refutes the principle of the rock which finds utility in suffering. West praises the Slav peasants repeatedly for both material and spiritual "extravagant" behavior. She says of these people, "These people hold that the way to make life better is to add good things to it, whereas in the West we hold that the way to make life better is to take bad things away from it" (*BLGF* 80). West connects the peasant generosity with their art:

> Peasants, more than any other class in the modern community, persistently produce and appreciate art which is simply the presentation of pleasing forms. ... They had never forgotten the *idea of magnificence*, which is a valuable moral idea, for it implies that the duty of man is to make a superfluity beyond that which satisfies his animal needs and turn it to splendid uses ... gold and silver, not as wealth, not as mintable material, but as glory to be used for shining ornament. (*BLGF* 784, emphasis added)

West describes a dinner that shares this superfluity.

> We ate and drank enormously. Valetta said in my ear, "You really must eat, you know. They will think you dislike their food if you do not. It is our Slav custom to give our guests too much to eat, as a kind of boastfulness, and of course out of good-will, and the guests show how strong they are by eating it. We are really a very primitive people, I am afraid." (*BLGF* 80)

The extravagance of Slav peasant embroidery and hospitality is essentially unselfish. West reveals the ultimate power of art in her discussion of the second factor that fosters human change: goodness. Her promotion of human goodness would seem naive if she did not demonstrate its resilience amidst her interminable portraits of blood baths and human cruelty. West locates "goodness" in many places, but it is most emphatically to be found in the Slav peasants. She demonstrates the power of an unsentimental, stoic kindness in the Slav peasants she encounters throughout her trip. These people possess vitality and strength in spite of physical suffering and material degradation because they are sustained by a connection with nature and with their rich cultural traditions. Their devotion to their culture and their religion—a communal good outside themselves with no apparent "usefulness"—also bolsters them. This selfless investment in community contrasts with the egotistic, Western individualism that makes Westerners susceptible to the power of the rock. She describes the peasants' victory in the face of a Macedonian woman at Mass, a ceremony which she calls "a supreme masterpiece of communal art" (*BLGF* 638). The Easter Mass is the goal of West's and her companions' epic quest. It is fitting that this emblematic figure appears in this scene at this moment. West admires the woman whose "face was unresentful, exulted, sensitive to her sorrows yet preoccupied by that which she perceived to be more important, *magnificence* and its adoration" (*BLGF* 639, emphasis added). The "magnificence and its adoration" that preoccupy this woman have—of course—no utilitarian value. West contrasts the Slav's generosity with Western economy: "These people, who had neither wealth nor security, nor ever had had them, stood before the Creator, and thought not what they might ask for but what they might give" (*BLGF* 65).

This selfless attention to something beyond the self also undermines any divisive or exclusive threat of nationalism. Adhering to one's cultural roots does not mean a denial of or an oppression of the other. According to legend, the Slavs lost the battle of Kosovo because they "were divided among themselves" (*BLGF* 902). This division could have been avoided. The alliances (examined in our discussion of the travel chronicle) of people who come together in fusions that infuriate possess this type of goodness.

Her contemporary British working class join the Yugoslav peasants in the ranks of epic heroes. West believes that many European urban poor have become alienated (like Luccheni), but that Londoners have escaped the curse of dislocation because of their connection with nature and with their national cultural and artistic tradition:

> In Italy and Germany and Austria this class [the lower class] fell into the extreme destitution and degradation represented by Mussolini and Hitler, and in France its inertia did much to promote the state of political banditry which led to the tragedy of 1940. In England it was controlled by a national tradition, which transcends the traditions of town and country, and by this was kept from the shame which comes of ignorance and [sic ?] good and evil. (*BLGF* 1129)

She describes the heroic British response to aerial bombing to demonstrate the power of goodness and to vest goodness in the working class.

> Bombs dropped; many were maimed and killed, and made homeless, and all knew the humiliating pain of fear. ... Now, though their knees knocked together,

> though their eyes were glassy with horror, they joked from sunset, when the sirens unfurled their long flag of sound, till dawn, when the light showed them the annihilation of dear and familiar things. ... They worked, they fought like soldiers. ... In this sobriety, men and women went out and dug among the ruins for the injured while bombs were still falling, and they turned on fire, which it is our nature to flee, and fought it at close range. (*BLGF* 1130)

The response of the British and other Europeans (including the Yugoslavians) to the crises of 1940 "gave [West] a promise that life can transcend itself, that we are not bound to repeat a limited pattern" (*BLGF* 1131). "The power of the rock"—the idea that pain induces virtue—is really a principle of fixity and limits. West finds that both goodness (as she discovers it in the Londoners of the blitz) and art exceed fixity and limits.

The Londoners' response also transforms the Battle of Kosovo and the meaning of Tsar Lazar's act for West. This transformation finally affirms the power and potential of art. The words of the Kosovo poem apply to West's contemporary situation. The poem applies because of what West refers to in *Black Lamb and Grey Falcon* and other works as the "prodigiousness" of art. This is an excessiveness that gives art an indeterminacy that refuses to be fixed and that allows art to exceed its bounds—just as *Black Lamb and Grey Falcon* esthetically and formally exceeds all bounds. Art shares the peasant's lavishness. She explains:

> It applies; and the secret of its application lies in the complex nature of all profound works of art. An artist is goaded into creation ... to find out where the truth lies among divergent opinions on a vital issue. His work, therefore, is often a palimpsest on which are superimposed several incompatible views about his subject; and it may be that which is expressed with the greatest intensity, which his deeper nature finds the truest, is not that which has determined the narrative form he has given to it. The poem of the Tsar Lazar and the grey falcon tells a story which celebrates the death-wish; but its hidden meaning pulses with life. (*BLGF* 1145)

This description of art's attempt to discover truth "among divergent opinions on a vital issue" validates West's works—like *Black Lamb and Grey Falcon*—as hybrid genres which come together to create a "contact zone" where these divergent opinions can interact to transformational ends. In *Black Lamb and Grey Falcon* West brings together subversive interpretations of the travel chronicle, the travel guidebook, and the epic in order to transform her contemporary world and to change its values. West reinterprets the poem to discover that "it was their resistance [of the Serbians under Lazar], not their defeat, which appeared to them as the sacred element in their ordeal." She concludes using language that transforms her language describing violence at the Sheep's rock:

> Goodness is adorable and it is immortal. When it is trodden down into the earth it springs up again, and human beings scrabble in the dust to find the first green seedling of its return. The stock cannot survive save by the mutual kindness of men and women, of old and young, of state and individual. (*BLGF* 1146)

Like the art that she promotes, *Black Lamb and Grey Falcon* esthetically and formally exceeds all bounds. This prodigiousness is the book's achievement and its promise.

Notes

Chapter 1

1 "Both these phases can be found in a single work of art, if it is of the highest order. Both of them can be found in an artist's output as a whole. ... Sometimes an artist performs the first part of the process, and another the second" (*EE* 305).

2 See Stetz: "She had cut her teeth (intellectually speaking) on the suffrage movement at the turn of the century and would remain a crusader for the rights of women, even after abandoning organized political action as the means to achieve these rights" (Stetz 1994: 53).

3 *Sunflower* combines a political satire, a *roman à clef*, and a symbolist poem.

Chapter 2

1 The words "culture" and "civilization" need to be enclosed in quotation marks precisely because of the skeptical consciousness the war engendered.

2 And he convinces us of the war's sustaining influence: "Indeed a striking phenomenon of the last twenty-five years is the obsession with the images and myths of the Great War among novelists and poets too young to have experienced it directly. They have worked it up by purely literary means, means which necessarily transform the war into a 'subject' and simplify its motifs into myth and figures expressive of the modern existential predicament" (Fussell 1975: 321).

3 "Of course women lived through the First World War, and suffered; and many served on the Western Front. Yet although the First World War is seen and presented as the main determinant of modern British culture, the crucial area of that War, the experience of trench warfare and of battle in particular, was a zone forbidden to women. ... That means, if Fussell can substantiate his thesis, that women were prohibited from direct participation in their national culture. ... For an understanding of 'modern understanding' we remain dependent on men" (Tylee 1990: 8).

4 See Cohen: "It is perhaps in the home front works written during the war that traditional paradigms of war narrative can more definitively be rewritten—indeed, must be rewritten, since the lack of a resolution denies the author any standard valediction" (Cohen 2002: 2).
5 This delay is typical of literature of many wars. One thinks of the relative neglect of the Vietnam War by literature or film until the flood of films and novels that were unleashed in the mid- to late-1980s.
6 Misha Kavka discusses Chris's choice in one of the most insightful articles on *The Return of the Soldier,* "Men in (Shell-)Shock: Masculinity, Trauma, and Psychoanalysis in Rebecca West's *Return of the Soldier*" (Kavka 1998). Kavka argues that in choosing Margaret, Chris is choosing the "passionate woman" but she does not prove her contention with evidence from the text. While Chris and Margaret's spiritual love is passionate, West's emphasis is clearly on the spirituality of the relationship more than the passion.
7 "For the modern imagination that last summer has assumed the status of a permanent symbol for anything innocently but irrecoverably lost" (Fussell 1975: 24).
8 See Virginia Woolf: "On or about December, 1910, human character changed," in "Mr Bennett and Mrs Brown" (Woolf 1984: 194).
9 Peter Wolfe describes West's use of "the idea of sexual ambivalence to combine the best of male and female strains." West praises Charlotte Bronte's "power to speak of 'what is man in woman'" (Wolfe 1971: 10).
10 The ambiguous ending is typical of a Jamesian narrative, but there is also a deliberate political motive in this ambiguous ending. Works that were stridently pacifist or opposed to the war were censored or banned under the aegis of the Defence of the Realm Act. See Grayzel's discussion of Rose Allatini's *Despised and Rejected* which was banned under DORA (Grayzel 1999: 36 ff).
11 West's use of specific flora is deliberate in this novel. For the resonance of her association of the cedar with Baldry Court, see Robert Lerner's *The Powers of Prophecy: The Cedar of Lebanon Vision from the Mongol Onslaught to the Dawn of the Enlightenment*: "Cedars of Lebanon grow thick in the Bible ... [with] both good and bad connotations. They could be fine, godly trees because of their great height, spreading foliage, perennial greenness, and durable wood, but the same qualities made them excellent symbols of pride before a fall. ... In the Psalms, for example, (Ps. 37:34-35), the Lord 'cuts off the wicked' who spread himself like a cedar, and in Ezechiel, Chapter 31, He strikes down the vainglorious Assyrian, who is described as 'a cedar of Lebanon.' [In] the Book of Isaiah ... the prophet warned that ... 'the day of the Lord of hosts shall be upon everyone that is proud and lofty, and upon everyone that is lifted up ... and upon all the Cedars of Lebanon that are high and lifted up'" (Lerner 1983: 17–18).
12 Squires (1974) refers to John F. Lynen as discriminating this feature of pastoral in *The Pastoral Art of Robert Frost* (1960).

13 Many of these plants are traditional to the pastoral and have special and multiple symbolic import. For example, Jenny remarks that the hawthorne stood out in both Margaret's and Chris's memories. The hawthorne appears frequently in the pastoral and is associated with the moon, Athena (see Chris and Margaret's love scene), magic, and innocence. It was the wedding flower of the Greek marriage ceremony. Chris and Margaret's mutual, yet unspoken, devotion to it seems to seal their love.
14 Note that West draws attention to the fact that Monkey Island does not have an artificial border.
15 Note that a traditional pastoral motif is the ceremony of gift-bringing.
16 Fussell says of literature of the Great War: "The Golden Age posited by Classical and Renaissance pastoral now finds it counterpart in ideas of 'home' and 'summer of 1914.'" However the parallel is not apt. Classical and Renaissance artists knew that the Golden Age never existed.
17 For example, "Past these marched the poplar and lifted their strong yet tremulous silver spires on each side of the gravel slope ... there stood a white hawthorne" (*RS* 72).
18 This contrast between rustic simplicity and generosity with urban artificiality and corruption is traditional in the pastoral. Frank Kermode says of Ben Jonson: "When Jonson turned from Satire to Pastoral, at the end of his career, he lamented the death of an order as old, he thought, as the countryside; a way of life in which generosity, in the fullest sense of that word, accompanied purity of life and pleasure which the Juvenalian town had exchanged for disease, obscurantism, affectation, and bigotry" (Kermode 1952: 38).

Chapter 3

1 Raub's statistical study of popular fiction focuses on the 1920s, but her generalizations apply to the surrounding decades.
2 Shirley Peterson describes West as a "New Woman": "Society both celebrated and derided Rebecca West as the era's consummate 'New Woman.' ... She was brash, intellectually sharp, quick-witted, and an emblem of the modern sexual revolution" (Peterson 1997: 106).
3 *The Sentinel, Adela, The Judge, Sunflower*, and *Harriet Hume*.
4 This label is implicit in Ann Norton's discussion of the tension between Ellen's ambitions and social codes of beauty in "Beauty and Tragedy in *The Judge*" (Norton 1991).
5 Pykett is alluding to Grant Allen's New Woman novel, *The Woman Who Did* (1895).
6 In her Introduction to the 1980 edition of *The Judge,* Jane Marcus recognizes the novel's gothic potential in calling Marion "a great Bronte-esque figure" (Marcus 1980: 6).

7 See the comments on the gothic in *Novel Beginnings* by Patricia Meyer Spacks: "The uneasiness presumably experienced by characters and readers alike perhaps reflects that of a nation recently defeated by its own colonies, torn by political dissension, and frightened by revolutionary developments across the channel" (Spacks 2006: 192).

8 Kitty, for example, embodies the values of a masculinist and capitalist system in *The Return of the Soldier.*

9 This sexual harassment in the workplace figures importantly in Bonnie Kime Scott's interpretation of *The Judge* (1991).

10 Many writers have been influenced by Radcliffe's definitions. Stephen King, for example, states, "I recognize terror as the finest emotion and so I will try to terrorize the reader. But if I find that I cannot terrify, I will try to horrify, and if I find that I cannot horrify, I'll go for the gross-out. I'm not proud" (King 1981: 87). He also calls this third term, "revulsion."

11 See Rogers: "Radcliffe relates picturesque scenes to her characters' emotional awareness: only sensitive, virtuous characters like her heroines experience heightened, transcendent reactions to nature" (Rogers 2007: 41).

12 Likewise, *The Return of the Soldier* can only be fully understood if one analyzes it as a pastoral. Chris rejects the artifice of the ornamental gardens at Baldry Court and thrives in the wild nature that surrounds Baldry Court. Monkey Island represents a pastoral ideal of nature combined with art.

13 The words "overarching figure" are Scott's (1991: 172).

Chapter 4

1 *Harriet Hume* must have come as a surprise to readers of *The Judge.* Late-twentieth-century readers and twenty-first-century readers have the advantage of reading *Sunflower,* a posthumously published unfinished novel that also treats a New Woman artist, politics, and imaginative visions.

2 Of Ferdinand's political enemies: "By the time he had passed through his twenties he had made an army of personal enemies, which he constantly increased by his intemperate and uninstructed political habits" (*BLGF* 336). Of his rogue allies: "The manners of Franz Ferdinand did worse for him than make him enemies. They made him gangster friends that may become enemies at any moment with the deadly weapon of a friend's close knowledge" (*BLGF* 341).

3 In writing about West's criticism, Stetz also notes West's "organicism" which blends art and nature: "Underlying all of her writing on the arts was a philosophy of organicism—of connection between art and nature—that was also deliberately antihierarchical and democratic" (Stetz 1994: 53).

4 "It acquires, therefore, this fantasy, a domination over the individual which could not be surpassed and which is not normally ever broken" (*SN* 62).
5 Charles Perrault wrote his fairy tales for the court of Louis XIV.
6 Margaret D. Stetz elaborates on Wilde's influence upon West in her essay "Rebecca West, Aestheticism, and the Legacy of Oscar Wilde" (Stetz 2006).
7 Proleptically, West uses the words "marvel" and "marvelous" frequently to describe Harriet and also to describe Harriet and Arnold's relationship. For example, in the first chapter Harriet declares, "Indeed we are marvellous, and should be able to command marvellous things" (*HH* 31). See also *HH* 32 and 35.
8 Todorov's continuum rejects what he calls either "poetic" or "allegorical" readings of the marvelous. The poetical or allegorical lie outside the bounds of his concerns because the reader "realizes that he is not to take them [supernatural phenomenon] literally" (Todorov 1975: 32). Harriet's fairy tales especially lend themselves to allegorical readings as we can see in essays by Jane Marcus and Debra Rae Cohen. The use of fantasy in *Harriet Hume* could prompt us to ask whether or not *all* works of literature are "poetical" or "allegorical." We might also interrogate the mystical or spiritual status of what we consider the "real" world.
9 This is the scene in which "he felt his intention to rise in the world like lead in his bosom" (*HH* 60).
10 There are quite a few occasions when Arnold finds himself in darkness or death-like spaces or when he appears death-like. As he crosses London in Chapter 5, he wonders if he is blind, but concludes "No tis a general wreckage. ... Look, how the dark lies like a great cat in the yard and how darkness sits on the clouds. ... Something is swallowing up the world" (*HH* 231). In Chapter 2 as Arnold wanders through a park, he wonders if "he and Harriet had already made their embarkations [to the underworld?], and that other selves of theirs than could be seen were even now drifting down a dark stream, their faces pale in a colder and a later hour than this that chilled them now" (*HH* 81).
11 "There was no entrance to Harriet's abode. So hastily had the old house been converted to feed the house-hunger that raged after the Great War ... that some problems of architecture had inevitably gone unsolved" (*HH* 13).

Chapter 5

1 Pavlov received a 1904 Nobel Prize for his work. *Conditioned Reflexes* had been translated into English in 1927.
2 Laura Heffernan argues that "The Strange Necessity" should be considered a "work of modernist criticism" in order for us to understand a line of modernist

criticism that considered artwork in its network of social relations and not only according to internal formal characteristics (Heffernan 2008: 311).

3 Nattie Golubov's "Rebecca West's 'Strange Necessity': Literature, Love, and the Good" is a humane, capacious interpretation of "The Strange Necessity." Nonetheless, my interpretation of "fantasy" as an individual's attempt to create a pattern from his analysis and synthesis of experience treats the word "fantasy" more generously than Golubov who emphasizes fantasies as "illusions" and states, "'fantasy' is the word used by West to name the distorting and blinding, because self-centered attitude of man" (Golubov 2006: 213).

4 "There are a million million manifestations of bad art ... they do not represent processes of analysis and synthesis of experience terminating in the creation of excitatory complexes, but are attempts to make excitatory complexes out of the crude factual elements of experiences" (*SN* 181).

5 "[Yeats] produces a vision of the universe which is far madder in effect than that presented by William Blake, who was not nearly so sane as he is ... but who was embedded in England; who held in his hand an unbroken mystical tradition" (*SN* 169–70).

6 This sense of art as a part of a culture or what Heffernan and Bourdieu would call a "social field" supports Heffernan's arguments for the theoretical importance of "The Strange Necessity" in modernist estimations of art (Heffernan 2008).

7 The desire for a lost cultural unity would in some modernist cases result in a conservative nostalgia for conformity. West's emphasis on unity in "The Strange Necessity," like her character Harriet Hume's, seeks to bring together diverse elements, not suppress different elements that threaten a homogeneous unity.

8 T. S. Eliot: "In the seventeenth century a dissociation of sensibility set in from which we have never recovered" (Eliot 1975: 64). Eliot's description of ordinary, but disparate events which a unified consciousness can assimilate is reminiscent of West's list of ordinary events which help form a tradition: "The ordinary man's [experience] is chaotic, irregular, fragmentary. The latter falls in love, or reads Spinoza, and these two experiences have nothing to do with each other, or with the noise of the typewriter or the smell of cooking; in the mind of the poet these experiences are always forming new wholes" (Eliot 1975: 64).

9 "In England art and science have in the main been carried on by a middle class which is unafraid to examine the nature of the universe and subject it to the change that comes of knowledge because it was change in the nature of the universe which lifted their stock out of the working classes. The aristocracy was on the whole averse from the responsibility of conducting any such researches, because they were where they wanted to be, and change might put them somewhere else" (*SN* 168).

10 "He writes down these strings of words as if they corresponded to the stream of one's consciousness, as if, should one resolve to describe one's impressions as they come, one would produce isolated words and phrases which would not cohere into sentences. Yet there is nothing more certain than that sentences were used by man before words. ... They, and not words, are the foundation of all language" (*SN* 32).

11 "And it is true that for all their talk of art they produced nothing but one good farce and a cartload of such weak, sweet verse as schoolgirls copy into exercise-books. ... And yet, for all its fruitlessness, that prattle about art gave them a valid claim on our respect" (*HJ* 80–1).

12 G. B. Shaw (1856–1950), H. G. Wells (1866–1947), Arnold Bennett (1867–1931), John Galsworthy (1867–1933). West frequently invents hereditary fictions. Concerned by the threatening political situations of the 1930s, the Hogarth Press engaged West and other famous figures to write a letter to a person of one's choice. The majority of the letters in this series were addressed to political and literary figures, including Adolf Hitler, Madame Blanchard, an Archbishop, Virginia Woolf, and W. B. Yeats. West interpreted the assignment by creating an imaginary family whose members have a hereditary gift for mystical visions. West's letter—*A Letter to a Grandfather* (1933)—is from a granddaughter to her grandfather about their gift.

13 West uses the metaphor of a "jewel" to describe the beauty, brilliance, and infrangibility of art as early as her biography *Henry James* (1916).

14 "Society" can be defined as "companionship or association with one's fellows: friendly or intimate association; cooperation."

15 Clarissa Dalloway's thoughts echo Septimus Smith's thoughts in *Mrs Dalloway*: "looking at the flowers, at the trees with the smoke winding off them and the rooks rising, falling. ... Heaven only knows why one loves it so, how one sees it so, making it up, building it round one, tumbling it creating it every moment afresh ... what she loves; life; London; this moment in June" (Woolf 1925a: 3). Septimus has a similar moment of being: "The elm trees rising and falling, rising and falling with all their leaves alight" (Woolf 1925a: 32).

16 "That was his [Mr Carmichael's] way of looking, different from hers [Mrs Ramsay]. But looking together united them" (Woolf 1927: 97).

17 For a discussion of the various uncles' reaction to *The Strange Necessity*, see Collier 2006.

18 This denunciation of "lowbrow" genres is connected to the dismissal of hybrid genres.

19 "Irked by West's account of shopping for a dress and hats in Paris while reflecting on Joyce's work, Beckett goes on to say, 'When Miss Rebecca West clears her decks for a sorrowful deprecation of the Narcissistic element in Mr Joyce by

the purchase of 3 hats, one feels that she might very well wear her bib at all her intellectual banquets, or alternatively, assert a more noteworthy control over her salivary glands'" (Briggs 1996: 84). "And like Beckett, Joyce, too, was distressed by West's hats ... [which resulted in] 'forty bonnets,'" in the *Wake* (Briggs 1996: 85).

Chapter 6

1 The Sino-Japanese War began in 1937, but the Japanese invasion of Manchuria was in 1931.
2 Bloomsday in James Joyce's *Ulysses* is in June and Mrs Dalloway's party in the eponymous novel by Virginia Woolf takes place in June. Both these works contain their own sorts of modernist visions. West may be making a parallel between C. B.'s journey across Paris and these other modernist journeys through Dublin and London. *Mrs Dalloway*, like *A Letter to a Grandfather*, also combines tragedy (Septimus Smith's death) and celebratory vision ("moments of being" and Clarissa's party).
3 "*Beau*" = "fair." "*Champ*" = "field."
4 See Rollyson: "West lavished so much attention on the relationship between Augustine and his loving mother, Monnica, that reviewers and later commentators have both praised and blamed her for her pioneering Freudian approach" (Rollyson 1998: 99). West's Wikipedia entry draws attention to her psychoanalytical approach in its claim that her biography of Saint Augustine is the "first psycho-biography of the Christian Church Father."
5 For West the imagination nurtures empathy as she explains at length in "The Strange Necessity."
6 Several critics, including Wolfe and Norton, remark the obvious allusion to Isabelle Archer. No one comments that West's mother's name is Isabella. It is likely that many of Isabelle's good traits—her nurturing nature and her dignity in the face of tragedy—are a tribute to West's mother. West's middle name is also "Isabel."
7 Caesar's lines to Brutus in Shakespeare's *Julius Caesar* do *not* apply to *A Thinking Reed*. "The fault, dear Brutus, is not in our stars,/But in ourselves, that we are underlings" (*Julius Caesar* I, ii, 140–1).
8 "If we examine ourselves carefully we cannot claim to have free will. We exercise what looks like a free faculty of choice, but the way we exercise that faculty of choice depends on our innate qualities and *our environment*, and these always bind us in some way or another to the neuroses which compel us to choose death rather than life. ... Augustine's view that we are all full of original sin, that we do not enjoy the free use of our wills, and must link ourselves to the eternal if we are to be saved, is at least a symbolic interpretation of something that the most secular-minded must allow to be true" (*SA* 121–1, emphasis added).

9 See Bermel, "Farce, then, can animate other kinds of drama, and they can animate farce. ... Where can the territory of farce end and the other territories begin? ... Farce might be said to exist on the ludicrous fringes of tragedy" (Bermel 1990: 58).

10 See Bermel, "In farce we laugh at the characters, not with them" (Bermel 1990: 54).

11 See Bermel, "Sennett repeatedly spoke ... about the 'fall of dignity' in his pictures. Most often he accomplished it by obliterating visible evidence of class differences. Tarred, floured, or drenched people look alike. Dignity might fall in literal fashion ... especially into a liquid" (Bermel 1990: 161).

12 Again see Bermel discussing Sennett's belief that the turbulence created by speed is essential to farce: "As the performers hustle toward their partners or put distances between themselves and their opponents—or try to close those distances—the frenzy invokes a sense of danger, for speed can only end in deceleration ... or in collisions" (Bermel 1990: 163).

13 There is the possibility that Isabelle's rage for reason and control has been the result of her parents' deaths when she was a child. Her embrace of Marc could also be an acceptance of her parents' death and a necessary grieving that she never allowed herself.

14 See my discussion of Bonnie Kime Scott's argument that Joyce and West countered the modernist wasteland with an affirmation of natural cycles in her article "Refiguring the Binary, Breaking the Cycle: Rebecca West as Feminist Modernist" in Chapter 4.

15 "Indissoluble Matrimony" was published in Wyndham Lewis's Vorticist journal *BLAST* (1914) and thus helped established West's place in early modernism.

Chapter 7

1 See Fussell: "To canvas merely the titles of works between the wars is to sense the permeation of the 'travel spirit'" (Fussell 1980: 53). And Hynes: "[The journey] is the most insistent of 'thirties metaphors. ... one might say that the travel books simply act out in the real world, the basic trope of the generation" (Hynes 1976: 229). And Vesna Goldsworthy: "West's *magnum opus* therefore plays a major part in the movement to establish a new role for travel writing" (Goldsworthy 1997: 2).

2 Mary Louise Pratt defines these forms according to their narrative points of view. The guidebook, to her, has an impersonal "manners and customs figure" and the travel chronicle has a more personally invested "sentimental figure" (Pratt 1992: 201).

3 Indeed, West went to Yugoslavia in the first place with a sort of "civilizing mission": the British Council sent her to Yugoslavia to give a series of cultural lectures. There is no trace of her "civilizing mission" in her final book.

4 West's campaign against imperialism in *Black Lamb and Grey Falcon* and other works is widely acknowledged. Surprisingly fewer critics have recognized her resistance to postcolonial narratives and conventions. Zofia P. Lesinska does "interpret West's representation of interwar Yugoslavia as the space of postcolonial difference within Europe" (Lesinska 2002: 137).

5 Paul Fussell's tourist also has motives of self-aggrandizement in *Abroad: British Literary Travelling Between the Wars* (Fussell 1980: 42).

6 See Schweizer: "Before discussing West's presentation of Serb history, it is necessary to point out the questionable historical premises of her argument. ... Historians have challenged ... the wholesale condemnation of Turkish rule" (Schweizer 2001: 137). And Lesinska: "West's critical attitude towards imperialism guards her work against condescending Orientalism. ... Still ... [she risks a] twofold orientalizing trap. On the one hand, she frequently demonizes Turkey and the advances of Islam in Europe during the Middle Ages. ... On the other hand she often romanticizes the cultural heritage of the South Slavs" (Lesinska 2002: 140). See also Montefiore (1996: 192).

7 West's insistence on having "faith in what is entirely hidden and unknown, to cast away all the acquisitions and certainties" gives this chapter its title. This ambition actually informs all of West's works studied in this book.

8 Harper quotes Susan Morgan: "Women's accounts placed value on personal lived experience and this validated the writers' voices and accomplishments. ... Women ... are more likely to show identification with other people" (Harper 2001: 17).

9 See Part 5 of this chapter section for West's gendered definitions of "lunatic" and "idiotic" visions.

10 This celebration of simplicity is the opposite of the validation of the bourgeois that prevails in much travel writing. See Pratt in *Imperial Eyes*: "The discourses that legitimate bourgeois authority and delegitimate peasant and subsistence lifeways ... can be expected to do this ideological work within Europe as well as in Africa or Argentina" (Pratt 1992: 10). I disagree here with Schweizer's interpretation of *Black Lamb and Grey Falcon* as an epic because of its elevated style and substance (Schweizer 2002: 84).

11 In this I differ from Schweizer who believes that West has an orientalist bias: "West's discourse displays any number of 'male' traits, specifically the 'mastery' of foreign societies by appeal to discourses of history, politics, and anthropology as well as an orientalist bias that could pass as a symptom of masculine cultural arrogance" (Schweizer 2001: 81).

12 Constantine is based on her guide Stanislav Vinaver. Although there are many factual similarities between Constantine and Stanislav, Gerda is for the most part West's fictional construction.

13 In "Rebecca West and the Meaning of Exile," Schweizer reminds us that West's "deep anxiety about and abhorrence of exile contrasts with the more positive modernist (and postmodernist) approaches to the issue" (Schweizer 2010: 390).

14 My interpretation of West's nationalism is the opposite of Loretta Stec's in "Nostalgic Nationalism." Stec believes that West's nationalism "participates in a nostalgic logic of gender domination" (Stec 1997: 139). As my discussion of West's dismantling of binaries will show, I believe that Stec reads gender dualism in West that West's text disproves.

15 The subversive potential of a liminal space is implicit in many different theoretical frames. Zofia P. Lesinska uses Homi Bhabha and Jacques Lacan to theorize West's postcolonial critique. The Bhabha/Lacan lens can be applied to Stowe's sense of the disruptive potential of the "tribal liminal" or borders: "Drawing on Lacan, Bhabha argues that a temporal break with symbolic synchronicity which produces a truth outside of the knowledge of the subject 'happens in the liminal moment of the ego deprived of subjectivity'" (Lesinska 2002: 138).

16 See Janet Montefiore in *Men and Women Writers of the 1930s*: "*Black Lamb and Grey Falcon* is an easy book to get lost in ... in practice it remains irretrievably hybrid, mixing political history, travel, autobiography, meditation, art history, and even fiction ... the phrase 'loose baggy monster' does suggest itself" (Montefiore 1996: 179, 184).

17 West scholars are indebted to Ann V. Norton who devotes a whole work to contradictions in West's philosophy and artistic practice, *Paradoxical Feminism*. Norton sometimes sees tension and paradox as a failing and I do not.

18 See Steve Clark in *Travel Writing and Empire*: "Its perennially marginal position both grants a licence to idiosyncratic formal innovation, and allows the production of a self ... by means of perpetual detours into communal utterance, public codes" (Clark 1999: 1).

19 According to Anderson, "Women were not initially qualified for travel writing either" (Anderson 2006: 13).

20 See, for example, *Solitary Travelers* by Harper (2001).

21 See Stec: "She presents the voice of her 'husband' to give opinions and provide facts about significant issues. ... Through this rhetorical strategy West seems to be suppressing her authority in favor of that of a virile male. Some critics, most notably Mary Ellmann (114-15), have read this as literary submission" (Stec 1997: 152).

22 Anderson sees women travelers who oppose imperialism in a "double bind": in "exempting women from responsibility in the imperial effort [because they, too, are 'marginal'], we coincidentally negate women's agency" (Anderson 2006: 18). In sharing a "subject" position with men, West has solved Anderson's "double-bind" and kept her own agency while not objectifying Yugoslavia. Susan Bassnett

sees women's "exceptionality" as a way of marginalizing them: "The theory of the exceptional woman who is somehow different from other women and therefore empowered to perform feats no normal woman would be capable of carrying out has been one of the classic ways of marginalizing women's achievements" (Bassnett 2002: 228). West's role as wife and traveling companion "normalizes" her and protects her from the marginalization of the exceptional.

23 My argument that *Black Lamb and Grey Falcon* has "plural" protagonists is original and contradicts a long-standing scholarly tradition of treating Rebecca West herself as the individual heroine of her (often epic) quest. See Joanna Labon: "West makes herself the main character of the book" (Labon 1999: 213). See Schweizer: "In the case of Rebecca West, Karen Lawrence's argument that 'women writers of travel have tended to mistrust the rhetoric of mastery, conquest, and quest that has funded a good deal of male fictional and nonfictional travel' does not hold" (Schweizer 2001: 81).

24 I believe that West's movement between private and public creates a shifting, liminal space that strengthens the subversive potential of *Black Lamb and Grey Falcon.* The "private" or "public" nature of West's work is a contested area. Lesinska, for example, believes West prioritizes the private (West 2002: 136). Goldsworthy distinguishes *Black Lamb and Grey Falcon* from other travel narratives because of its personal, private voice (Goldsworthy 1997: 2). Mary Ellmann believes that "the person capable of describing idiocy or lunacy cannot herself be confined by either of them" (Ellmann 1968: 108). Cohen insists that West's voice is public. In drawing attention to the complexity of West's use of private and public voices, Cohen comments that people misread *Black Lamb and Grey Falcon* as private: "West's strategic use of genre in *Black Lamb* has often prompted unwitting reproduction of the very gendered generic expectations she seeks to exploit and critique" (Cohen 2009: 153).

25 Because her analyses of these two types of violence mark a turn in West's philosophy, they create new tensions in her work. We witness the struggles of a liberal intellectual in the 1930s who set out to understand modern civilization through a study of the First World War and who is suddenly confronted with the reality of the Second World War.

26 Schweizer summarizes what he calls West's "two epiphanies on the Sheep's Field and on the Field of Blackbirds" in one paragraph. Our interpretations agree. Nonetheless my further elaboration helps me give a context to my interpretation. See Schweizer: "The first epiphany was dominated by West's realization that sacrificing animals for the benefit of female conception was a triumph of the necrophile tendencies inherent in the masculine mind. The second epiphany involved the Christian dogma of atonement and its defeatist implications as celebrated in the poem about Tsar Lazar and the gray falcon" (Schweizer 2002: 96).

27 Schweizer believes that *Black Lamb and Grey Falcon* "features no journey to the underworld" (Schweizer 2002: 83).

28 "Nearly all writers dip their pens in inkwells tainted with this beastliness" (*BLGF* 830). Mozart, Jane Austen, and William Blake are exempt from its taint.

29 She has in mind, of course, Czechoslovakia.

30 Schweizer's chapter on *Black Lamb and Grey Falcon* is primarily devoted to West's critique of what he calls male heroism and her validation of her definition of female heroism. Schweizer and I agree on many points and my analysis reinforces his argument. My analysis does differ from Schweizer's in my assumptions about West's approach to heroism. I do not believe that she has a gendered binary approach to heroism. Gerda, for example, has all the qualities of Schweizer's "male hero." West offers a feminist alternative to the traditional epic hero—who has most often been a man. West recognizes that the epic's validation of individualism, violence, and power have often been located in men. In promoting a new definition of heroism that is based on feminist values, she is not suggesting that women are universally better than men. Rather she is suggesting that *all* people should be less egotistical, less individualistic, less power-hungry, less violent, less self-sacrificial, and less alienated. She promotes these cultural values for *all* people, not just for women.

References Cited

Aiken, Conrad (1929), Review of *The Strange Necessity*, by Rebecca West. *Bookman* 69: 211–12.

Anderson, Monica (2006), *Women and the Politics of Travel: 1870-1914*. Madison, NJ: Fairleigh Dickinson University Press.

Ardis, Ann L. (1990), *New Women, New Novels: Feminism and Early Modernism*. New Brunswick: Rutgers University Press.

Auden, W. H. (1961), "Il faut payer." *Mid-Century* 22 (February): 3–10.

—(1977), *The English Auden: Poems, Essays, and Dramatic Writings, 1927-1939*, edited by Edward Mendelson. New York: Random House.

Bassnett, Susan (2002), "Travel Writing and Gender." In *Cambridge Companion to Travel Writing*, edited by Peter Hulme and Tim Young. Cambridge: Cambridge University Press, 225–41.

Bermel, Albert (1990), *Farce: A History from Aristophanes to Woody Allen*. Carbondale: Southern Illinois University Press.

Bhabha, Homi (1987[1983]), "Of Mimicry and Man: The Ambivalence of Colonial Discourse." In *October: The First Decade, 1976-86*, edited by Douglas Crimp, Rosalind Krauss, and Annette Michelsen. Cambridge, MA: MIT Press, 317–25.

Bomarito, Jessica (2006), "Introduction." In *Gothic Literature: A Gale Critical Companion*, edited by Jessica Bomarito. Farmington Hills, MI: Gale Cengage. Microsoft reader ebook.

Botting, Fred (1996), *Gothic*. London: Routledge.

Bracco, Rosa Maria (1993), *Merchants of Hope: British Middlebrow Writers and the First World War, 1919-1939*. Oxford: Berg Publishers.

Briggs, Austin (1996), "Rebecca West vs. James Joyce." In *Joyce in the Hibernian Metropolis*, edited by Morris Beja and David Norris. Columbus: Ohio State University Press, 83–102.

Cavallero, David (2002), *The Gothic Vision: Three Centuries of Horror, Terror, and Fear*. London: Continuum.

Clark, Steve (1999), "Introduction." In *Travel Writing and Empire*, edited by Steve Clark. New York: St Martin's, 1–28.

Coe, Richard, Lorelei Lingard, and Tatiana Teslenko (2002), "Genre As Action, Strategy, and Difference: An Introduction." In *The Rhetoric and Ideology of Genre: Strategies for Stability and Change*, edited by Richard Coe. Cresskill: Hampton, 1–12.

Cohen, Debra Rae (2002), *Remapping the Home Front: Locating Citizenship in British Women's Great War Fiction*. Boston: Northeastern University Press.

—(2006), "Sheepish Modernism: Rebecca West, the Adam Brothers, and the Taxonomies of Criticism." In *Rebecca West Today: Contemporary Approaches*, edited by Bernard Schweizer. Newark: University of Delaware Press, 143–56.

—(2009), "Rebecca West's Palimpsestic Praxis: Crafting the Intermodern Voice of Witness." In *Intermodernism: Literary Culture in Mid-Twentieth-Century Britain*, edited by Kristin Bluemel. Edinburgh: Edinburgh University Press, 150–67.

Collier, Patrick (2006), *Modernism on Fleet Street*. Burlington: Ashgate.

Cunningham, A. R. (1973), "The New Woman Fiction of the 1890s." *Victorian Studies* 17 (December): 177–86.

Davis, Jessica Milner (1978), *Farce*. London: Metheun & Co.

Deakin, Motley (1980), *Rebecca West*. Boston: G. K. Hall and Co.

Derrida, Jacques (1978), "Violence and Metaphysics: An Essay on the Thought of Emmanuel Levinas." In *Writing and Difference*, translated by Alan Bass. Chicago: University of Chicago Press, 79–153.

Dimock, Wai Chee (2007), "Introduction: Genres as Fields of Knowledge." *PMLA* 122.5 (October): 377–88.

Eliot, T. S. (1975a), "The Metaphysical Poets." In *Selected Prose of T. S. Eliot*, edited with an introduction by Frank Kermode. New York: Harcourt, Brace, & World, 59–67.

—(1975b), "Tradition and the Individual Talent." In *Selected Prose of T. S. Eliot*, edited with an introduction by Frank Kermode. New York: Harcourt, Brace, & World, 37–44.

Ellis, Markman (2000), *The History of Gothic Fiction*. Edinburgh: Edinburgh University Press.

Ellmann, Mary (1968), *Thinking about Women*. New York: Harcourt, Brace & World.

Empson, William (1974), *Some Versions of Pastoral*. New York: New Directions.

Farley, David G. (2010), *Modernist Travel Writing: Intellectuals Abroad*. Columbia, MO: University of Missouri Press.

Freadman, Anne (2002), "Uptake." In *The Rhetoric and Ideology of Genre: Strategies for Stability and Change*, edited by Richard Coe, Lorelei Lingard, and Tatiana Teslenko. Cresskill, NJ: Hampton Press, 39–53.

Friedman, Susan Stanford (2003), "Modernism in a Transnational Landscape: Spatial Poetic, Postcolonialism, and Gender in Césaire's *Cahier/Notebook* and Cha's *Dictée*." *Paideuma: Studies in American and British Modernist Poetry* 32.1–3: 39–74.

Frigerio, Francesca (2002), "Under West(ern)Eyes: Rebecca West Reads Joyce." *Journal of Modern Literature* 26 (Fall): 66–72.

—(2006), "Music and Feminine Art of Detail in Rebecca West's *Harriet Hume*." In *Rebecca West Today: Contemporary Approaches*, edited by Bernard Schweizer. Newark: University of Delaware Press, 125–42.

Fussell, Paul (1975), *The Great War and Modern Memory*. Oxford: Oxford University Press.

—(1980), *Abroad: British Literary Traveling between the Wars*. New York: Oxford University Press.

Garnett, Edward (1928), "Channels and Sandbanks." Review of *The Strange Necessity*, by Rebecca West. *The Saturday Review of Literature* (November 10): 335.

Glendinning, Victoria (1987), *Rebecca West, a Life*. New York: Knopf.

Goldsworthy, Vesna (1997), "*Black Lamb and Grey Falcon:* Rebecca West's Journey through the Balkans." *Women: A Cultural Review* 8.1: 1–11.

Golubov, Nattie (2006), "Rebecca West's 'Strange Necessity': Literature, Love, and the Good." In *Rebecca West Today: Contemporary Approaches*, edited by Bernard Schweizer. Newark: University of Delaware Press, 206–22.

Grayzel, Susan R. (1999), *Women's Identities at War: Gender, Motherhood, and Politics in Britain and France during the First World War*. Chapel Hill: University of North Carolina Press.

Guilhamet, Leon (1987), *Satire and the Transformation of Genre*. Philadelphia: University of Pennsylvania Press.

Hallie, Philip (1982), *Paradox of Cruelty*. Middletown, CT: Wesleyan University Press. Quoted in Ray, Philip E. (1988), "*The Judge* Reexamined: Rebecca West's Underrated Gothic Romance." *English Literature in Transition, 1880-1920* 31.3: 297–307.

Harper, Lila Marz (2001), *Solitary Travelers: Nineteenth-Century Women's Travel Narratives and the Scientific Vocation*. Madison: Fairleigh Dickinson University Press.

Heffernan, Laura (2008), "Rebecca West's *The Strange Necessity* and the Aesthetic 'System of Relations.'" *Tulsa Studies in Women's Literature* 27.2 (Fall): 309–25.

Hogle, Jerrold E. (2002), "Introduction." In *Cambridge Companion to Gothic Fiction*, edited by Jerrold E. Hogle. New York: Cambridge University Press, 1–20.

Homer (1967), *The Odyssey*, translated by Richard Lattimore. New York: Harper & Rowe.

Howe, Irving (1990), "Farce and Fiction." *Threepenny Review* 43 (Autumn): 5–6.

Hughes, Leo (1956), *A Century of English Farce*. Princeton: Princeton University Press.

Hynes, Samuel (1976), *The Auden Generation: Literature and Politics in England in the 1930s*. Princeton: Princeton University Press.

—(1977), "Introduction." In *Rebecca West: A Celebration*, edited by Rebecca West. London: Macmillan, ix–xviii.

—(1991), *A War Imagined: The First World War and English Culture*. New York: Atheneum.

Irwin, W. R. (1976), *The Game of Impossible: A Rhetoric of Fantasy*. Urbana: University of Illinois Press.

Jackson, Rosemary (1981), *Fantasy: The Literature of Subversion*. Methuen: New Accents.

James, Henry (1920), *The Letters of Henry James*. Vol. 2, edited by Percy Lubbock. New York: Scribner.

Joyce, James (1963), *Stephen Hero*, introduction by Theodore Spencer. New York: New Directions.

—(1986), *Ulysses*. New York: Random House.

Kavka, Misha (1998), "Men in (Shell-) Shock Masculinity, Trauma, and Psychoanalysis in Rebecca West's *Return of the Soldier*." *Studies in Twentieth Century Literature* 22 (Winter): 151–71.

Kermode, Frank (1952), *English Pastoral Poetry*. London: George G. Harrup and Co.

King, Stephen (1981), *Danse Macabre*. Pickering, Ontario: Beaverbooks.

Kucich, John (1996), "Curious Dualities: *The Heavenly Twins* (1893) and Sarah Grand's Belated Modernist Aesthetics." In *The New Nineteenth Century: Feminist Readings of Underread Victorian Fiction*, edited by Barbara Leah Harman and Susan Meyer. New York: Garland Publishing, 195–204.

Labon, Joanna (1999), "Come in from the Cold War: Rebecca West and Storm Jameson in 1930s Europe." In *Women Writers of the 1930s: Gender, Politics, and History*, edited by Maroula Joannou. Edinburgh: Edinburgh University Press, 205–16.

Laing, Kathryn S. (1997), "Addressing Femininity in the Twenties: Virginia Woolf and Rebecca West on Money, Mirrors and Masquerade." In *Virginia Woolf and the Arts: Selected Papers from the Sixth Annual Conference on Virginia Woolf*, edited by Diane F. Gillespie and Leslie K. Hankins. New York: Pace University Press, 66–75.

—(2006), "Rebecca West's *The Sentinel, Adela,* and *The Judge*." In *Rebecca West Today: Contemporary Approaches,* edited by Bernard Schweizer. Newark: University of Delaware Press, 170–88.

Landre, Jeanne (1917), *L'école des marraines.* Michel. Quoted in Grayzel, Susan (1999), *Women's Identities at War: Gender, Motherhood, and Politics in Britain and France during the First World War*. Chapel Hill: University of North Carolina Press.

Lerner, Robert (1983), *The Powers of Prophecy: The Cedar of Lebanon Vision from the Mongol Onslaught to the Dawn of the Enlightenment.* Berkeley: University of California Press.

Lesinska, Zofia P. (2002), *Perspectives of Four Women Writers on the Second World War: Gertrude Stein, Janet Flanner, Kay Boyle, and Rebecca West.* New York: Peter Lang.

MacKay, Marina (2002), "Immortal Goodness: Ideas of Resurrection in Rebecca West's *Black Lamb and Grey Falcon*." *Renascence* 54.3 (Spring): 177–95.

Mao, Douglas (2008), *Fateful Beauty.* Princeton: Princeton University Press.

Marcus, Jane (1980), "Introduction." In *The Judge*, by Rebecca West. New York: Dial, 1–10.

—, ed. (1982), *The Young Rebecca: Writings of Rebecca West, 1911-17*. New York: Viking Press.

—(1984), "Wilderness of One's Own: Feminist Fantasy Novels of the Twenties: Rebecca West and Sylvia Townshend Warner." In *Women Writers and the City*, edited by Susan Merrill Squier. Knoxville: University of Tennessee, 134–60.

McFarland, Thomas (1972), *Shakespeare's Pastoral Comedies*. Chapel Hill: University of North Carolina Press.

Mellen, Joan (2000), *Magic Realism*. Vol. 5 of *Gale Study Guides to Great Literature: Literary Topics*. Detroit: Thomson Gale.

Mills, Sara (1991), *Discourses of Difference: an Analysis of Women's Travel Writing and Colonialism*. London: Routledge.
Moi, Toril (1985), *Sexual/Textual Politics: Feminist Literary Theory*. London: Methuen.
Montefiore, Janet (1996), *Men and Women Writers of the 1930s: the Dangerous Flood of History*. London: Routledge.
Morris, David B. (1985), "Gothic Sublimity." *New Literary History* 16.2, *The Sublime and the Beautiful: Reconsiderations* (Winter): 299–319.
Norton, Ann V. (1991), "Beauty and Tragedy in *The Judge*." *English Literature in Transition, 1880-1920* 34.3: 295–308.
—(2000), *Paradoxical Feminism: the Novels of Rebecca West*. Lanham, MD: International Scholars Publications.
Orel, Harold (1986), *The Literary Achievement of Rebecca West*. New York: Macmillan Palgrave.
Owen, Stephen (2007), "Genres in Motion." *PMLA* 122.5: 1389–93.
Pare, Anthony (2002), "Genre and Identity: Individuals, Institutions, and Ideology." In *The Rhetoric and Ideology of Genre: Strategies for Stability and Change*, edited by Richard M. Coe, Lorelei Lingard, and Tatiana Teslenko. Cresskill, NJ: Hampton Press, 39–53.
Pater, Walter (1910), *The Renaissance: Studies in Art and Poetry*. Reprint, London: Macmillan, 1977.
Paxton, Nancy (2006), "Renegotiating the Public and Private Divide." In *Rebecca West Today: Contemporary Approaches*, edited by Bernard Schweizer. Newark: University of Delaware Press, 189–205.
Peterson, Shirley (1997), "Modernism, Single Motherhood, and the Discourse of Woman's Liberation in Rebecca West's *The Judge*." In *Unmanning Modernism: Gendered Re-Readings*, edited by Elizabeth Jane Harrison and Shirley Peterson. Knoxville: University of Tennessee Press, 105–16.
Pratt, Mary Louise (1992), *Imperial Eyes Travel Writing and Transculturation*. London: Routledge.
The Princeton Encyclopedia of Poetry and Poetics (2012), Princeton: Princeton University Press.
Punter, David (1998), *Gothic Pathologies: The Text, the Body, and the Law*. New York: Macmillan.
Puttenham, George (1936), *Arts of English Poesie*, edited by G. D. Willcock and A. Walker. Cambridge: Cambridge University Press.
Pykett, Lyn (2000), "Writing Around Modernism: May Sinclair and Rebecca West." In *Outside Modernism: In Pursuit of the English Novel, 1900-30*, edited by Nancy L. Paxton and Lynne Hapgood. London: St. Martin's Press, 103–22.
Radcliffe, Ann (1826), "On the Supernatural in Poetry." *New Monthly Magazine* 16.1: 145–52. Electronic pdf. http://academic.brooklyn.cuny.edu/english/melani/gothic/radcliffe1.html.

Rainer, Dachine (1965), "The New Meaning of Treason." Review of *The New Meaning of Treason,* by Rebecca West. *Commonweal* 81 (January 15): 525–6.

Raub, Patricia (1994), "A New Woman or an Old Fashioned Girl? The Portrayal of the Heroine in Popular Women's Novels of the Twenties." *American Studies* 35 (Spring): 109–30.

Ray, Philip E. (1988), "*The Judge* Reexamined: Rebecca West's Underrated Gothic Romance." *English Literature in Transition, 1880-1920* 31.3: 297–307.

"Rebecca West" (2014), http://en.wikipedia.org/wiki/Rebecca_West, accessed January 30.

Robbins, Bruce (2007), "Afterword." *PMLA* 122.5 (October): 1644–51.

Rogers, Deborah D. (2007), *The Matrophobic Gothic and Its Legacy: Sacrificing Mothers in the Novel and in Popular Culture.* New York: Peter Lang.

Rollyson, Carl E. (1995), *Rebecca West: a Saga of the Century.* London: Hodder & Stoughton.

—(2007), *The Literary Legacy of Rebecca West.* Lincoln, Nebraska: International Scholars Publication.

Sartre, Jean-Paul (1962), *Imagination: A Psychological Critique*, translated by F. Williams. Ann Arbor: University of Michigan Press. Quoted in Jackson 1981.

Schweizer, Bernard (2001), *Radicals on the Road the Politics of English Travel Writing in the 1930s.* Charlottesville: University of Virginia Press.

—(2002), *Rebecca West: Heroism, Rebellion, and the Female Epic.* Westport, CT: Greenwood Press.

—, ed. (2006), *Rebecca West Today: Contemporary Critical Approaches.* Newark: University of Delaware Press.

—(2010), "Rebecca West and the Meaning of Exile." *Partial Answers: Journal of Literature and The History of Ideas* 8.2 (June): 389–407.

Scott, Bonnie Kime (1987), "The Strange Necessity of Rebecca West." In *Women Reading Women's Writing*, edited by Sue Roe. New York: St. Martin's Press, 263–86.

—, ed. (1990), *The Gender of Modernism: A Critical Anthology.* Bloomington: Indiana University Press.

—(1991), "Refiguring the Binary, Breaking the Cycle: Rebecca West as Feminist Modernist." *Twentieth Century Literature* 37: 169–91.

Showalter, Ellen (1977), *A Literature of their Own.* Princeton: Princeton University Press.

Snyder, Carol L. (1991), "Introduction." In *Gender and Genre in Literature: Female Heroism in the Pastoral*, edited by Gail David. New York: Garland, xi–xii.

Spacks, Patricia Meyer (2006), *Novel Beginnings: Experiments in Eighteenth-Century English Fiction.* New Haven: Yale University Press.

Squires, Michael (1974), *The Pastoral Novel: Studies in George Eliot, Thomas Hardy, and D. H. Lawrence.* Charlottesville, VA: University Press of Virginia.

Stec, Loretta (1997), "Female Sacrifice: Gender and Nostalgic Nationalism in Rebecca West's *Black Lamb and Grey Falcon*." In *Narrative of Nostalgia, Gender, and Nationalism*, edited by Suzanne Kehde and Jean Pickering. New York: New York University Press, 138–58.

Stern, Ernesta de Hierschel (1916), *Le bapteme du courage*. Paris: Editions de "La Nouvelle revue." Quoted in Grayzel 1999.

Stetz, Margaret D. (1994), "Rebecca West's Criticism: Alliance, Tradition and Modernism." In *Rereading Modernism: New Directions in Feminist Criticism*, edited by Lisa Rado. New York: Garland, 41–66.

—(2001), *British Women's Comic Fiction, 1890-1990*. Burlington, VT: Ashgate.

—(2006), "Rebecca West, Aestheticism, and the Legacy of Oscar Wilde." In *Rebecca West Today: Contemporary Approaches*, edited by Bernard Schweizer. Newark: University of Delaware Press, 157–69.

Stowe, William W. (1994), *Going Abroad: European Travel in Nineteenth-Century American Culture*. Princeton: Princeton University Press.

Sutherland, W. O. S. (1965), *The Art of the Satirist: Essays on the Satire of Augustan England*. Austin: University of Texas Press.

Thomas, Sue (1987), "Virginia Woolf's Septimus Smith and Contemporary Perceptions of Shell Shock." *English Language Notes* 25.2 (December): 49–57.

Time (1941), Unsigned review of *Black Lamb and Grey Falcon* (November 17): 94–8.

TLS (1922), Unsigned review of *The Judge*, by Rebecca West (June 29): 427.

Todorov, Tzvetan (1975), *The Fantastic: A Structural Approach to a Literary Genre*. Ithaca, NY: Cornell University Press.

Toliver, Harold E. (1971), *Pastoral Forms and Attitudes*. Berkeley: University of California Press.

Tylee, Claire M. (1990), *The Great War and Women's Consciousness: Images of Militarism and Womanhood in Women's Writings, 1914-64*. Iowa City: University of Iowa Press.

West, Rebecca (1915), "Miss Sinclair's Genius." In *YR* Marcus. Reprint, New York: Viking Press, 1982.

—(1916), *Henry James*. Port Washington, NY: Kennikat Press, 1968.

—(1918), *The Return of the Soldier*. New York: Dial Press, 1980.

—(1922), *The Judge*. New York: Carroll & Graf, 1995.

—(1928a) *The Strange Necessity*. London: Jonathan Cape, 1931.

—(1928b), "High Fountain of Genius." *The New York Herald Tribune* 1 (October 21): 6.

—(1929a), "Elegy." In *Legion: The Book of the British Legion*, edited by Humphrey Cotton Michin. Garden City, New York: Doubleday, Doran & Co., 213–34.

—(1929b), *Harriet Hume: A London Fantasy*. New York: Dial Press, 1980.

—(1930), "A Last London Letter." *Bookman* 71: 513–22.

—(1931), *Ending in Earnest: A Literary Log*. New York: Doubleday, Doran & Co.

—(1932), "What is Mr T. S. Eliot's Authority as a Critic?" *Daily Telegraph* (September 30): 6. Reprinted in *The Gender of Modernism: A Critical Anthology*, edited by Bonnie Kime Scott (1990). Bloomington: Indiana University Press, 587–92.

—(1933a), *A Letter to a Grandfather.* London: Hogarth Press.

—(1933b), "Mrs Pankhurst." In *The Post-Victorians*, edited by W. R. Inge. London: Ivor Nicholson & Watson, 479–500.

—(1933c), *St Augustine.* New York: D. Appleton and Co.

—(1935), *The Harsh Voice.* New York: Doubleday, Doran & Co., 1936.

—(1936), *The Thinking Reed.* New York: Viking.

—(1940), "I Believe." In *I Believe.* London: George Allen & Unwin, 369–90.

—(1941), *Black Lamb and Grey Falcon: A Journey through Yugoslavia.* New York: Penguin, 1982.

—(1957), *The Court and The Castle.* New Haven: Yale University Press.

—(1977), *Rebecca West, a Celebration*, edited by Samuel Hynes. New York: Viking.

—(1982), *The Young Rebecca: Writings of Rebecca West, 1911-17*, edited by Jane Marcus. New York: Viking.

Williams, Anne (1995), *Art of Darkness: A Poetics of Gothic.* Chicago: University of Chicago Press.

Williams, William Carlos (1929), "A Point for American Criticism." In *Our Exagmination Round His Factification for Incamination of "Work in Progress,"* edited by Samuel Beckett, Marcel Brion, Frank Budgen, Stuart Gilbert, Eugene Jolas, Victor Llona, Robert McAlmon, Thomas McGreevy, Elliot Paul, John Rodker, Robert Sage, and William Carlos Williams. London: Faber and Faber Limited, accessed February 24, 2014. http://zehfilardo.files.wordpress.com/2012/09/our-exagmination-round-his-factification-for-incamination-of-work-in-progress-searcheable.pdf.

Wolfe, Peter (1971), *Rebecca West: Artist and Thinker.* Carbondale: Southern Illinois University Press.

Woods, Katharine (1941), "Rebecca West's Brilliant Mosaic of Yugoslavian Travel." Review of *Black Lamb and Grey Falcon*, by Rebecca West. *New York Times Book Review* (26 October): 4+. Print.

Woolf, Virginia (1925a), *Mrs Dalloway.* Reprint, London: Harcourt, Brace & World, 1953.

—(1925b), "Modern Fiction." In *The Common Reader*, edited by Virginia Woolf. Reprint, New York: Harcourt, Brace & World, 1953, 150–8.

—(1927), *To the Lighthouse.* Reprint, London: Harcourt, Inc, 1981.

—(1976), "A Sketch of the Past." In *Moments of Being: Unpublished Autobiographical Writings*, edited by Jeanne Schulkind. London: Harcourt, Brace Jovanovich, 61–139.

—(1984), "Mr Bennett and Mrs Brown." In *The Virginia Woolf Reader*, edited by Mitchell A. Leaska. San Diego: Harcourt Brace Jovanovich, 192–212.

Wordsworth, William (1798), "Lines Written on the River Wye above Tintern Abbey." In *Lyrical Ballads, with a Few Other Poems.* London: J & A Arch.

—(1807), "I Wandered Lonely as a Cloud." In *Poems, In Two Volumes*. London: Longman.

Yeats, W. B. (1961), "The Symbolism of Poetry." In *Essays and Introductions*. New York: Collier Books, 153–64.

Young, David (1972), *The Heart's Forest: A Study of Shakespeare's Pastoral Plays*. New Haven: Yale University Press.

Zipes, Jack (1983), *Fairy Tales and the Art of Subversion*. New York: Methuen.

Index

Aaron's Rod 155
Adela 12, 49
Aiken, Conrad 105, 106
Ardis, Ann 51
Aristotle 89, 92
"Ash Wednesday" 111, 130
Auden, W. H. 38, 149

Babbitt, Irving 92–4, 119
Bakhtin, Mikhail 9, 78
Bermel, Albert 121–2, 126, 175nn. 9, 12
biography 1, 16, 107, 113–16, 173n. 13
Black Lamb and Grey Falcon 2, 3, 9, 10, 11, 12, 69, 70, 91, 92, 133–65
- as anatomy of violence 156–8
- art in 161 5
- contradictory genre expectations in 148–52
- epic conventions in 153–65
- imperialism in 135–40
- integrative nationalism 141–8
- liberal nationalism 140–1
- principle of the rock 157–60, 162–5
- as travel chronicle 134–5
- violence of the dispossessed 140–1, 156, 160, 163

Blake, William 91
Bluemel, Kristen 3, 107
Bomarito, Jessica 56
book reviews 12, 15–16, 94–6
Bracco, Rosa Maria 18
British Women's Comic Fiction, 1890-1990: Not Drowning, But Laughing 3–4
Brittain, Vera 10, 19
Burke, Edmund 59
Burke, Kenneth 9
burlesque 107, 111–13, 131

Cantos 153
Capone, Al "Scarface" 4, 115, 140, 141
Cecil, Viscount 107
City Lights 121
The City of God 114
Clarion 13, 31, 34, 37
classicism 9–10, 129
Coe, Richard 8, 9
Cohen, Debra Rae 3, 11, 19, 35, 168n. 4, 178n. 24
Collier, Patrick 3, 106
Conditioned Reflexes 88–9
"contact zones" 7, 11, 15, 44, 51, 56, 74, 79, 104, 146–9, 152, 164
Coward, Noël 121
cultural traditions 4, 91, 92,102, 115, 142, 162
Cunningham, A. R. 48–9, 65

Deakin, Motley 20, 21, 32
Defence of the Realm Act 44, 168n. 10
Derrida, Jacques 67–8, 71, 72, 73, 84
"dialogism" 9
différance 72, 74, 75, 84, 85
Dimock, Wai Chee 8
Dostoevsky, Fyodor 90, 91
dove 109

"Elegy" 7, 10
- analysis of 5–6
- summary of 4–5

Eliot, T. S. 14, 16–17, 53, 89, 92, 99, 110–11, 121, 130, 149, 153, 172n. 8
Ellmann, Richard 88
Empson, William 38, 43
epic 11, 92, 105
- conventions in *Black Lamb and Grey Falcon* 153–65, 176n. 11, 178n. 23, 179n. 30

epiphanies 98, 100, 102, 178n. 26
essays 2, 12, 13–15
- see also *The Strange Necessity*

Fairfield, Cicely Isabel *see* West, Rebecca
fairy tales 78–9, 83

fantastic 10
in *Harriet Hume* 79–84
The Fantastic: A Structural Approach to a Literary Genre 79
fantasy 10, 11, 78
in *Harriet Hume* 67, 77–85
in "The Strange Necessity" 78, 80
in *The Thinking Reed* 129
farce 10, 113, 175n. 9–12
in *The Harsh Voice* 131
in *The Thinking Reed* 120–30
Farley, David 133
fascism 93–4, 141
female gothic 54, 57
in *The Judge* 57–66
nature in 62
terror in 58
feminism 10, 13–14, 31, 50
Ferdinand, Franz (Archduke) 69–70, 138, 170n. 2
Forster, E. M. 107
Four Quartets 149
Freadman, Anne 7, 146, 148
The Freewoman 10, 13
Friedman, Susan Stanford 49, 153–4
Fussell, Paul 18, 21, 29, 30, 31, 33–4, 38, 42, 133, 139, 149, 155, 167n. 3, 169n. 16

Garnett, Edward 104–5
genres
conservative 8, 9
of fantasy 79–83
features of West's hybrid 10–11
feminist goals 10
inclusion of one "unreal" genre 10–11
social class issues 11
marginalized 149
pastoral *see* pastoral genres
"process" over "product" promotion 4, 9, 143, 159, 161
theoretical construct for, West's subversive hybrid 6–10
variety of 1–2
see also *specific individual genres*
Going Abroad 147
Golding, Louis 107
Good-bye to All That 19
Grand, Sarah 65
Graves, Robert 19
Grayzel, Susan R. 18–19, 20, 22–3, 25, 26, 168n. 10
The Great War and Modern Memory 18, 33
The Great War and Women's Consciousness 18
Grey, Edward 30
guidebooks 134–6, 156, 161, 164, 175n. 2
Guilhamet, Leon 70

Hall, Radclyffe 19
Hamilton, Cicely 21
Harper, Lila Marz 150
Harriet Hume 1, 3, 10, 12, 67–85
conclusion in 82
dualism 74–6
irony of character's names in 70–1
masculinist and capitalist system in 71–2
as political satire 67–77
spirituality and imagination in 76–7
synopsis 68
use of fantasy in 77–85
fantastic 79–84
marvelous 79, 171n. 7
uncanny 79–80
Western metaphysics 72–3
The Harsh Voice 11, 107, 131–2
tragic spirit in 131
Heath, Stephen 8
Heffernan, Laura 148
Henry James 16–17, 97, 173n. 13
Hitler, Adolph 108
"home front" 18–19, 20, 29, 168n. 4
Howe, Irving 120–1
Hughes, Leo 112
Hugo, Victor 98
Hynes, Samuel 1, 2, 19, 20, 21, 22, 24, 29, 30, 113, 175n. 1

Imperial Eyes: Travel Writing and Transculturation 7
integrative nationalism 141–2
as a "fusion that infuriates" 141–2
examples of 142–6
theorizing 146–8
intermodernism 3, 107
The Irish Guards in the Great War 21
irony 15, 21, 29, 32, 70, 113, 114, 128, 130, 131
Irwin, W. R. 78

James, Henry 16–17, 22, 30, 36, 82, 97, 116, 173n. 13
jouissance 85
A Journal of Impressions in Belgium 22
Joyce, James 4, 53, 65, 87, 88, 92, 94–6, 98, 100, 103–6, 108, 140, 153, 155, 174n. 2
The Judge 10, 49–66, 67, 79, 87, 116, 169n. 6
  ending in 64–6
  as female gothic terror 57–66
  as gothic novel 52
  hybrid of new woman novel 49–51, 62–3
  male gothic reading of 52–7
  mother-daughter kinship relationship in 59, 63, 66
  portrayal of nature in 60–2, 66, 69
The Judge Reexamined: Rebecca West's Underrated Gothic Romance 52

Kavka, Misha 30, 31, 168n. 6
Kipling, Rudyard 21, 91, 115, 140
Kucich, John 65

Laing, Kathryn 49, 105–6
Landre, Jeanne 25
La vieillée des armes 26
Lawrence, D. H. 155
Le baptê me du courage 26
L'école des marraines 25
A Letter to a Grandfather 10, 92, 107–13, 130, 173n. 12
  carnival worker 112–13
  desire for filiation in 108
  stretched consciousness in 109–10
  tragic sense of life in 110–12
  visions in 108–9
Lewis, Sinclair 131
liberal nationalism 140–1
"liminal space" concept 147–8, 177n. 15
"Lines Written a Few Miles above Tintern Abbey" 60
Lingard, Lorelei 9
locus amoenus 33, 38, 39

McFarland, Thomas 39
MacKay, Marina 148–9
male gothic 54, 56, 59, 64, 65
  horror in 58
  reading of *The Judge* 52–7
Mao, Douglas 32
Marcus, Jane 10, 13, 82, 169n. 6
marginalized genres 149
Marriage 16
Marsden, Dora 10
Memoirs of an Infantry Officer 19
Memories of a Fox-Hunting Man 19
Merchants of Hope: British Middlebrow Writers and the First World War 1919–39 18
metaphor 8, 15, 28, 31, 42, 100, 101, 129, 146, 148, 155, 173n. 13
"The Metaphysical Poets" 92
A Midsummer's Night Dream 39, 43, 45
Miller, Carolyn 7
Mills, Sara 137, 150–1, 155
"Modernism in a Transnational Landscape" 154
Modernist Travel Writing 133
Modern Times 121
Montefiore, Jam 2
Moore, George 91
More, Paul Elmore 92–4, 119
Morris, David B. 55
Mrs Dalloway 19, 87, 88, 99, 173n. 15, 174n. 2

narcissism 96
"The Necessity and Grandeur of the International Idea" 142
New Picture of Rome's 135
"New Woman" fiction 48–53, 56, 62–5, 169n. 2
Norton, Ann V. 64, 75, 82, 118, 128, 177n. 17

"On the Supernatural in Poetry" 55, 58
orientalism 138–9
Orlando 85
Owen, Stephen 8, 9

Pare, Anthony 8
pastoral genres 10, 168n. 12, 169n. 13, 170n. 12
  in *The Return of the Soldier* 32–45
    as nostalgia for rural life 33–8
    renaissance 38–45

Pater, Walter 97–9, 100, 101–3
Pavlov, Ivan 87, 88, 104, 171n. 1
Paxton, Nancy 53
Peterson, Shirley 50, 51, 57
"Philosophy of the Same" 71–2
Portrait of a Lady 116
A Portrait of the Artist as a Young Man 155
Pound, Ezra 89, 153
Pratt, Mary Louise 7, 51, 137, 146–7, 148, 152, 175n. 2
The Princeton Encyclopedia of Poetry and Poetics 42
Prothalamion 34
Punter, David 53
Puttenham, George 45
Pykett, Lyn 4, 50, 51, 52, 64, 65, 169n. 5

Radcliffe, Ann 55, 58, 59, 62
Radicals on the Road 2, 134
Raub, Patricia 48
Ray, Philip E. 52, 53, 54–5, 56, 57
Rebecca West: A Celebration 1
Rebecca West: Heroism, Rebellion, and the Female Epic 2–3, 153
Remapping the Home Front 19
The Renaissance 97
renaissance pastoral 38–45
The Return of the Soldier 10, 11, 109
  British class system in 37–8
  "divine life" and "outer life" 28–9
  ending in 32
  landscapes description in 36–7
  materialistic attitude of characters in 26–8
  metaphors in 31
  neglect of women's experiences of war 18–19
  nostalgia for ruralism 34
  pastoral as nostalgia for rural life in 33–8
  renaissance pastoral 38–45
  synopsis 19–20
  theme of absence in 20–1
  war romance plot 22–5
  war's negative presence in 20–2
  woman's war novel 18–32
Robbins, Bruce 8
Rogers, Deborah D. 59, 170n. 11
Rollyson, Carl 2, 11, 19, 82, 88, 104, 141, 174n. 4
romanticism 3, 9–10, 42, 59–62, 66, 129

Said, Edward 137
St Augustine 107, 109, 110, 113–16
  cultural traditions 115–16
  dualism 114–15
  free will 115
  irony 114
  tragic sense of life in 111–12, 114–15
Sartre, Jean-Paul 11
Sassoon, Siegfried 19
satire 5, 67–77, 112, 121, 122, 131, 169n. 3
Schweizer, Bernard 2–3, 133, 134, 142, 153, 154, 176nn. 6, 11, 177n. 13, 179n. 30
Scott, Bonnie Kime 2, 48, 65, 76, 82, 175n. 14
sentimentalism 95–6
The Sentinel 12, 49
Shaw, George Bernard 13, 88, 97, 103, 173n. 12
Showalter, Elaine 23, 45, 64
Sinclair, May 22
Snyder, Carol L. 8
social class issues, as feature of West's hybrid genres 11
Solitary Travelers 150
Some Versions of the Pastoral 38
Spacks, Patricia Meyer 15, 170n. 7
Spenser, Edmund 34
Stern, Ernest 26
Stetz, Margaret D. 3–4, 5–6, 76, 97, 98, 142, 167n. 2, 170n. 3, 171n. 6
The Strange Necessity 2, 3, 11, 12, 78, 87–106, 108, 115, 117, 119, 140, 148, 160, 171n. 2, 172n. 7
  "blazing jewel" of art in 100–1
  book review of *Ulysses* 94–6
  critical reception of 103–6
  cultural nationalism 90–2
  genres in 87
  hybrid advantage 94
  nationalism *vs.* imperialism 93–4
  as novella 88
  pater familias 96–103
  as poetics 89–94
  as scientific analysis 88–9

scientists and artists, similarities between 89–90
threat of isolation 101–2
Stowe, William W. 135–8, 147–8, 151
Sunflower 12, 49, 87, 167n. 3, 169n. 3, 170n. 1
Sutherland, W. O. S. 74

The Tempest 39, 43
Teslenko, Tatiana 9
The Testament of Youth 10, 19
The Thinking Reed 10, 107, 112, 113, 114, 116–30, 174n. 7
climactic scene of 124–6
farce in 120–30
lives of sport in 117–18
money's influence 118
romanticism in 129
synopsis 116
tradition in 118–19
tragic spirit in 116–20, 126
Thomas, Sue 31–2
Tinayre, Marcelle 26
Todorov, Tzvetan 79–80, 82–3, 171n. 8
Toliver, Harold E. 39
Tolstoy, Leo 115
To the Lighthouse 98, 100, 102
"Tradition and the Individual Talent" 17, 92
tragedy 10, 14, 44, 47, 63, 64, 66, 92, 174n. 2, 175n. 9
see also tragic spirit and tragic sense in *A Harsh Voice*, *A Letter to a Grandfather*, and *The Thinking Reed*
travel chronicle 1, 134–5, 137, 147, 156, 161, 175n. 2
travel writing 2–3, 7, 147, 149, 176n. 10, 177n. 18
in 1930s 133–4
guidebook and travel chronicle 134–5
"The Turn of the Screw" 82
Tylee, Claire M. 18, 23–4, 32

Ulysses 53, 87, 88, 94–6, 100, 103, 105, 153, 156, 174n. 2
unreal genre, as feature of West's hybrid genres 10–11
"uptake" concept 7, 56, 104, 146, 147, 148, 149

Walpole, Hugh 55, 107
The Waste Land 53, 92, 111, 130, 153
The Well of Loneliness 19
Wells, H. G. 16, 97
West, Rebecca 1
Black Lamb and Grey Falcon 133–65
book reviews 15–16, 94–6
early journalism 13–16
"Elegy" 4–6
essays 14–15
features of hybrid genres 10–11
feminist politics of 13–14
Harriet Hume 67–85
The Harsh Voice 131–2
Henry James 16–17
"Indissoluble Matrimony" 131, 175n. 15
The Judge 47–66
A Letter to a Grandfather 107–13
The Return of the Soldier 17–45
St Augustine 113–16
The Strange Necessity 87–106
theoretical construct for, subversive hybrid genres 6–10
The Thinking Reed 116–30
variety of genres 1–2
works of 1
Williams, Anne 54, 56, 58
Williams, William Carlos 2, 103, 105
Wolfe, Peter 1, 80, 82, 84, 116, 143, 150, 168n. 9
Women and the First World War 18
Women and the Politics of Travel: 1870–1914 150
Women's Identities at War: Gender, Motherhood, and Politics in Britain and France during the First World War 18
Woolf, Virginia 19, 30, 85, 87, 88, 98, 99–100, 101, 102, 107, 173n. 12, 173n. 15, 173n. 16, 174n. 2
Wordsworth, William 34, 59–61, 89
Wright, Andrew 54

Yeats, W. B. 28–9, 89, 91, 108, 112, 115, 140, 153–4, 173n. 12
Young, David 39
The Young Rebecca 13

Zipes, Jack 78
Zweig, Paul 155